The Latent World of Architecture

MW00790817

This book features thirteen essays by the late architect, philosopher and teacher Dalibor Vesely (1934–2015). Vesely was a leading authority on philosophical hermeneutics and phenomenology in relation to architecture worldwide, and influenced a generation of thinkers, teachers and practitioners. This collection presents the full range of his writing, drawing primarily from the history of art and architecture, as well as philosophy, theology, anthropology and ecology, and spanning from early antiquity to modernism. It composes a multifaceted and globally relevant argument about the enduring cultural role of architecture and the significance of its history. The book, edited and introduced by Vesely's teaching partner at Cambridge Peter Carl and former student Alexandra Stara, and with a foreword by David Leatherbarrow, brings to light new and hard-to-access material for those familiar with Vesely's thought and, at the same time, offers a compelling introduction to his writing and its profound relevance for architecture and culture today.

Alexandra Stara is associate professor and reader in the history and theory of architecture at Kingston University London and a qualified architect in her native Greece, with Masters degrees from UCL and the University of Cambridge, and a PhD from the University of Oxford. She has been lecturing and publishing on art and architecture for the past three decades.

Peter Carl taught graduate design and the graduate programme in the history and philosophy of architecture at the University of Cambridge with Dalibor Vesely for 30 years. He then established the PhD programme in architecture at London Metropolitan University, where he was professor until his retirement. He has lectured and taught internationally, publishing a body of work that interprets architectural and urban order in terms of phenomenological hermeneutics.

The Latent World of Architecture

Selected Essays

Dalibor Vesely

Edited by Alexandra Stara and Peter Carl

Routledge
Taylor & Francis Group

LONDON AND NEW YORK

Cover image: Guarino Guarini, *Disegni di architettura civile ed ecclesiastica*, 1737, Plate 2. Plan for the chapel of the Holy Shroud (detail). Getty Research Institute.

First published 2023
by Routledge
4 Park Square, Milton Park, Abingdon, Oxon OX14 4RN

and by Routledge
605 Third Avenue, New York, NY 10158

Routledge is an imprint of the Taylor & Francis Group, an informa business

© 2023 selection and editorial matter, Alexandra Stara and Peter Carl; individual chapters, the contributors

British Library Cataloguing-in-Publication Data
A catalogue record for this book is available from the British Library

Library of Congress Cataloging-in-Publication Data
Names: Vesely, Dalibor, author. | Stara, Alexandra, 1967- editor. | Carl, Peter, editor.
Title: The latent world of architecture: selected essays / Dalibor Vesely; edited by Alexandra Stara and Peter Carl.
Description: Abingdon, Oxon: Routledge, 2023. | Includes bibliographical references and index. | Identifiers: LCCN 2022009197 (print) | LCCN 2022009198 (ebook) | ISBN 9781032223254 (hardback) | ISBN 9781032223261 (paperback) | ISBN 9781003272090 (ebook)
Subjects: LCSH: Architecture.
Classification: LCC NA27 .V47 2023 (print) | LCC NA27 (ebook) | DDC 720--dc23/eng/20220715
LC record available at https://lccn.loc.gov/2022009197
LC ebook record available at https://lccn.loc.gov/2022009198

ISBN: 978-1-032-22325-4 (hbk)
ISBN: 978-1-032-22326-1 (pbk)
ISBN: 978-1-003-27209-0 (ebk)

DOI: 10.4324/9781003272090

Typeset in Galliard
by KnowledgeWorks Global Ltd.

Contents

Acknowledgements

There were many people with whom Dalibor Vesely maintained conversations and collaborations on philosophy, history and architecture throughout his life. They have significantly contributed to his research and design teaching, and therefore also helped give the essays in this collection their direction. Vesely has appropriately thanked them in his book, and we would like to do this here, also.

We would never have been able to complete the editing of this collection without the assistance of the following people, who are owed our profound gratitude. David Leatherbarrow helped us with several philosophical and architectural questions, as well as writing the beautiful Foreword. Fabio Barry was immensely helpful with Classical, Early Christian and Medieval sources; and Kate Spence pointed us to recent scholarship on New Kingdom obelisks. Robin Middleton provided his usual acute guidance on some eighteenth and nineteenth century issues. The Czech material required the assistance of Dagmar Motycka-Weston, Irena Murray and Tomáš Vlček, whose collective knowledge of the history, terminology and sources was invaluable for us. Daphne Becket clarified Vesely's contributions to the Religion, Science and Environment symposia. We are deeply grateful to José de Paiva for his contribution to sourcing Vesely's writings and for important conversations at the early stages of the book; to Nicholas Temple for his guidance and encouragement with publishing; and to Fran Ford and her team at Routledge for their consistent support. We are also deeply grateful to Stuart Arrandale, a former music colleague of Vesely, for his generous financial support for the acquisition of images.

This book is dedicated to Dalibor's brother, Drahosh Vesely, who embodies the generosity, wit and profound ethical sense of Czech culture of which he is as knowledgeable as he is about the practices of contemporary scientific research, and who was Dalibor's constant support and companion throughout their lives together.

Foreword

David Leatherbarrow

A voice in conversation echoes through the pages of this book, one that must be, of course, silently understood. The echoes are silent in a second sense; this is a posthumous publication. You won't find line-by-line transcriptions or faithful reports of in-person dialogue on these pages; instead, something like reverberations or the after-effects of conversations, maybe also prompts for their sequel. In some cases, Vesely communicates with his contemporaries. More frequent are conversations with architects and authors from past decades, previous centuries, or the very remote past. Unsurprisingly, his interlocutors also include works of art and architecture, quasi-subjects one might say, paintings, buildings, landscapes and cities, with and against which he tests and develops his ideas and arguments. All this can be called conversational because topics of reciprocal interest are in play, through back-and-forth questions and replies, assumptions and corrections, points and counterpoints. Just because we die individually doesn't mean we must live and think that way. Here, the movement of thought is paced by the movement of discussion, real or imagined, alternately fast and slow in its progress, occasionally reversing its advances or repeating its points, and stopping now and then in order to renew itself through yet another question or reply.

These essays not only echo conversational thought, they render it a little more coherent and more durable. Although spontaneity and sociability are less in evidence, one doesn't regret the scripted version—despite what Plato said about writing chaining ideas—for these collected texts will now be widely available. And now that they're on our desks and under our eyes we can easily favour ourselves with the impression that the questions they pose and pursue are ones we ourselves would have asked, as if by some miracle of foresight Vesely had discovered that our interests are rather like those that concerned him.

Under what conditions can a conversation between a contemporary thinker and a distant building or text take place? What disposition or intermediary would be required for a fair and productive reading?

According to Pascal's Law, a change in pressure at any point in an enclosed fluid at rest is transmitted undiminished to all points in the fluid, no matter how many or what shapes its different containers may take. This principle gave rise to a corresponding observation about *communicating vessels*: hydrostatic pressure maintains a single and shared level of liquid in separate but connected bottles. In place of the piston that provided Pascal's experiments with pressure, André Breton, whose surrealism was so warmly received in Czech *avant-garde* circles, pointed to the forces that weighed down modern culture as sufficient pressure for the establishment of a common level. In his *Communicating Vessels*, published in Paris in 1932 and Prague two years later, the many and varied pressures of prosaic life, powerful as they had become, prompted direct communication between understanding and emotion, reason and passion.[1] As for the intermediary, dreams and poetic images would, he thought, form the 'capillary tissue' between every-day and desired conditions, or the world as given and imagined, or, again—as in conversation—statements made and questions asked, each otherwise a separate vessel. Breton's ease with exaggeration even allowed him to envisage communication of great intensity, love, between complete strangers on the streets of Paris, a conversation no less difficult to imagine and achieve than one between a modern architect and a Baroque building or ancient text, such as we see in this book.

The conversing and questioning that animates these essays make their way along a two-way street. When Vesely asks about the sense of a text or built project, he treats the work under consideration as an answer to a question posed by its author or designer. The methodological premise here is that comparable pressures give rise to comparable questions, the architect's or author's and Vesely's. But that thesis gets us ahead of ourselves. First, we need to note that the interlocutors are rarely forthcoming about why the say what they do. In all likelihood, they will not have given their motivations much thought, assuming them to be obvious, which is to say silently understood. This means the documents this book considers are viewed as answers to unstated questions—a building by Janák, a painting by Altdorfer or a Platonic dialogue. Recovering the motivating question requires restoring the context in which it emerged. Some homework is necessary for that, hence the abundant historical material in this book. When the works or statements being questioned are from another time, or set forth in another language, the articulations are typically ambiguous and almost always fragmentary. Thus, intertwined with the work of contextualisation is that of translation. Both involve seeing things that really aren't on display or hearing what was never actually said, only implied, as when a gesture or intonation expresses another person's sense of a subject more fully than the words they have spoken. Much of the text you have in your hands resonates with the apprehension of what was never explicitly stated but is for that reason all the more valuable, having been discerned and described.

The voice I've called conversational is also European. In one sense, that simply means multi-lingual, as will be obvious if you turn from these few pages to the book's notes and review the works that have been cited. But a range of languages does not a continent make. Europe is commonly understood geographically. It is where several nations have their place. Yet, insofar as the borders that enclose today's states are not what they once were—have shifted, will continue to do so, and at some points never existed at all—it would be a mistake to limit one's conception of European identity to geographical or political definitions. No less misleading would be the identification of a language and the culture it embodies with one or another country. Adolf Loos, Franz Kafka and Edmund Husserl weren't the only moderns who were born into Czech families but worked and wrote in German. Language and location are important, but not everything. There is also the little issue of what one does with them. The voice echoing through the words and images of this book is European in a different sense. Another Czech, Jan Patočka, argued that the single most important characteristic of a European voice is its 'care for the soul', a vocation, he argued in *Plato and Europe*, that has sounded its call through the centuries in different locations, but was first articulated on the streets of ancient Athens, though also silenced there.[2]

In a lecture on the Danube River, Vesely argued that 'it was and remains a vital *space of communication* where the most heterogeneous peoples have found a source of identity and solidarity.'[3] This coupling of singularity and sharing is very striking, today almost impossible to understand. Difference seems much more prominent.

Before Martin Heidegger[4] embarked on his interpretation of Friedrich Hölderlin's great river poem, *The Ister* (Ἴστρος in Greek, Ister in Latin, Donau in German, Danube in English), he devoted a few lines to the opening of a poem called *Voice of the People*. The philosopher's sense of what the poet had in mind parallels what our architect-author observed about the Danube and other European rivers. The key lines from the first and second stanzas of Hölderlin's poem are these:

> Unconcerned with our wisdom
> The rivers still rush on, and yet

> Who loves them not? And always do they move
> My heart, when afar I hear them vanishing[5]

Heidegger neglected the rather deflating allusion to the limits of 'our wisdom' and the river's indifference to human affairs, concentrating instead on fluvial movement, locomotive in its advance one might say, though one suspects the philosopher wouldn't like the metaphor. He discovered something of a paradox in a river's powerful forwarding: having been formed out of many tributaries its singularly defined a place (Europe), but also departed. Its absence, however, did not prevent it from attracting the affection of those who resided nearby—a rather extensive nearby given its territorial reach. Thus, the poet's plaintive question: Who loves them not? All do, at least all Europeans. Insofar as what the rivers once were remains no longer—they absent themselves—the same can be expected for what's to come, tomorrow they won't be what they are today. That's true also for nations too. Can the same be said for European art and architecture, this book's subject matter? Later in the poem, Hölderlin described a river's effect on built settlements:

> So rivers plunge—not movement but rest they seek—
> Drawn on, pulled down against their will from
> Boulder to boulder—abandoned, helmless—

> ... Chaotic deeps attract, and whole peoples too
> May come to long for death, and valiant
> Towns that have striven to do the best thing.

> ... these too
> A holy end has stricken, the earth grows green...

As it happens, the poet's sense of the future of European towns anticipated a blunt prognosis from the philosopher whose thought guided Vesely's. Patočka wrote: 'Europe, that two-thousand-year-old construction... is definitely at an end.'[6] Yet, on the next page the 'European' task was recalled. Despite everything, there is still the need to 'care for the soul'.

After he assumed the presidency in 1989, the poet-playwright Václav Havel repeated Patočka's demand. Failing that, the Czech lands specifically and Europe more broadly would never hold their ground between the attractions and dangers of the two superpowers. Care for the soul meant resisting all that puts its well-being at risk and doing so as a matter of personal responsibility. The manager of a fruit and veg shop is the protagonist in one of Havel's greatest texts, 'The Power of the Powerless' (1978).[7] The pages of this book voice a corresponding understanding of care and responsibility, for rivers and towns of course, landscapes and architecture, but also, and no less importantly, the lives that try to sustain themselves these days with some measure of personal dignity and civility.

Conversational and situated, the voice that echoes through these pages is perforce embodied. Minds don't talk with one another, voices do. The articulation of thought requires embodiment, spoken words in some cases, writings like these in others, but also, and no less often, non-verbal expressions—let's say incorporations—which are surely at play when we make sense of buildings, but also, and no less commonly, when full understanding (agreement or disagreement) is achieved between two or more of us. I had this in mind above when I recalled that intentions and expressions can be silently understood, as when a gesture or throated intonation qualifies the common sense of a word or phrase. Voices—voicings—can be hard or soft, rough or smooth. Before long, a dry voice becomes unbearable. Exchanges can be heated or cool. In the absence of intonation, songs with the best of lyrics are very dull. In *Architecture in the Age of Divided Representation*, Vesely wrote: 'it is the concreteness and the richness of the lower order that gives power and meaning to the higher'.[8] Setting off on its way to an auditor, voiced thought departs from the lungs, and while on route carries with it the qualities of the air they had made use of.

With the concreteness of the book's echoes in mind, let me give my third and last image of voices in communication.

Before a person with a question was allowed to enter into conversation with the oracle at Delphi, the proper hermeneutical context had to be established. First there was a cave, the lowest part of which, the *adyton*, was associated with Apollo. On some accounts that was the spot where he killed a great serpent, Pytho, understood to be a son of the earth, Gaia. Nevertheless, within the cave was a cleft in the ground, a *chasma* (χάσμα), from which cold vapours rose, capable of inducing intoxication. Placed over the cleft was a wooden tripod, and then, on top of that, a seat for the prophetess, a girl of honourable birth whose preparations for the conversation included a bath, lining her hair with gold and covering herself with simple dress hung from her shoulders. Though one imagines sunlight rarely entered the cave, a supplicant would also find there an ancient bay tree. Laurel seems to have been hung from the ceiling. The same leaves encircled the visitor who'd come with a question. Despite these preparations, the Pythia's answers were often obscure or enigmatic. They always required translation.

The voice, however, is what concerns me; specifically, its concreteness, or perhaps situatedness. It was the unique combination of breath and vapour from the crevices of the earth that provided answers to the supplicant's question. In short, the oracle's expressions were earthed. Vesely's sense of 'situation' includes physical settings, as they combine outcomes of designed construction and the workings of the natural word, but also the habituated and institutional practices they accommodate and represent. The story of cave conversations at Delphi might also provide a useful analogue to what's at play in the participatory sense of situations. No sense would have been made of the enigma without the questioner's involvement in the event of articulation. 'The figuration of meaning', Vesely wrote, 'is directly related to the movement of our body and hands, which may be seen as a work (*ergon*).' He could have added the voice to his short list of instruments of articulation. Your voice is unique, also mine, certainly his. Sometimes utterances are enigmatic. When it comes to reading the tradition of art and architecture, that's often the case. At the same time, they are potentially communicative, when the conditions are right. This book (re)constructs those conditions as they've been established in architecture and experienced in life.

Notes

1 André Breton, *Communicating Vessels*, trans. Mary Ann Caws & Geoffrey T. Harris, Lincoln, NE: University of Nebraska Press, 1990.
2 Jan Patočka, *Plato and Europe*, trans. Petr Lom, Stanford, CA: Stanford University Press, 2002. See especially 'Care of the Soul and the Heritage of Europe', pp. 86–90.
3 Dalibor Vesely, 'Danube and Europe', lecture at the Danube River Symposium, part of the Religion, Science and the Environment

Symposia, 17–26 October 1999. http://www.rsesymposia.org/more.
php?catid=101&pcatid=48
4 Martin Heidegger, *Hölderlin's Hymn 'The Ister,'* trans. William
McNeill and Julia Davis, Bloomington, IN: Indiana University Press,
1984.
5 This is Heidegger's translation; ibid, 27ff. I have also consulted a more
recent and authoritative bi-lingual publication: *Friedrich Hölderlin Poems & Fragments*, trans. Michael Hamburger, London: Anvil,
1994. 'Voice of the People (second version)' is found on pages 183–8
of Hamburger's translation.
6 Patočka, op. cit., p. 9.
7 Václav Havel, 'The Power of the Powerless,' in *Living in Truth*, London: Faber and Faber, 1987, pp. 36–122.
8 Dalibor Vesely, *Architecture in the Age of Divided Representation: The
Question of Creativity in the Shadow of Production*, Cambridge, MA:
MIT Press, 2004, p. 71.

Introduction

Peter Carl and Alexandra Stara

Dalibor Vesely's abiding concern was to understand the place of architecture in the culture, or the indebtedness of cultural possibilities to the embodying conditions of architecture. At his death in 2015, he was in the early stages of writing a book whose working title was *The Modernity of the Baroque*. Although Baroque architecture from seventeenth century Rome to mid-eighteenth-century Central Europe, together with the associated philosophical and theological texts, were certainly part of the historical material,[1] it seems Vesely's intention was to propose 'Baroque' as a metaphor for a possible 'Modernity'. A sentence from the beginning of one of the fragments for this book gives the sense of what was at issue: 'The main tendency in the formation of Baroque was the overcoming of the disintegration and fragmentation of the traditional culture and a search for the unity and universality of the shared world.'[2]

This statement makes clear that we are to consider how the culture as a whole is embodied; in effect, we are asked to consider the conditions for an honest understanding of the nature of our place in reality. By way of situating the particular studies in this book, we will attempt to reconstruct how his understanding of Baroque culture may have guided his thinking with respect to modernity. We will begin by sketching the context in the discipline when Vesely began his research and then outline his urban, architectural and philosophical concerns with respect to our own fragmented culture for which universality currently solicits less approval than does difference.

In many ways, Baroque culture was that against which revolutionary Modernism reacted, for reasons political and philosophical as well as architectural. Emil Kaufmann's famous *Von Ledoux bis Le Corbusier*[3] placed the origins of Modernist architecture in the eighteenth-century Enlightenment. Even the vilification of Modernist

DOI: 10.4324/9781003272090-1

architecture that was Pier Paolo Pasolini's *Salò* followed this model.[4] Adolf Loos' famous essay, 'Ornament and Crime',[5] testified to the distance Modernist architects sought to create from Baroque concerns, even in Vienna. The complex ambiguities and visual opulence of European Baroque architecture[6] contrasted with the austerity of another inspiration from the seventeenth century, Katsura, by which refined Japanese architecture conferred a dignity upon planar simplicity and tectonic clarity, a decorum deemed appropriate for new forms of collective dwelling (and industrial production). Twentieth-century Modernism divided the *Zeitgeist* between technological futurism and 'primitive' craft production (Behrens embraced both); but neither included the Baroque. In *Vers une architecture*, Le Corbusier included Mannerist and Baroque interiors among 'The Rome of Horrors'.[7] Against this background, Vesely's appeal to the modernity of the Baroque appears quite radical.

For architects of the early twentieth century, 'modernity' promised freedom from the burden of history or, like Siegfried Giedion's interpretation of Nietzsche's 'eternal present', permitted reducing the history of architecture and its several cultures to a few formal attributes.[8] The stimulus of technology offered, at one extreme, emancipation from history and tradition in pursuit of the city as system and, at the other extreme, the lyric mysticism of Constructivist propositions. Le Corbusier's indebtedness to tradition was acknowledged mostly after World War II; but his proclivity for deriving moral lessons from ancient or traditional architectures did not involve profound understanding of the cultures from which they came. This motif was still present in Colin Rowe's discovery of Mannerism in modern architecture,[9] whose formalist comparisons were a legacy of the art history of the generation of Heinrich Wölfflin and Alois Riegl fortified by Structuralism. The recovery of history began in the late nineteen sixties, including the Essex course run by Joseph Rykwert (history) and Vesely (philosophy).[10] However, none of the participants in the 1978 *Roma interrotta* exhibition looked deeper historically than the eighteenth century date of the Nolli Plan of Rome on which the exhibition was based; and only the catalogue introduction of Giulio Carlo Argan managed to evoke Rome's sedimented 'composite of epic and idyll, within a chthonic matrix'.[11]

In the façades of the *Strada Novissima* of the 1980 Biennale di Venezia, it became obvious that 'recovery of history' had narrowed to play with historicist iconography. Conforming to Venturi's semiotic field of quotable fragments,[12] it was seen at the time as emblematic of a more cosmopolitan city; but actually, it was symptomatic of the great opportunity lost in the period's re-engagement with the traditions of European cities. If the turn away from C.I.A.M urbanism had been heralded by Team 10 in the previous decade, but the bottom-up analysis of Jane Jacobs[13] went largely ignored, the dominant understandings of urban order revolved around either the figure-field interpretation of Rowe (which overvalued the distinction between public and private) or the typological approaches arising from Aldo Rossi (which valued the architectural configurations over the nature of typicality in urban life and accorded undue prominence to monuments). Manfredo Tafuri sought to preserve through 'operative criticism' the ethical and political aspirations of the early modern manifestoes, if not always the architecture, in response to the 'critical eclecticism' required to address the contributions emerging from disciplines such as anthropology, linguistics, structuralism, Marxism, philosophy, etc.[14] Manifesto-writing had anyway long since given way to architectural theory and history (the standard course designation in architecture schools), which continued to blossom with ever more refined species of critical discourse in the succeeding decades.

To Vesely, the generally well-intentioned, if vague, quality of this work was often compromised by the theoretical attitude, which sought too quickly to convert cultural insights—concepts—into design procedures.[15] The earliest example of this in architecture is Vitruvius, who converted the moral scope of decorum into rules of composition and proportion;[16] and of course architectural theory adhered to compositional rules from the Renaissance onwards, within the parameters of the 'idealised and highly homogenized world' of perspective.[17] The paradigm of theory-practice was one of the principal legacies of the Enlightenment; and its home had been experimental science and technology since the time of Galileo and Francis Bacon, supported by Cartesian, Idealist and Positivist philosophies and subsequently exported to the social sciences.[18] This procedure not only made architecture seem easier to design than it really was, the milieu of its execution in the radical generalisations of 'space' (which proposed to accommodate everything from higher mathematics and nuclear physics to personal psychology) and 'form' (in fact shapes arranged according to rules, typically tectonic-geometrical) had the effect of flattening the results to highly ambiguous fragments. The intuition held by every beginning student of architecture that the discipline was some sort of combination of the sciences and the humanities was typically expressed as an exchange between technics and aesthetics, both of which had long since converged upon methods for 'getting it right' in the material and moral domains, respectively.[19] Conversely, however, 'getting it wrong' in the aesthetic domain had been an important vehicle of radical thinking at least since the Fauves and *Décadence*; but it remained obscure how this motive could be allied to the desiderata of social inclusion and political empowerment of disenfranchised citizens, let alone to any more profound culture, humanist or otherwise. As Vesely remarked, 'the task [was] not only to invent a particular building from one's own cultural resources, but also to invent a culture which would make the building meaningful'.[20]

Understanding of the physical metabolism of cities has improved in the succeeding forty years—ranging from, e.g., sustainability protocols to bottom-up urban acupuncture—but the cultural metabolism appears to have remain stranded in what Charles Jencks and Jean-François Lyotard had named 'post-Modernism',[21] persisting well after the abandonment of historicist iconography in architecture.[22] Insofar as the term described an ambiguous milieu of fragments and their references providing multiple opportunities for both profound insight and delusion, Vesely realised that further speculation at the conceptual (theoretical) level would only amplify the problem,[23] whereas addressing the embodying conditions of the culture, where architecture prevailed, offered a renewal of orientation. For Vesely, 'architecture represents the most elementary mode of embodiment that enables the more articulated levels of culture, including numbers and ideas, to be situated in reality as a whole'.[24]

To attach the term 'Baroque' to such an endeavour possibly strikes the reader as a nostalgic appeal to pre-Revolutionary orthodoxies managed by princes and priests indulging in richly ornamented palaces and churches, hosting elaborate ceremonies with their sophisticated music, drama, literature, theology and philosophy above the heads of ordinary citizens. However, for Vesely, the European Baroque was not simply an historical period enshrined in an architectural style of formal attributes involving curves, diagonals and metamorphic ornament obeying complex iconographic programmes.[25] Rather, the actualities of the period in Europe were marked by the effort to recover orientation within the fragmenting, 'divided representation' of progressive secularisation, individualism and the emerging contest between symbolic and instrumental understandings of reality.[26] At the same time, the mathematics and geometry of, for example, Balthasar Neumann's vaults and of astronomy were more related to each other than they are now.[27] Indeed, Vesely calls attention to the reciprocity between mystical and conceptual modes of interpretation in the period;[28] and the Baroque commitment to architecture and to its rites and ceremonies made architecture one of the principal vehicles of reconciliation of thematic conflicts in the understanding of reality. For Vesely, recovering Baroque symbolic hermeneutics offered contemporary collective existence—with each other, with nature, with technology—a creative understanding of profound themes within an ethical orientation.

In this respect, 'Baroque' named an interpretative ethos—a poetics, according to the last chapter of Vesely's book[29]—which he also found in, for example, works from ancient Crete as well as from the European Middle Ages or Surrealism. Whether or not one can subtract from the historical actuality of the Baroque period such aspects as the development of absolutism, the Inquisition, the Wars of Religion or the colonisation of the Americas, Vesely had little patience for totalitarian politics, having grown up in the Czech Republic under both the Nazi and Soviet regimes before leaving for England in 1968. Life under these dispensations was marked by the familiar Orwellian distortions as well as by the replacement of civic solidarity with mutual suspicion, but subversive art could escape the imaginations of the censors. This combination seems to have stimulated an avoidance of explicit politics in Vesely's writings in favour of the deeper and more enduring truths embodied in poetics. It is possible that his conversations with Václav Havel helped to encourage this attitude,[30] although it conformed also to the famous dictum of Aristotle that poetry is more true than history.[31]

However, Vesely also makes poetics political. He displaces poetics from the expression of individual freedom which we currently expect from artists, by situating poetics within the customs and mores of a culture, as the ethically oriented comportment associated with *praxis*.[32] In these terms, poetics represents a rich or profound understanding of civic behaviour. Implied here, however, is the possibility that civic life provides a sufficiently trustworthy matrix to be able to situate oneself with respect to the fundamental natural conditions (cosmos), a form of understanding that attracts the term 'symbolic'. Any city is like a symbol—it remains the same through constant reinterpretation in history; *Gilgamesh* teaches us that a city is more immortal than its heroes. Explicitly symbolic cities, such as that of Plato 'laid up in heaven',[33] or Augustine's City of God interpreting John of Patmos's Heavenly Jerusalem, have long animated European

thinking and conditioned the paradigmatic value attached to certain earthly cities, notably Jerusalem, Athens and Rome, much later
challenged by the City Beautiful, the Garden City, the Radiant City,
etc. Indeed, John Cassian's use of Jerusalem to demonstrate the four
levels of Christian hermeneutics—historical (the actual city in the
Levant), allegorical (the community of Christians, or Ecclesia), tropo-
logical (morality of the soul) and anagogical (Heavenly Jerusalem, the
completion of meaning at the eschaton)[34]—is evidently a particularly
Christian version of how anyone would move from everyday practical
life to profound reflection. The motif of a stratified understanding
itself was first mooted in Plato's rendering of the potential participation of the soul in the Highest Good in his *Politeia*, or *Republic*[35]—
that is, within the context of urban life. The Baroque city commended
itself to Vesely as the end of the ancient tradition of the symbolic
city, before the rupture of the Enlightenment and the persistent claim
upon Modernist imaginations of possible revolutions.[36]

A rethinking of current conditions from the bottom up is itself
characteristic Enlightenment procedure; and Baroque as metaphor
for an ethico-poetic orientation calls for a more radically profound
interpretation than, for example, reviving Classical details or striving to restore ancient gods or cults. A living tradition is a vehicle
for reinterpretation of primary collective themes in history, whereas
a dead tradition has been made into arbitrary dogmatic rules that
could be enforced (by which standard the creative theology and theatre of the Counter Reformation are compromised by the Index and
Inquisition). Reinterpretation of a tradition is necessarily collective,
collaborative and indebted to the given conditions; but Vesely's concern is that the hermeneutics appropriate to the inevitable conflicts
respect the universality of our existence in common. In this light,
it merits observing that Vesely's European emphasis in his examples and characterising of a tradition are less indicative of a putative
Eurocentrism than it is of needing to understand the nature of cultural depth and richness. Most important is orientation with respect
to the fundamental conditions, common-to-all; and in this respect
traditional cultures have more in common with each other than any
of them do with post-Enlightenment capitalism, individual freedom,
experimental science and technology.[37] The task, therefore, is less a
Nietzschean overcoming or another revolution than it is one of reconciling the virtues of the two cultural conditions.

The task is made difficult by the great scale, dispersion and overall
evenness of many contemporary urban topographies. Most of these

are very new, and the sprawl might eventually develop clusters of intensity, as has happened in Los Angeles and Tokyo. However, the tendency to regard cities like systems that might be managed digitally (so-called 'smart cities') stands in opposition to Philo of Alexandria's exhortation to contemplate 'the greatest of cities, namely, this world [cosmos]' as a preliminary apprehension of the divine (transcendent conditions of human freedom).[38] Against the belief that the field of fragments is precisely what is most appropriate to current conditions, phenomena such as the climate crisis remind us of our obligation to a larger whole, the common ground against which all relativisms are measured.

Vesely arrived in England with a living experience in Prague of both continuity[39] and discontinuity between the traditional and post-Enlightenment city. Although he well understood what historians divide into periods—Medieval, Mannerist, Baroque, Modern, etc.—of greater interest to him was the historical reinterpretation of what remained essentially the same. What remained the same were characteristic situations of conflict, negotiation, accommodation and collaboration as well as face-to-face discourse, loving, hating and so forth; and Vesely became the leading proponent of the understanding of architecture as the setting for situations.[40] The term 'situation' had arisen in phenomenology, in particular the work of Merleau-Ponty, where it connoted activities with their decorum and their fields of reference, which Vesely developed as 'typicality of situations'.[41] Situational typicality, for Vesely, was rooted in custom and habit in dialogue with cultural contexts—the resonances with music, literature, the visual arts, etc., through recurring activities like discussing, judging, farming, fighting, governing, worship. The narratives of these situations could be traced back to the compact representation of myth, where they held an orienting value for a people, what Vesely termed 'paradigmatic'. Narrative (*mythos*), in turn, was the principal constituent of tragic drama, according to Aristotle, whose rendering of the dramatic situation as the *mimesis* [interpretation, or hermeneutics] of *praxis* attracts the theatric implications of the term 'setting'.[42] Accordingly, the design of a building did not depend upon adapting form to behaviour, as it did in functionalism, but was already implicated in the life of the culture.[43] Similarly, the depth of a configuration from street to garden and from earth to sky invoked venerable themes. The architecture was not supporting an iconography, rather the references were embodied in the architectural dispositions of situations; and, in these terms, the city may be regarded as an extended topography of embodiment for possible cultures.

This conformed to Heidegger's strife of earth and world (embodying conditions and cultural possibilities), a formulation with a long history reaching back through Enlightenment matter-mind or matter-spirit controversies (arising from more ancient body-soul, sensible-intelligible speculations) to the Incarnational symbolism of Aquinas and John of Damascus to the Aristotelian *physis* (nature) and *nomos* (custom, norms).[44] For the visual arts of the Baroque period this reciprocity had established itself in terms of the Mannerist *concetto* (both conceit and concept),[45] the synthesis of image (perspective) and word (rhetoric), which allowed the visual topography to communicate with texts culled from the corpus of Classical and Christian literature. Vesely's interpretation of the abbey church at Zwiefalten (1739–47, frescoes completed 1753) takes account of this interpretative protocol in order to demonstrate, through the structuring of material metaphor and allegory, the movement from the body of the building through its rocaille ornament to the themes of the frescoes, as a leading example of what he terms 'rhetorical' or 'communicative' space.[46] He also describes this as a movement from sensible to intelligible, from embodiment (earth) to articulation (world). Although, in this case, the frescoes orient the movement, it is evident that a setting has been created which resonates with the time-out-of-time[47] of the rites and ceremonies—and their movements, liturgy, oration, music,[48] etc.—and in turn with the seasonal cycles and their associated activities (in which practical life such as planting and harvesting is co-ordinated with religious festivals). Both the richness and coherence depend upon the parallel, mutually-reinforcing rhythms of embodiments;[49] and the thematic continuity across the several levels and temporalities of embodiment will be named 'ontological movement' in Vesely's later writings.

Such a rhythmic order could be adduced for traditional Islamic architecture,[50] for example, although, as we've said, Vesely remained within the European context with whose languages and cultures he was familiar. However, the question is raised regarding the necessity of Christian theology to the coherence and depth of 'Baroque' in its ethico-poetic sense in addition to its historical manifestation (where, for example, Descartes, Kepler, Leibniz and Newton all needed the Christian God to complete their metaphysical speculations). Certainly, it is characteristic of traditional cultures to accord divinity to the highest meanings, even if the continuity and 'universality of the shared world' has yielded a plurality of gods. The Baroque reforms strive to preserve the great stratification of Being inherited from the Medieval theologians, because, without that, one's poetics are restricted to experiences of the sublime or to endowing quotidian fragments with an aesthetic sanctity.[51] However, the communication between philosophy, theology and poetics is ancient, having a common basis in fundamental, persistent human questions of orientation and meaning; and it is these which provide Vesely with the basis for regaining continuity with European traditions. Gadamer remarks that 'meanings [...] are like a space in which things are related to one another'.[52] There are particular complexities to the European history of this transaction between philosophy, theology and poetics such as the role of Greek philosophical terms in Christian theology (translated into Latin in the Western Church), or the largely Lutheran background to German philosophy from Leibniz to Gadamer, or the role of embodying conditions with respect to formulations in language. However, Vesely's focus on the hermeneutics of *praxis* addresses the conditions from which any particular philosophy or theology or poetics might arise, and he could value the echoes of myth in certain works of Surrealism, for example.[53] This commitment to what is common to all is also the ethical basis of Vesely's concerns, although the transcendence of Being[54] arises within the nature of spatiality itself.

Spatiality depends upon our modes of involvement in the embodying conditions; and, whilst Heidegger's development of the worldhood of world[55] displaced this involvement from subject-oriented perspectivity, the most profound understanding of this phenomenon was that of Maurice Merleau-Ponty. Building on the work of figures such as Kurt Goldstein and Erwin Strauss, Merleau-Ponty's leading motif was 'perception'; and, inspired by Edmund Husserl, he sought to demonstrate that perception was not an intellectual processing of subject-object relations, but rather modes of participation in the world. He regularly found that patients suffering from aphasia or apraxia, etc., were not experiencing defects in psycho-physical systems; rather they did not 'have' a complete world.[56] This places the emphasis upon content or meaning—the Husserlian 'all experience [perception] is experience of something'[57]—for which one's culturally situated body is the medium.[58] The question of content considered in terms of perception immediately raises the question of hallucination, from which, according to Merleau-Ponty, we are saved not by our 'critical powers' but by the 'structure of our space'.[59]

Architects typically hear the design of a room in these words, but Merleau-Ponty is actually discussing the depth, richness and structure of our involvement with cultural themes which Vesely developed as 'communicative space'.[60] This led Merleau-Ponty to declare that one 'never wholly lives in varieties of human space, but is always ultimately rooted in a natural and non-human space'[61] (which Vesely would also call the cosmic conditions'). Spatiality, then, for Merleau-Ponty is a characteristic of the world, identifying the kinds of remoteness exhibited in the structure of references, ultimately rooted in the natural, non-human world, which grants objectivity, and which Vesely, inspired by Jan Patočka, treated under the rubric of 'latent world'.[62] The term 'latent' speaks of the embodying conditions for possible articulation; and these conditions are always already articulated as the deep history of customs and behaviours, their settings and the meanings associated with typical situations, originally disclosed in cosmological myth.[63]

The spatiality underlying the transcendence of Being has both an extensive, ontic dimension—manifest in the topography of embodying claims and affordances, from objects ready-to-hand to furniture to architecture to urban or rural context—and an intensive, ontological dimension—manifest in the movement or communication between embodiment and articulation (bearing echoes of movement between chthonic and celestial). Both the ontic and ontological dimensions of spatiality—the latent world—have their source in the fundamental natural conditions; and both involve movement in the comprehension of their intervals or relations, whereby traversing temporal distance is experienced as content rather than as simple duration (the hour of one's wedding is not the same as an hour asleep, or an hour in the life of a mayfly, grapevine or brick). Again inspired by Patočka,[64] Vesely spoke of 'ontological movement' as the nature of an order in which we participate.[65] Central to this, and important to place alongside modernity's fascination with change and progress, are the recurring temporalities of rite, ceremony, drama, festival, whereby general orientation is recovered through reinterpretation of original conditions (exemplary manifestations of 'mimesis of praxis').

The perspectival theatre, which has been so influential upon our intuitions of spatiality, seeks to capture this festival or ceremonial temporality with everyone and everything arranged for ideal communication to a viewer. In *Divided Representation*, Vesely vividly describes perspective representation from the late fourteenth century discovery of dramatic situations informed by Medieval light metaphysics, culminating the following century in those of Nicholas

Cusanus,[66] and its subsequent descent into a succession of construction routines from painting to architecture, eventually formalised into systematic routines such as that of J.N.L. Durand.[67] Stimulated in part by developments in physics,[68] such procedures left architects with a 'space' that presented itself as an infinite plenum in which psychological effects could be achieved through geometric manipulation of signifying forms. The results aspired to be a species of inhabited sculpture, appreciated visually; and the 4-screens of our CAD software preserve the coordination of plan, section/elevation, perspective argued by Raphael and Castiglione in their famous letter to Pope Leo X in the sixteenth century.[69]

The general predominance of sight in our understanding the relation of Being to 'space' dates back at least to Plato, where its association with light, intellection and with proportional harmony (*analogia*)[70] remained a compelling symbol for centuries; but, particularly under the influence of Neoplatonism, it could degenerate from a symbol to an instrumental concept, bestowing inordinate value upon compositional geometries, for example.[71] In this respect, Vesely's emphasis in his essays upon the modalities of *praxis* in terms of the Husserlian 'earth which does not move'[72] suggests a fundamentally new relation of Being to spatiality that is more concrete, that builds up from the communication within multiple kinds and levels of embodiment rather than downwards from concepts or intellection, and that is therefore more redolent of the character of Being itself.

On this reading we should regard Zwiefalten, for example, less as elaborate display of a top-down argument regarding Marian orthodoxy and more as a visually intense, intelligent and carefully worked-out result of the collaboration of praxes involved in its creation and use. This collaboration begins as embodied tradition, in the settlements, fields and workshops before it enters the arena of design and construction of the church, which involves successful communication between theologians, architects, masons and carpenters, stucco-masters (both stucco-lustro and moulding ornament), sculptors, fresco-artists and then celebrants, musicians, composers, etc.[73] The sympathy one detects between Baroque architecture and Baroque music shares the ontological movement from popular dance figures to complex polyphony, where the *basso continuo* establishes the basic cosmological harmonics (equivalent to the architectural plan) and the melody or *aria* represents the vulnerability of human finitude (equivalent to the ornament and frescoes). The *Psalmodia Christiana* (1665) of Hector Mithobius declared that 'God cannot be praised artificially enough',[74] indicating the glimpse of transcendence inherent in the medium itself. This sort of continuity from local agricultural rhythms through celebration to theological interpretations of infinity—orientation in reality or situatedness, properly speaking—is apparently not possible in the current cultural conditions (although we recognise it when we see it);[75] but having once been possible, it evidently lies dormant within our latent world.

Looking for 'Baroque' poetics in Vesely's design-studio teaching[76] for the contemporary culture of referential fragments, we find the theatrics of transcendence are less important than the basic conditions for 'creativity', as he called it in the title of his book. Creative attunement to the latent world embodied in urban configurations gives rise to intimations of the transcendence inherent in metaphoric spatiality. Vesely would set projects in European cities exploring the possibilities of communication across disciplines or fields of endeavour typically regarded as distinct in contemporary culture (divided representation), notably between the sciences and the humanities. Taking advantage of the existing institutional structure of *praxis*, groups normally in conflict or simply distant from each other—for example, medical ethics and an animation studio—would be set within an urban block structure offering the potential for discovering common ground in, typically, political rooms and performance spaces addressing a shared interior garden. In his essay included here on ecology, Vesely argues the case for a common language or means of representation between the sciences and the humanities, which would provide a basis for reconciling so-called 'value-free' experimental science with ethics.[77] In this we find an echo of Tesauro's centrality of metaphor to Baroque culture; and indeed, the images of critical settings for these projects cultivate a material metaphoricity ultimately rooted in the shared gardens. Eschewing both the benign, everything-works-summer-evening ethos that is characteristic of many professional renderings, on the one hand, and, on the other, the sentimental piety others derive from their reading of Heidegger, the images sought inspiration in the darkness, wit and collage techniques of contemporary Czech Surrealism. This orientation to chthonic metamorphosis—to earth—acknowledges the one world of which we are all part; and the embodying conditions generally hold the memory of what is always already there. However, the current cultural context prevents the sort of full articulation of our place in transcendence that Vesely finds in Baroque culture, where, for example, libraries and churches could share fundamental similarities. We can assemble the fragments of continuity with traditions,[78] as the basis for reinterpretation and a possible renewal, a possibility for which architecture can provide the conditions.

Notes on the essays

The essays published here represent roughly a quarter of the surviving texts of Vesely's research, though many of these are fragments or incomplete. Our main criteria for inclusion in the present volume were completeness and a desire to provide an overview of Vesely's contributions to architectural, historical and philosophical understanding. Our editing focused on two areas. The availability of different drafts in Vesely's archive gave us the opportunity to revisit all essays, including those previously published, to make often small and occasionally larger emendations, which, we believe, further illuminate the texts. Additionally, we retraced the majority of references correcting, completing and clarifying them. Vesely drew from a remarkable breadth of material, and we sometimes required the assistance of colleagues mentioned in the Acknowledgements; any remaining errors or omissions are entirely our own responsibility. Vesely was in the habit of re-using passages, occasionally lengthy with minor word changes, in different contexts, re-qualifying their significance or developing a wider frame of reference. He did this on the authority of Gadamer, who remarked to Vesely that it was fine to repeat oneself because readers might not always grasp the full meaning on the first reading; and we have let these passages stand. Where possible, we have followed Vesely's indications for illustrations, sometimes having to interpolate from lecture slides or image collections, which were generally much larger than the present publication could accommodate. We eschewed providing abstracts of each essay, since Vesely's prose is so clear and vivid on its own; we felt it best to allow Vesely's voice to speak for itself.

Chapter 1, 'Architecture and the Limits of Modern Theory', was originally published in *Architektur weiterdenken: Werner Oechslin zum 60.Geburtstag*, ed. Sylvia Claus et al., Zurich: Gta Verlag, 2004; it is currently out of print.

Chapter 2, 'Architecture and the Question of Technology', was originally published in *Architecture, Ethics and Technology*, ed.

Louise Pelletier et al., Montreal: Carleton University Press, 1994. The book is out of print and the publishers no longer exist.

Chapter 3, 'The Architectonics of Embodiment', was originally published in *Body and Building: Essays on the changing relation of body and architecture*, ed. George Dodds et al., Cambridge, MA: MIT Press, 2002; it is currently out of print.

Chapter 4, 'The Relation of Religion and Science', is an unpublished essay from 2013. Between 1995 and 2006, Vesely participated in the symposia organised by Religion, Science and Environment, a non-governmental organisation created in 1993, which seeks to provide common ground among the worlds of religion, science and the environment in the interest of protecting the environment. At the 1999 symposium on the Danube, Vesely presented a paper, 'The Role of the Danube in the Formation of Europe' (unpublished). The present chapter was written, or re-written, some years after the 2006 Symposium on the Amazon. For further information on the RSE, see http://www.rsesymposia.org/more.php?catid=29.

Chapter 5, 'Architecture and Ethics in the Age of Fragmentation', is an unpublished essay from 2013. It returns to the theme of the fragment, which Vesely explored in various other texts, combining aspects of those texts with original material. We judged this combination to be the most illuminating and appropriate for inclusion in this volume.

Chapter 6, 'The Hermeneutics of the Latent World of Architecture', 2009, is an unpublished text for a keynote lecture presented at the Second Architecture and Phenomenology International Conference, Kyoto Seika University, Japan 26–29 June 2009. The Appendix to the text published here comprises the concluding passages from the text of a lecture titled 'The Natural World - the Latent Ground of Architecture', delivered at De Montfort University, Leicester, in 2011, the beginning of which repeats material from the Kyoto Lecture.

Chapter 7, 'Architecture as a Humanistic Discipline', was originally published in *The Humanities in Architectural Design: A Contemporary and Historical Perspective*, ed. Soumyen Bandyopadhyay et al., London: Routledge, 2010.

Chapter 8, 'Elements of Architecture and their Meaning', was originally published in *Column, Vase, Obelisk*, ed. Thomas Vlček, Prague: Národní galerie, Kontinuum Library, 2005, pp. 23–57. The essay was also published in a Czech version of this edition, entitled *Sloup, váza, obelisk*; both are currently out of print.

Chapter 9, 'Mathesis Universalis in the Jesuit tradition', was originally published in *Bohemia Jesuitica 1556–2006* vol. 2, ed. Petronilla Cemus et al., Prague: Univerzita Karlova V Praze Nakladatelstvi Karolinum, 2010, pp. 701–15.

Chapter 10, 'Surrealism and the Latent world of Creativity', was originally published in *Umeni/Art: Journal of the Institute of Art History Academy of Sciences of the Czech Republic*, no. 3–4, 2011; Vesely stated in that publication that the text was an expanded and revised version of 'The Surrealist House as a Labyrinth and Metaphor of Creativity', in *The Surreal House: Architecture of Desire*, ed. Jane Alison, New Haven, CT: Yale University Press, 2010, pp. 34–41.

Chapter 11, 'Czech New Architecture and Cubism', was originally published in *Umeni/Art: Journal of the Institute of Art History Academy of Sciences of the Czech Republic*, no. 6, 2005, pp. 586–604.

Chapter 12, 'Spatiality, Simulation and the Limits of the Technological Imagination' is a revised and expanded version of 'Space, Simulation and Disembodiment in Contemporary Architecture', published in *OASE*, no. 58, 2002.

Chapter 13, 'Between Architecture and the City', is Vesely's last publication, in *Phenomenologies of the City: Studies in the History and Philosophy of Architecture*, ed. Henrietta Steiner and Max Sternberg, London: Routledge, 2015, pp. 151–65.

Notes

1 Evident in the surviving manuscript fragments. Vesely's PhD dissertation was devoted to Jan Santini Aichel (1667–1723), whose fusion of Gothic and Classical motifs was quite different from that of his contemporaries in Protestant England, Christopher Wren and Nicholas Hawksmoor. However, the scope of Vesely's research ranged from Archaic Greece to the present, as is evident in his book, *Architecture in the Age of Divided Representation: The Question of Creativity in the Shadow of Production* (Cambridge, MA: MIT Press, 2004), where the principal treatment of Baroque culture appeared in Chapter 4, 'The Age of Divided Representation'. He maintained a deep interest in Baroque architecture and culture, supervising several dissertations in this area as well as carrying on a lively discussion with colleagues (notably Karsten Harries) and he also contributed regularly to the annual seminars on the Baroque organised by Werner Oechslin, held in his library at Einsiedeln, Switzerland.

2 Vesely, *The Modernity of the Baroque*, unpublished manuscript fragment 14.6, 2014, p. 1.

3   Emil Kaufmann, *Von Ledoux bis Le Corbusier, Ursprung und Entwick-
    lung der autonomen Architektur*, Vienna: Passer, 1933. Vincent Scully
    makes a point of separating the Baroque from the Modern in *Modern
    Architecture*, New York: George Braziller, Inc., 1966, p. 11. Sigfried
    Giedion begins *Space, Time and Architecture, the Growth of a New Tra-
    dition* (Cambridge, MA: Harvard University Press, 5th Edition, 1966)
    with the Italian Renaissance ('Our Architectural Inheritance', pp. 29
    ff.). William J.R. Curtis begins with 'The Idea of Modern Architec-
    ture in the Nineteenth Century', in *Modern Architecture Since 1900*,
    London: Phaidon Press, 1996, pp. 21 ff, as, of course, had Nikolaus
    Pevsner before him, *Pioneers of Modern Design*, Harmondsworth: Pen-
    guin, 1960.
4   Pier Paolo Pasolini, *Salò o le 120 giornate di Sodoma*, 1975, which,
    in striving to include Modernist architecture within what Pasolini
    considered a pervasive bourgeois Fascism, is set in a Neoclassical villa
    furnished with works from, among others, Mackintosh, Leger, Sironi,
    Carrà, Gris, etc.
5   Now collected in Adolf Loos, *Ornament and Crime selected essays*,
    ed. and intro Adolf Opel, trans. Michael Mitchell, Riverside: Ariadne
    Press, 1998, pp. 167–76; but see the complicated publication history in
    footnote 1 of Jimena Canales and Andrew Herscher, 'Criminal skins:
    Tattoos and Modern Architecture in the work of Adolf Loos', *Archi-
    tectural History* 48, 2005, p. 251. Hanno-Walter Kruft traces this
    motive to Loos' time in Chicago in *A History of Architectural Theory*,
    New York: Zwemmer, 1994, p. 365. This said, Vesely was interested
    in the sequential nature of the *raumplan*; and David Leatherbarrow
    reminds us that Loos expressed appreciation of Fischer von Erlach and
    of Andreas Schlüter. See also Chapter 4, 'The Promise of Ornament'
    in Karsten Harries, *The Ethical Function of Architecture*, Cambridge,
    MA: MIT Press, 2000, pp. 50–68, where Harries moves from Loos to
    ornament's relation to style understood as 'belonging … to a commu-
    nity enduring through time' (p. 63).
6   As a generic descriptor, 'Baroque' could be applied to nineteenth
    century eclectic examples such as Charles Garnier's Opera in Paris
    (1875); see, for example, C.L.V. Meeks' effort to reclassify Wölff-
    lin's five categories of the Baroque under 'Picturesque Eclecticism',
    The Art Bulletin, 32, no. 3, September 1950, pp. 226–35. Carl J.
    Friedrich traces the origins of the term 'Baroque' as an aesthetic
    style to the generation of Winkelmann, but rightly notes its appear-
    ance in sixteenth-century scholastic texts as *barocco*, a particularly
    complex figure in formal logic in his *The Age of the Baroque*, New
    York: Harper Torchbooks, 1952, pp. 38–47. More recently, Rob-
    ert Hudson Vincent concurs, with examples: 'Barocco, The Logic
    of English Baroque Poetics', *Modern Language Quarterly*, 80, no. 3,
    September 2019, pp. 233–59, also mentioning the possible influ-
    ence of the Portuguese jeweller's term for an irregularly shaped pearl
    (p. 234). However, Vincent sides with Enlightenment critics who
    use the term to identify 'anything … that exhibits outlandish com-
    plexity or absurd confusion' (p. 255). This is inadequate to describe

a period that saw in architecture both Borromini and Perrault, in painting both Rubens and Poussin, in philosophy both Leibniz and Descartes, not to mention the conflicts and reciprocities between Roman Catholicism and Protestantism, or those between theology and the emerging experimental sciences; and the term 'divided representation' coined by Vesely seems most appropriate. For a good summary of the 'rehabilitation' of Baroque and Rococo in architecture, see Karsten Harries, *The Bavarian and Rococo Church*, New Haven, CT: Yale University Press, 1983, pp. 2–9.

7 Le Corbusier, *Towards a New Architecture*, trans. Frederick Etchells, London: The Architectural Press, 1927, p. 161: 'To send architectural students to Rome is to cripple them for life'. He includes in this category the facade of Guglielmo Calderini's Palazzo di Giustizia, completed in 1910.

8 Sigfried Giedion, *The Eternal Present: The Beginnings of Architecture*, Pantheon Books, New York: Bollingen, 1964.

9 The title of his famous essay published in *The Architectural Review*, May 1950, pp. 289–99, following prompts from Nicholas Pevsner (whose PhD was devoted to the Baroque architecture of Leipzig), 'Architecture of Mannerism', *Mint*, London, 1946, pp. 116–38, and Anthony Blunt, 'Mannerism in Architecture', RIBA lecture, 1949, in the context of the then developing literature on Mannerism. Rowe's use of sixteenth century architecture in his critiques of Modernist architecture was not as frequent as his advocacy of the nineteenth century city.

10 The course at the University of Essex ran from 1968 to 1978; Vesely then moved to the University of Cambridge, Rykwert joining him two years later, first as Slade Professor then as Reader in Architecture; and the Essex course was reconstituted as the graduate programme in the History and Philosophy of Architecture in 1983. Accounts of this teaching can be found in Jorge Otero-Pailos, *Architecture's Historical Turn Phenomenology and the Rise of the Postmodern*, Minneapolis, MN: University of Minnesota Press, 2010; and Joseph Bedford, *Creativity's Shadow: Dalibor Vesely, Phenomenology and Architectural Education (1968–1989)*, PhD. Dissertation, Princeton University, 2018. The rubric of 'history and philosophy' had two objectives. First, it was meant to indicate a methodological difference from the ubiquitous 'history and theory' courses, in which phenomenological hermeneutics was seen to offer more profound insights into the nature of architectural and urban phenomena, as well as into the continuity between historical and modern concerns. Second, the concrete details of architectural and urban history were taken as seriously as was the 'universality of the shared world', for the communication between which (effectively a dialogue between history and tradition), again, phenomenological hermeneutics offered the most substantial framework for interpretation.

11 Giulio Carlo Argan, 'Introduction' to *Roma interrotta*, Incontri internazionali d'Arte, Rome: Officina, 1978, pp. 11–13.

12 Robert Venturi, *Complexity and Contradiction in Architecture*, New York: The Museum of Modern Art Press, 1966; with Denise Scott Brown and Steven Izenour, *Learning from Las Vegas*, Cambridge, MA: MIT Press, 1972, where the semiotic argument is presented explicitly; see also Venturi and Scott Brown, *Architecture as Signs and Systems: for a Mannerist Time*, Cambridge, MA: Harvard University Press, 2004.

13 Jane Jacobs, *The Death and Life of Great American Cities*, New York: Random House, 1961.

14 See Manfredo Tafuri, 'Introduction,' in *Theories and Histories of Architecture*, trans. Giorgio Verrecchia, St. Albans: Granada Publishing Limited, 1976, pp. 1–9. The disorientation he feels with respect to the methodology of interpreting contemporary architecture is absent from his subtle readings of Italian Renaissance Rome.

15 See Vesely, Chapter 1 in this volume.

16 Following the precepts of Ciceronian rhetoric; on the subsequent vicissitudes of Vitruvian decorum, see Vesely, *Divided Representation*, op. cit., pp. 365 ff.

17 Vesely, *Divided Representation*, op. cit., p. 192, where perspectivity is seen to contribute to the development of both Cartesian and the 'absolute' space of Newtonian physics. Vitruvius was an exemplar of Hellenistic perspectivism with its origins in Ptolemaic Alexandria.

18 Against which Wilhelm Dilthey reacted; see Hans-Georg Gadamer, *Truth and Method*, trans. William Glen-Doepel, London: Sheed and Ward, 1975, Second Part, I.2, pp. 192–214.

19 On the vicissitudes of aesthetics, see ibid., First Part, I, pp. 5–90; note also in Vesely's essay, 'The Nature of the Modern Fragment and the Sense of Wholeness' (in *Fragments, Architecture and the Unfinished: Essays presented to Robin Middleton*, ed. Barry Bergdoll and Werner Oechslin, London: Thames and Hudson, 2006) the distinction he draws between poetics and aesthetics (p. 49), and his observation that the *Gesamtkunstwerk* is inappropriately applied to Baroque architecture because it is an aesthetic concept rather than ontologically situated poetics (p. 53).

20 Vesely, Chapter 3 in this volume.

21 Charles Jencks, *The Language of Post-Modern Architecture*, New York: Rizzoli, 1977; Jean-François Lyotard, *The Postmodern Condition*, trans. Geoffrey Bennington and Brian Massumi, Minneapolis, MN: University of Minnesota Press, 1984.

22 Generally marked by the 1988 Deconstructivist Exhibition at MOMA. One of themes that gained prominence at this time was the notion of 'autonomous architecture', which ranged in meaning between the adaptability of types (Aldo Rossi) to a conception of architecture as constituted in geometric transformations (Peter Eisenman). It bears remarking that Robin Evans, a graduate of the Essex course run by Rykwert and Vesely, rejected iconography and analogy in favour of what he termed a 'projective' order rooted in geometry, construction and perception in his book *The Projective Cast: Architecture and its Three Geometries*, Cambridge, MA: MIT Press, 1995. This conception of a projective order therefore partially overlaps, but also significantly differs from, the projective order Vesely was developing in his study

of Baroque architecture, which emphasised the analogical possibilities and the communication with, for example, theology. See the treatment of this phenomenon in José de Paiva, *Fragments towards a Theology of Architecture*, London: Hinterland, 2015, particularly Chapter 6.

23 This, for example, was his concern with Gilles Deleuze, *The Fold, Leibniz and the Baroque*, trans. Tom Conley, Minneapolis, MN: University of Minnesota Press, 1993.

24 Vesely, Chapter 3 in this volume.

25 Vesely, *Divided Representation*, op. cit., p. 212: 'I am thinking not about stylistic or formal correspondences, but rather of the intrinsic structure of space and its specific role in the articulation of intelligible (divine) reality'.

26 This is the central drama of *Divided Representation*; in several respects it takes its point of departure from Edmund Husserl, *The Crisis of European Sciences and Transcendental Phenomenology*, trans. David Carr, Evanston, IL: Northwestern Press, 1970. Symptoms of the more general problem include the breakdown of the ontological structure of analogy (*Divided Representation*, op. cit., p. 180 and note 15, p. 427), as well as the gradual supplanting of symbolic infinity, associated with divinity, by actual infinity, as developed by the mathematicians (ibid., pp. 207–14). He accounts for the Heideggerian 'forgetfulness of Being' as the replacement of implicitly articulated levels of reality by explicit representation (ibid., p. 189).

27 On the collaboration between the arts and sciences in the period, an effort largely coming from the artists, humanists and theologians (although certainly not absent from the speculation of Kepler or Newton), see Vesely on Emanuele Tesauro's *Il Cannochiale Aristotelico* (*The Aristotelian Telescope*, 1670), a comprehensive treatment of metaphor, in particular the 'continuous metaphor,' *Divided Representation*, op. cit., pp. 222–6, and Jon R. Snyder, 'Art and Truth in Baroque Italy, or the Case of Emanuele Tesauro's *Il cannochiale aristotelico*', *Moden Language Notes*, 131, no. 1, January 2016, pp. 74–96. Because of the centrality of perspective to Baroque representation, the new optical instruments, such as the telescope and microscope, attracted significant interest from figures like Gottfried Wilhelm Leibniz (e.g., Svetlana Alpers, *The Art of Describing: Dutch Art in the Seventeenth Century*, Chicago, IL: University of Chicago Press, 1984). For the largely Jesuit efforts to preserve the symbolism of geometry in the face of the purely instrumental mathematics of Descartes, see José de Paiva, *Fragments*, op. cit. For the phenomenon in literature, see Robert Hudson Vincent, 'Baroque Optics and Luis de Góngora's Polifemo', *Moden Language Notes*, 133, no. 2, March 2018, pp. 224–41. Vesely declares Leibniz 'a Baroque thinker par excellence' (*Divided Representation*, op. cit., p. 176) for his intelligent mediation of mathematics, physics and theology, similar to Guarini (ibid., pp. 194 ff.), a motive that spread beyond German speaking lands after Schelling's *Naturphilosophie* (Iain Hamilton Grant, *Philosophies of Nature After Schelling*, London: Continuum, 2006; John Tresch, *The Romantic Machine*, Chicago, IL: Chicago University Press, 2012).

28 Vesely, *Modernity*, op. cit., p. 18.
29 Vesely, *Divided Representation*, op. cit., Chapter 8.
30 See, in Jan Vladislav, ed., *Václav Havel or Living in Truth*, London, Faber and Faber, 1987, the two essays by Havel, 'The Power of the Powerless' (dedicated to Jan Patočka, trans. Paul Wilson) and 'Six asides about culture' (trans. Erazim Kohák), pp. 36–135. On Vesely's reading lists was also Richard Sennet, *The Uses of Disorder*, New York: Alfred A. Knopf, 1971.
31 Aristotle, '… poetry is something more philosophical and serious than history, because poetry tends to give universal truths while history gives particular facts,' *The Poetics*, trans. W. Hamilton Fyfe, Loeb Classical Library, Cambridge, MA: Harvard University Press, 1927, 1451b3.
32 Vesely, Chapter 5 in this volume, and in *Divided Representation*, op. cit., pp. 82–83, 372–3. On *praxis*, see Gadamer, *Truth and Method*, op. cit., Second Part, II, pp. 235–341, and the three essays on practice in Gadamer, *Reason in the Age of Science*, trans., Frederick G. Lawrence, Cambridge, MA: MIT Press, 1981, pp. 69–138. Also influential on Vesely's teaching in this area were Richard Sennet, *The Fall of Public Man*, New York, Alfred A. Knopf, 1977; and such works of Jürgen Habermas as *The Structural Transformation of the Public Sphere*, trans. Thomas Burger and Frederick G. Lawrence, Cambridge, MA: MIT Press, 1989, and *Knowledge and Human Interests*, trans. Jeremy Shapiro, London: Heinemann, 1972. Vesely shared Eric Voegelin's aversion to political aspirations for 'intramundane salvation' (e.g., utopia); for an introduction to this theme in Voegelin's extensive writings, see *Science, Politics and Gnosticism*, Chicago, IL: Regnery Gateway, Inc., 1968.
33 Plato, *Republic*, trans. Paul Shorey, Loeb Classical Library, Cambridge, MA: Harvard University Press, 1930, 592a-b. Colin Rowe and Fred Koetter ended their *Collage City* (Cambridge, MA: MIT Press, 1979) with this famous passage.
34 John Cassian (ca. 360–435), *Conlationes (Conferences)*, trans. Edgar C.S. Gibson, *A Select Library of Nicene and Post-Nicene Fathers of the Christian Church*, New York, 1894, Vol. 11, Conference 14, 'The First Conference of Abbot Nesteros, On Spiritual Knowledge', Chapter VIII, p. 222.
35 Plato, *Republic*, op. cit., 496b–511a (the Divided Line). Plato's stratification was subsequently systematised by Plotinus and the Neoplatonists, including Christian theologians such as St. Augustine and Dionysos Areopagita. For most of the Christian Middle Ages, Platonism was effectively Neoplatonism. Positively, the Medieval Neoplatonic stratification of reality (cf. Arthur O. Lovejoy, *The Great Chain of Being*, Cambridge, MA: Harvard University Press, 1936) preserved the dependence of higher-order articulations upon the lower-order, embodying conditions, an insight important to phenomenology. Negatively, Medieval theologians concentrated upon the apex of this hierarchy, creating the conditions for the priority of conceptual thought in later centuries. It appears Vesely wishes to restore the full scope of the

articulation between the open potential of the conditions and the universality of the shared world, since, without that, we are constrained to the relativistic, flattened poetics of everyday fragments.

36 Vesely, Appendix to Chapter 6 in this volume.

37 Of the four ontologies offered by Phillipe Descola—Animism, Totemism, Analogism, Naturalism—only the last takes a stance outside the fundamental natural conditions (*Beyond Nature and Culture*, trans. Janet Lloyd, Chicago, IL: University of Chicago Press, 2013, p. 304 and adjacent discussion). However, Descola is more accurate when referring to the largely Western distinction between nature and culture as enshrined in Hellenistic and then Enlightenment natural sciences and technology, than when discussing the Aristotelian inheritance (note 44, below), since for Aristotle *nomos* was an interpretation of *physis*.

38 Philo of Alexandria, *The Special Laws*, I.34–35, trans. Charles Duke Yonge, *The Complete Works of Philo of Alexandria*, Hastings: Delphi Classics, 2017, p. 1623.

39 'Continuity' is an important term for Vesely, carrying not only the sense of preservation of primary themes in conditions of historical change, but also, for example, continuity in architectural sequences (and see notes 35 and 78). Vesely was a member of a group called The Continualists in Prague, and the title of the first publication of works from his design-teaching (with Mohsen Mostafavi) was *Architecture and Continuity* (*Themes 1*, London: Architectural Association, 1982). This raises the question, 'continuity of what?'. In the first place would lie the typical situations enacted within the natural conditions. From within this reservoir of *praxes* and their narratives arise the collective phenomena usually designated by 'culture', marked by ethical obligations but also by histories of stability and conflict, within which play out rites, ceremonies, performances, along with attention to gestural and linguistic usage, metaphor and analogy, etc. If, roughly speaking, this provides the framework for understanding the transaction between the universality of the shared world, on the one hand, and individual difference and historical accident, on the other, Vesely's term 'creativity' pertains to a collective hermeneutics which would honestly and properly acknowledge this condition.

40 The centrality to Vesely's argument of the phenomenological situation is evident in the frequency of its appearance in the essays in this volume.

41 Vesely, *Divided Representation*, op. cit., pp. 77ff., 104, 377ff. This is the larger field on which depends the more narrow architectural conception of type, which is limited to characteristic layouts of architectural and urban configurations.

42 Vesely, *Divided Representation*, op. cit., pp. 366ff. The phrase 'mimesis of praxis' comes from Aristotle's *Poetics*, op. cit., 1451b9, *mimeitai de tas praxeis*, identifying the primary representational character of tragic drama.

43 Nor did a building depend upon 'circulation' for its order, as did functionalist designs, a trait inherited from the *marche* and axes of the

École des Beaux-Arts; similarly, Vesely decried the frontalities rooted in perspective, favouring the development of corners and sequences.

44 Martin Heidegger, 'The Origin of the Work of Art', in *Basic Writings*, ed., David Farrell Krell, London: Routledge, 1993 edition, pp. 139–212; Thomas Aquinas, *The Summa Theologiæ of St. Thomas Aquinas*, Third Part, Question 2 – 'The Mode of Union of the Word Incarnate', trans. Fathers of the English Dominican Province, Second and Revised Edition, 1920, https://www.newadvent.org/summa/4002.htm; John of Damascus, *On the Divine Images*, First Apology, 16, trans. David Anderson, Crestwood: St. Vladimir's Seminary Press, 1980, p. 23. Aristotle, *Nichomachean Ethics*, trans. Harris Rackham, Loeb Classical Library, Cambridge, MA: Harvard University Press, 1934, V.vii.1.

45 Erwin Panofsky, *Idea: A Concept in Art History*, trans., Joseph J. S. Peake, New York: Harper & Row, 1968, pp. 82 ff., from emblematics and the *impresa*, Robert Kline, *Form and Meaning*, trans. Madeline Jay and Leon Wieseltier, New York: Viking Press, 1979, pp. 3 ff. Tesauro put the principle succinctly: 'the figure forms the motto, and the motto forms the figure', cited in Snyder, op. cit., p. 80.

46 Vesely, *Divided Representation*, op. cit., pp. 214–26; see also below, note 60.

47 See, in Gadamer, *The Relevance of the Beautiful and other essays*, ed. Robert Bernasconi, trans. Nicholas Walker, Cambridge: Cambridge University Press, 1986, the essays, 'The Relevance of the Beautiful', pp. 1–53, 'The Festive Character of Theatre', pp. 57–65, and 'Aesthetic and Religious Experience', pp. 140–53. These essays develop material in Gadamer, *Truth and Method*, op. cit., First Part, II.1.b-d, pp. 99–119. See also the essays collected in Alessandro Falassi, *Time Out of Time*, Albuquerque NM: University of New Mexico Press, 1987. 'Time-out-of-time' refers to the recurring sameness of the rites, ceremonies, drama or musical or poetic performance, at the same time always renewed or reinterpreted in history, which institutes a live dialogue between history and the primordial conditions.

48 Indeed, for Baroque culture one cannot ignore the significance of dance movement, not only to musical genres (*gavotte, passacaglia*, etc.) but also to public ceremony and its decorum, and therefore to architectural orchestration of sequences, layout of gardens, etc.

49 Vesely Chapter 3 in this volume.

50 See Gulru Necipoglu, *The Topkapi Scroll: Geometry and Ornament in Islamic Architecture*, Santa Monica CA: The Getty Center for the History of Art and the Humanities, 1995; and in the multi-volume *Epistles of the Brethren of Purity*, Oxford: Oxford University Press, as follows: *On Arithmetic and Geometry*, ed. and trans. Nader El-Bizri, 2012, Epistle 2, on geometry, pp. 101 ff., and *On Composition and the Arts*, ed. and trans. Nader El-Bizri and Godefroid de Callataÿ, 2018.

51 For example, the distribution of symbolic artefacts like bowls, towels, lilies, etc., referring to Mary in the Burgundian domestic setting of the Annunciation scene of the Merode Altarpiece (ca. 1420, attributed to Robert Campin) can be seen to anticipate the semi-sacred

allusions in the still-life paintings by Pieter Claesz two centuries later and, from there, such works as Juan Gris' famous collage, *Le petit déjeuner* of 1914.

52 Gadamer, *Truth and Method*, op. cit., Third Part, 2.c, p. 392.

53 Vesely, 'Surrealism, Myth and Modernity', *Architectural Design*, nos. 2/3, 1978, pp. 87–95; and Chapter 10 in this volume.

54 Heidegger, in the 1947 'Letter on Humanism' asserts that 'Being is the *transcendens* pure and simple' (*Basic Writings*, op. cit., p. 240), referring explicitly to the Introduction to *Being and Time*, trans. John Macquarrie and Edward Robinson, Oxford: Blackwell, 1980, H 3.

55 In general, inspiration from Heidegger in both the studio work and graduate seminars was centred around his ontology of worldhood of world, in *Being and Time*, op. cit., H 63–H 113. See also Vesely's observations regarding the neglect of embodiment by Heidegger in Chapter 6 in this volume.

56 Maurice Merleau-Ponty, *Phenomenology of Perception*, trans. Colin Smith, London: Routledge & Kegan Paul, 1962.

57 Husserl required all three books of the *Ideas* to explicate this sentence. The primary conditions are established in *Ideas I*: within the world-horizon the (non-psychological) 'mental processes' of an eco-logical body (individual and collective), move between the natural atti-tude of experience/perception and eidetics, disclosing the two forms of objectivity that arise—actual objects in the former, the entities of mathematics and geometry in the latter (absolute ideality), with lan-guage, having characteristics of both, providing a medium of exchange between them (*Ideas Pertaining to a Pure Phenomenology and to a Phe-nomenological Philosophy, First Book*, trans. Fred Kersten, The Hague: Martinus Nijhoff Publishers, 1983). For present purposes, note Merleau-Ponty's use of *Ideas II*, regarding the importance to Hus-serlian phenomenology of the pre-reflective 'world before a thesis' and of the earth, in *Nature, Course Notes from the Collège de France*, compiled by Dominique Séglard, trans. Robert Vallier, Evanston, IL: Northwestern University Press, 2003, pp. 70–79.

58 There is a popular misconception regarding experience and its relation to phenomenology, whereby one hears 'phenomenological' applied to personal experience, usually involving an element of tactility, thereby preserving the subject-object stance which phenomenology was designed to replace. The emphasis in phenomenology is upon the claim of the contexts—physical, linguistic, cultural—upon individ-ual freedom (human finitude), apprehended spontaneously in experi-ence, invoking the pre-reflective 'world before a thesis' (see note 57). Being-experienced implies openness to what Gadamer calls 'negative experience', that is, adjusting one's fore-understanding or prejudices, learning: 'The concept of experience is the epistemological basis for all knowledge of the objective'. See Gadamer, *Truth and Method*, op. cit., First Part.I.2.b.ii-iii, pp. 55–63 and Second Part.II.3.b, pp. 310–25. To this should be added Michael Polanyi, *The Tacit Dimension*, Chicago, IL: Chicago University Press, 1966.

59 Merleau-Ponty, op. cit., p. 291

60 Vesely, *Divided Representation*, op. cit., Chapter 2 in addition to note 46, above.
61 Merleau-Ponty, op. cit., pp. 291–3; see also Vesely, *Divided Representation*, op. cit., pp. 76ff.
62 Before leaving Prague for England, Vesely studied with Patočka. See Jan Patočka, *Body, Community, Language, World*, trans. Erazim Kohák, Chicago, IL: Open Court, 1998, pp. 113–8 & 122–34; and *The Natural World as a Philosophical Problem*, trans. Erika Abrams, Evanston, IL: Northwestern University Press, 2016, Chapter 3.
63 André Breton: 'We emphatically disagree with the view that it is possible to create a work of art or even, for that matter, do anything at all worthwhile by striving to express only the *manifest content* of a period. What surrealism sets out to do, by contrast, is to express its *latent content*.' 'Nonnational Boundaries of Surrealism', in *Free Rein*, trans., Michel Parmentier and Jacqueline D'Amboise, Lincoln, NB: University of Nebraska Press, 1995, p. 13, emphasis original.
64 Patočka, *Body, Community, Language, World*, op. cit., the Seventeenth and Eighteenth Lectures, pp. 143–61.
65 in Vesely, *Divided Representation*, op. cit., ontological movement is called 'communicative movement', pp. 70, 90–91, 345.
66 Ibid., Chapter 3.
67 Ibid., Chapter 5; see also Alberto Pérez-Gómez, *Architecture and the Crisis of Modern Science*, Cambridge, MA: MIT Press, 1983.
68 As per Max Jammer, *Concepts of Space: The History of Theories of Space in Physics*, Cambridge, MA: Harvard University Press, 1957.
69 See 'The Letter to Leo X by Raphael and Baldassare Castiglione, ca.1519,' in Vaughan Hart and Peter Hicks, *Palladio's Rome: A Translation of Andrea Palladio's Two Guidebooks to Rome*, New Haven, CT: Yale University Press, 2006, pp. 179–92. It is possible that Vesely's scepticism regarding the poetic potential of digital representation (see Chapter 12 in this volume) may be met by animated rendering software, which suppresses the orthogonal projections in favour of narrative disclosure of topographies (beyond glorified fly-throughs). For the most part, our involvement with architecture takes place in peripheral vision, a principle observed in literature, painting, cinema, drama, where emphasis is upon the situations.
70 Plato, *The Republic*, op. cit., 507c–509d; Merleau-Ponty, op. cit., p. 127: 'the symbolic function rests on the visual as on a ground; not that vision is its cause, but because it is that gift of nature which Mind was called upon to make use of beyond all hope, to which it was to give a fundamentally new meaning, yet which was needed, not only to be incarnate, but in order to be at all.'
71 See note 35, above; and the remarkable influence of Rudolf Wittkower's *Architectural Principles in the Age of Humanism* (New York: Random House, 1962), upon mid-century architects (see Henry Millon, 'Rudolf Wittkower, "Architectural Principles in the Age of Humanism": Its Influence on the Development and Interpretation of Modern Architecture', *Journal of the Society of Architectural Historians*, 31, no. 2, May 1972, pp. 83–91) was well-prepared by a

century of ambiguously plausible speculation on geometric ordering in design, archaeology and art history. The geometric algorithms remain the 'rational' moment in contemporary digital design which often seeks to appear to be the opposite.

72 Vesely, Chapter 6, this volume.
73 For an illuminating discussion of how one might think this sort of process in contemporary terms, and against the received vision of a conflict between nature and culture through the investment in technology, see David Leatherbarrow, *Uncommon Ground: Architecture, Technology and Topography*, Cambridge, MA, MIT Press, 2000.
74 Manfred F. Bukofzer, *Music in the Baroque Era*, London: J. M. Dent & Sons Ltd., 1947, pp. 410–11. See, in general, chapters 10–12 of Bukofzer's book.
75 This impossibility has at least three obvious sources. The gap between the humanities and the sciences is probably not as severe as that between the humanities and technology, whose centrality to economic and military desiderata and to nationalistic pride make its criteria of efficiency relatively invulnerable to scruples arising from the comparatively fractious humanities. Second, democratic societies rightly abhor the totalitarian regimes with which the recent large-scale experiments in reconciling tradition with modernity are associated, even if Mussolini's project to synthesise Marinetti futurism with *Mediterranietà* endorsed planning that was probably less destructive of the urban order underlying civic life than was C.I.A.M. urbanism, suggesting a distinction to be drawn between political regimes and urban topography. Thirdly, democratic societies place great value on both religious and artistic freedom, with originality holding a primary value in the latter; and this creates a centrifugal tension with whatever might be held in common.
76 Vesely taught graduate design studios for ten years at the Architectural Association, London, and then for thirty years at the University of Cambridge. See Chapter 13 in this volume.
77 Vesely, Chapter 4 in this volume.
78 On Vesely's notion of the 'positive fragment', see Chapter 5 in this volume, and *Divided Representation*, op. cit., Chapter 7, building on Tesauro's *agutezza* and metaphor's capacity 'to discover similarities between ideas, concepts, images, and meaningful gestures' (ibid., p. 225); see also his 'The Nature of the Modern Fragment and the Sense of Wholeness', op. cit., pp. 43–56.

1 Architecture and the Limits of Modern Theory

It would be interesting to know how many different meanings are associated today with the term 'theory'. In the more focused arguments, the term is used mostly in reference to theoretical knowledge. However, in a more spontaneous use, theory is used very loosely as a synonym for anything not practical, or any kind of reflective experience and a priori knowledge in general, including the knowledge of architecture.

The relationship between architecture and knowledge has a long history, which can be traced to its first explicit manifestation in the Greek notion of *techne*. As a knowledge, which can be described in modern terms as a 'know-how' of making (*poiesis*), *techne* was in the past closely linked not only with *poiesis* but also with the notion of creative interpretation (*mimesis*). In Classical thinking, *mimesis* was seen as a particular form of *poiesis* and the work of art, including architecture, as *mimesis* of *praxis*.[1]

It is true that we do not, as a rule, think about architecture as being a mimetic art. This has much to do with the well-established tradition in which architectural *mimesis* was reduced to the imitation of reified precedents, such as the primitive hut, the Solomonic temple, exemplary principles and buildings, etc., or to generalised notions such as the 'imitation of nature'. However, *mimesis* is not the same as imitation. As a form of creative interpretation, *mimesis* has much broader and deeper meaning related closely to the source of interpretation in the sphere of practical life (*praxis*).

The original meaning of *praxis* is living and acting in solidarity and in accordance with ethical principles. For a more specific understanding, it is better to see *praxis* as a situation where people are not only doing or experience something, but which also includes things that contribute to the fulfilment of human life.[2] Situations represent the

DOI: 10.4324/9781003272090-2

most complete way of understanding the condition of our experience of the surrounding world and the human qualities of the world. They also endow experience with durability, in relation to which other experiences can acquire meaning and can form memory and history. The temporal dimension makes the process of differentiation and stabilisation of situations more comprehensible. The deeper we move into history, the more situations share their common precedents until we reach the level of myth, which is their ultimate comprehensible foundation. Myth is the dimension of culture that opens the way to a unity of our experience and to the unity of our world. In its essence, myth is an interpretation of primary symbols which are spontaneously formed, and which preserve the memory of our first encounters with the cosmic condition of our existence. The mediated persistence of primary symbols, particularly in the field of architecture, contributes decisively to the formation of secondary symbols and finally to the formation of paradigmatic situations. The nature of paradigmatic situations is similar to the nature of institutions, deep structures or archetypes.

The presence of *praxis* (paradigmatic situations) in the depths of our culture has been overshadowed by the contemporary version of making, often reduced to technical innovation and aesthetic consideration, but this does not mean that the creative power of *praxis* is lost or dead. It is still alive in many areas of culture, including architecture, and most of all in the creative conditions and possibilities of practical life. The Classical notion of *praxis* belongs to the fundamental constitution of human beings and their situation in the world, and it is for this reason that it should not be confused with its modern equivalent, seen merely as an application of theoretical knowledge. *Praxis* does not depend exclusively on the abstract knowledge of norms but is always concretely, i.e., practically motivated: 'In every culture a series of things is taken for granted and lies fully beyond the explicit consciousness of anyone, and even in the greatest dissolution of traditional forms, mores and customs, the degree to which things held in common still determine everyone is only more concealed.'[3]

This is apparent to anyone taking seriously the creative possibilities of a design project, its programme or brief, which not only defines the content, but also anticipates the reception of the project. The close affinity between *praxis* and typical (paradigmatic) situations indicates that *praxis* always belongs to a world it articulates and thus brings about. Conversely, each human situation, even when it is more specifically or abstractly defined, is always practical. The practical nature of situations is revealed not only in the way people act, or in what they do in a particular setting, but also in the structure of the setting itself. We need to remember again that the practical situation is a place where people are not only doing or experiencing something, but that it also includes things that contribute to the fulfilment of human life. This includes everything associated with human activity, for instance, the table on which we take our daily meal, or the walls of a room that protect the intimacy of our conversation.

The spectrum of knowledge involved in any genuinely creative work includes not only inevitably a certain amount of theoretical rationalisation but also practical knowledge of skills, visual intelligence and deep experience of practical situations. It is difficult to see how such a rich and diverse spectrum of knowledge could be reduced to, and substituted by, one level of knowledge presented as theory. And yet this is exactly what has happened in modern times. Today we seem to have theories of almost anything, including a theory of architecture, judging by the ease with which the term is used in current publications, professional debates, and in the name of the research and academic departments. And yet, at the same time, we do not seem to have a plausible definition of architectural theory, to say nothing about agreement as to the content and meaning of the term.

It appears that one of the main sources of the current confusion is the unpredictable contamination (fusion) of the Classical theory (*theoria*) with the notion of theory borrowed from the modern natural sciences. The Classical *theoria* is an elevated vision of the essential, i.e., changeless and eternal, aspects of reality associated closely with the nature of the divine.[4] *Theoria* was not seen as independent and separated from the rest of knowledge, but always as rooted, not only in *praxis* but also in *techne*. This was clearly expressed in Aristotle's conclusion that *theoria* is the highest form of *praxis*.[5] The same is possible to say about any other kind of Classical or traditional knowledge, which even if it was not theoretical, was nevertheless pointing toward theory, but, and this is very important, preserving fully its specificity.

This is very well illustrated in our own field by the role of traditional theory in relation to the formation of architectural order. The primary principles of design and the resulting order originated very often in different areas of culture. It was quite common that not only the main principles but also a large part of the building programme originated in theology, philosophy, liberal arts, poetry and literature, theatre, painting, etc. (Fig. 1.1). With the exception of the theoretical sciences (physics, mathematics and metaphysics),[6] none of them were theoretical disciplines, and could therefore not be treated as theory.

1.1 Villard de Honnecourt, sketchbook, ca.1220–40. Diagrammatic figures.

What is common to all of them is not a common theory but a reference to a unifying framework, which, until as recently as the eighteenth century, was represented by cosmology. The reference to the
theoretical cosmological framework was always complemented by the
respect of the specificity of the non-theoretical disciplines. The nearest these disciplines came to theory was expressed in the well-known
statement *ars sine scientia nihil est*, where *ars*, the Latin version of

techne, is the knowledge of skills, while *scientia* represents in this case mathematical disciplines, mainly geometry (*scientia geometriae*).

Their relationship was described very clearly by James Ackerman in the conclusion to a long argument: 'The formulae of Gothic theory [*scientia*] establish generalities of form and structure as one, while the methods of Gothic "art" particularise them. The modern argument of form versus structure is as meaningless as the Medieval argument of *ars versus scientia*, for it likewise disrupts a partnership that can function only in happy union.'[7] In other words, the relationship of theory and practice is one of reciprocity or partnership, in which theory represents the universal context of practice, but does not exhaust or substitute its concreteness and richness.[8]

The traditional link between *praxis*, *techne* and *theoria* was challenged and disrupted during the seventeenth century, when a radically new form of theory was forged in the natural sciences, soon influencing the rest of culture. The main characteristic of modern theory is the constructed representation of reality, which follows very closely the mathematical form of reasoning.[9] In this kind of representation, reality is idealised and adapted to the means, possibilities and limits of representation, rather than presenting and revealing itself. The nature of modern theory can be well illustrated by two complementary examples. When Galileo speaks of the conditions of the free fall, he reaches the following conclusion: 'A more considerable disturbance arises from the impediment of the medium by reason of its multiple varieties. This is impossible to subject to firm rules, understood and made into science [theory]. No firm science can be given of such events as heaviness, speed, and shape, which are variable in infinitely many ways. Hence, to deal with such matters scientifically, it is necessary to abstract from them.'[10]

Modern theory was articulated in the relatively closed world of experimental dialogue. The imaginary nature of this dialogue and of the resulting world is well described by Descartes: 'For a short time, therefore, allow your thought to leave this world in order to come to see a wholly new one, which I shall cause to be born in the presence of your thought in imaginary spaces.'[11] Descartes also tells us what kind of science will be possible in such imaginary spaces: 'By science [theory] I understand skill at resolving all questions and in inventing by one's own industry everything in that science that can be invented by human ingenuity (*ars inveniendi*). Whoever has this science does not desire much else foreign to it, and indeed is quite properly called *autarches* - self-sufficient.'[12] (Fig. 1.2).

1.2 Sébastien Le Clerc, *The Academy of Sciences and Fine Arts*, 1698.

The constructed nature and self-sufficiency of theory make it an ideal vehicle for the conquest and control of reality, and in a sense, an 'unlimited power for calculating, planning and moulding of all things.'[13] Under the influence of modern theory, the creative possibilities of arts (*technai*) were transformed into a new kind of making based on the integration of *techne* and theory. As a result, the Classical *techne-poietike* was absorbed in the newly emerging *techne-theoretike*, the foundation of modern technology. The theoretical nature of modern technology reveals the radical discontinuity between the modern and traditional way of making. It distances itself from practical knowledge, spontaneous creativity and skill, in a process dominated by new goals, economy, efficiency, perfection of performance and, on a deeper level, by the acquisition of power and the desire to achieve the highest possible level of emancipation and autonomy. In that process, traditional theory as a vehicle of participation was transformed and reduced to productive knowledge and a vehicle of emancipation.

The new science as 'the theory of the real',[14] formed in the domain of natural science, became a model for the rest of culture. In our own field the new science allowed architecture to be treated as a discipline emancipated from the long tradition, its cosmology and metaphysics. Emancipated from the cosmic and metaphysical structure of the world, architecture became part of a historical development in which the cosmic paradigm of order was gradually replaced by a historical one. As a result, the vertical articulation of the world was subordinated to a horizontal articulation, in which the question of origins, speculation about the role of primitive precedents, historical styles and the possibility of utopia begin to dominate architectural thinking[15] (Fig. 1.3). Architecture became a discipline based on introverted experience, personal judgement and taste, and on anonymous constructions fulfilling only the most elementary or technically definable requirements.

The main characteristic of the new epoch is the growing reliance on theoretical knowledge. The traditional guilds and lodges were replaced by academies, and eventually by special centres of learning where architecture was taught together with other disciplines such as civil engineering, surveying, mechanics, etc.[16] The combination of theoretical knowledge and the new modes of representation that became possible owing to the development of technical drawings,

ÉLÉVATION DU CIMETIÈRE DE LA VILLE DE CHAUX.

1.3 Claude-Nicholas Ledoux, *L'architecture considérée sous le rapport de l'art*, 1804. Elevation of the cemetery of the town of Chaux.

new projective and descriptive geometries, transformed architecture into a highly formalised discipline.

   The historical understanding of architectural order reached a point when it seemed possible to see even history as a theoretical problem.[17] This is partly a fulfilment of the seventeenth century dream of representing the world as *mathesis universalis*, as a closed system, which is in no need of an explicit reference to the given natural or historical world.[18] Similar results were attained in the work of the so-called revolutionary architects, but especially in that of Jean-Nicholas-Louis Durand. It is generally accepted that Durand was the first to lay the foundation of an architectural order without direct reference to existing tradition, referring, instead to a state of architectural autonomy. If we study the pages of his *Recueil*, what unfolds before us is not a history of architecture, but a collection of systematically selected examples, organised into a comparative survey similar to the comparative studies and taxonomies of contemporary science[19] (Fig. 1.4). However, the set of images, drawn carefully to the same scale, were only a point of departure for the real task: the analysis of comparative material and the definition of principles and primary elements that would allow him to create a universal *mécanisme de la composition*. The process of design is discussed in Durand's

1.4 J.N.L. Durand, *Receuil et parallèle des édifices*, 1800. Frontispiece.

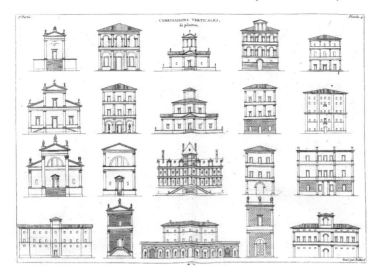

1.5 J.N.L. Durand, *Précis des leçons d'architecture*, 1802.
Vertical combinations of pilasters.

second and better-known treatise, the *Précis*[20] (Fig. 1.5). In the first
three sections he deals with architectural elements such as walls, columns, vaults, etc., with composition and with genres—public buildings, temples, triumphal arches, town halls, etc. The critical aspect of
the treatise is composition, which, like a grammar of a new language
is Durand's chief concern. He writes:

> We shall see how architectural elements should be combined with
> one another, how they are assembled each in relation to the whole,
> horizontally as well as vertically; and in the second place, how,
> through these combinations, a formation such different parts of
> the building as porticoes, atriums, vestibules, interior and exte-
> rior stairs, rooms of every kind, courts, grottoes and fountains is
> achieved. Once we have noted this part well, we shall then see how
> they combine in turn in the composition of the entire building.[21]

This new method of design, which was supposed to be the foundation of a new architectural order, was based upon several assumptions.
The first was that history had run its course and reached a standstill
at the end of the eighteenth century. History, therefore, could be
transformed into a new form of understanding: into a theory, which

would be a recapitulation and consummation of the past as well as the foundation of a new architectural order. The second, even more curious assumption was a belief that the new order could be based upon formal principles situated outside history. How was it possible to create a system that claimed to be self-referential, but which could be, at the same time, used as a framework for historical criticism and design? This dilemma was not addressed but quietly absorbed into the new ways of thinking inspired by the continuing success of the natural sciences and thus became a new, sophisticated form of self-deception.

Durand's attempt to create a universal method of design had a surprisingly broad influence, and in that sense was relatively success-ful, but as a meaningful method of design it was limited and naive. It could succeed only in a culture that had forgotten or suppressed its own tradition and history. An ideal vehicle for eclecticism, it was nevertheless useless in the face of a living history that, of course, did not stop. The main weakness of Durand's method was his belief that historical time could be arrested and encapsulated in a theory that would have a permanent validity.

The limits of Durand's achievement were recognised in the follow-ing generation, particularly by Gottfried Semper, who set himself a similar task. 'The Frenchman Durand', he writes, 'in his *Parallels* and other works on architecture came closer to the task [scientific architectural theory] than anybody else. But even he lost his aim [...]. He lost himself in tables and formulae, organised everything into series, and brought individual elements together in a mechani-cal way without demonstrating the organic law that establishes their relationship.'[22] Semper was better equipped and more sophisticated, and he seemed also to be aware, unlike Durand, that his goal was nothing less than a complex historical science of architectural design. In one of his earlier statements, he says:

> When I was a student in Paris I went often to the Jardin des Plantes, and I was always attracted, as it were, by a magic force from the sunny garden into those rooms where the fossil remains of the primeval world stand in long series ranged together with the skeletons and shells of the present creation. In this mag-nificent collection, the work of Baron Cuvier, we perceive the types for all the most implicated forms of the animal empire, we see progressing nature, with all its variety and immense rich-ness most sparing and economical in its fundamental forms and

motives l…]. A method, analogous to that which Baron Cuvier followed, applied to art, and especially to architecture, would at least contribute towards getting a clear insight over its whole province and perhaps also it would form the base of a doctrine of style and of a sort of topic or method, how to invent.[23]

I have quoted this passage at length because it illustrates very clearly the inspiration and main intentions behind Semper's own system. What such a system might be was determined by his faith in the redemptive role of science, in particular of biology, a science that could deal with change and purpose. He was influenced also by the contemporary belief that art is an expression of mysterious and still unknown powers in nature, no less than by his own belief that architecture should also refer to its own past. This led Semper to choose the primitive hut as a generative matrix of architectural order; this, however, he saw not only as a symbol and social phenomenon, but also as a formal structure constituted in the transformation of material and technical elements[24] (Fig. 1.6). Central to Semper's system was a vision of architecture as 'a conformity of artistic form with the history of its origin, with all the conditions and circumstances of its creation'.[25] This conformity, or harmony, was conceived as an analogy to a mathematical structure, where the work of art was meant to derive from a functional relationship between the individual conditions: material, technical, religious, political, etc., including individual talent and freedom.[26]

Semper's impressive but impossible task was never completed and in fact could not be completed. To do so, it would have been necessary to transform the whole culture to which architecture inevitably belongs into a transparent and verifiable understanding and make it part of a complete functional or relational system. The difficulty of such a task was probably recognised by Semper himself. What he did not recognise, however, and neither did his followers, was the self-defeating nature of the enterprise. Its success would have meant the transformation of architecture into an instrumental theoretical discipline with a formal purpose but with no explicit historical meaning, making it an instrument of pure *ars inveniendi*.

The dilemma and the limits of Semper's achievement illustrate a deeper dilemma in the very nature of modern architecture: how to reconcile the instrumental culture and requirements facing modern architecture with its humanistic purpose. Semper's attempt to formulate a new theory (science) of architecture as practical aesthetics did not resolve the dilemma but brought it to light. His own, very often poetic

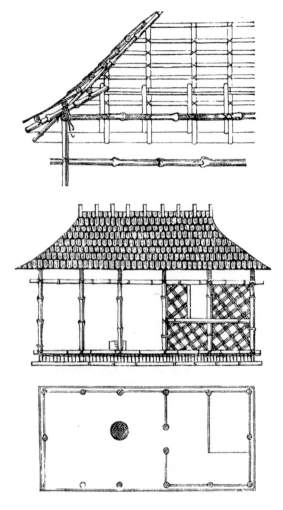

1.6 Gottfried Semper, *Der Stil in den technischen und tectonischen Künsten*, 1860–3. The Caribbean hut.

thinking, taking into consideration the role of ritual, metaphorical and symbolic transformations, broader cultural issues, etc. was in the last instance influenced by the methodical expectations of the time, and mostly lost in the problematic transparency of his 'system'.[27]

Methodical expectations illustrate the monologue of positivistic thinking, recognising only one standard of truth and one kind of theory regardless of the subject.[28] It is not surprising that the first attempt to challenge the methodical monologue came from the humanities and in particular from history, in its effort to overcome the dogma of historicism. The best example of such an attempt is the late work of Wilhelm Dilthey, who happened to appreciate Semper's *Der Stil*, which he describes as an 'enlightening model for how an important historical problem should be solved in aesthetics'.[29] There are many similarities between Semper's and Dilthey's thinking, such as the search for the simplest constituent elements of history, the use of comparative method, but most of all the search for the scientific theory (epistemology) of history and art. For Dilthey the paradigm of method (theory) and its scientific legitimacy was Kant's *Critique of Pure Reason*, which he tried to emulate with his own *Critique of Historical Reason*.[30] However, the result was not a success. Dilthey's articulation of 'historical reason' did not help to overcome the conflict between a recognition of the historicity of the human world and the attempt to develop a method which could grasp the phenomenon of historicity. As Hans-Georg Gadamer demonstrated, the second ambition cancels the first.[31] Dilthey's contribution, and in some sense Semper's as well, represent a turning point in the theoretical thinking about arts and humanities. Their search for the scientific method in these fields led, as we have seen, to the demonstration of the limits of such enterprise, and opened the door for a very different way of thinking about the humanities and the arts, including architecture.

The new way of thinking was cultivated mostly in the sphere of phenomenology and in contemporary hermeneutics.[32] In this tradition, method, epistemology and theory are not entirely dismissed, but are rather redundant. Their place is taken over by a more critical and subtle thinking, sensitive to the hermeneutical conditions of typical situations, reciprocity of their universal and particular meaning, formation of historical concepts and their creative interpretation.

It is not clear how long it will take to adopt this way of thinking and see the limits of modern theory and the sterility of its cultivation in such fields as architecture. The temptation to compete, or at least to come to terms with the dominating productive tendencies in our culture, supports very strongly the cultivation of modern theories as productive knowledge. However, we are also situated in the life world, which theoretical knowledge can never fully grasp. And, as Gadamer argues: 'We cannot escape the lifeworld as a fundamental condition. Our task remains to integrate and subordinate the theoretical knowledge and the technical possibilities of human beings to their praxis. It by no means consists in the transformation of the actual life world, which is just the world of praxis, into a theoretically justified technical construct.'[33]

Notes

1   Ernesto Grassi, *Kunst und Mythos*, Hamburg: Rowohlt Verlag, 1957, pp. 108–18.
    'It is mainly because a play is a representation (*mimesis*) of action (*praxis*) that it also for that reason represents people as doing something or experiencing something (*prattontes*).' Aristotle, *Poetics*, trans. Stephen Halliwell et al., Loeb Classical Library, Cambridge, MA: Harvard University Press, 1965, 1450b22.

2   *Praxis* includes people 'as acting' and all things 'as in act'. See Ernesto Grassi, *Die Theorie des Schönen in der Antike*, Köln: Du Mont, 1962, p. 127; Paul Ricoeur, *The Rule of Metaphor*, trans. Robert Czerny et al., London: Routledge & Kegan Paul, 1978, pp. 42–43; Aristotle, *Art of Rhetoric*, trans. John H. Freese, Loeb Classical Library, Cambridge, MA: Harvard University Press, 1975, 1411b24.

3   Hans-Georg Gadamer, 'What is Practice? The Conditions of Social Reason', in *Reason in the Age of Science*, trans. Frederick G. Lawrence, Cambridge, MA: MIT Press, 1981, p. 82.

4   Martin Heidegger, 'Science and Reflection' in *The Question Concerning Technology and Other Essays*, trans. William Lovitt, New York and London: Garland, 1977, pp. 163–64.

5   Aristotle, *Nicomachean Ethics*, trans. Harris Rackham, Loeb Classical Library, Cambridge, MA: Harvard University Press, 1968, X.vi.8–X.vii.4.

6   Ibid., VI.iii.2–VI.iv.6; see also Aristotle, *Metaphysics*, trans. Hugh Tredennick, Loeb Classical Library, Cambridge, MA: Harvard University Press, 1968, I.i.1–I.i.17, and VI.vii.4–VI.ix.8.

7   James S. Ackerman, '"Ars Sine Scientia Nihil Est": Gothic Theory of Architecture at the Cathedral of Milan', in *Distance Points: Essays in Theory and Renaissance Art and Architecture*, Cambridge, MA: MIT Press, 1991, p. 247.

8   I am using the term 'practice' to describe the link between *praxis, techne* and *theoria*. In the traditional context, practice had a character of mediation, while in modern times it became a direct application of theory.

9   Peter Dear, *Discipline and Experience: The Mathematical Way in the Scientific Revolution*, Chicago, IL: University of Chicago Press, 1995, pp. 151–80.

10   Ernan McMullin, 'The Conception of Science in Galileo's Work', in *New Perspectives on Galileo*, ed. Robert E. Butts and Joseph C. Pitt, Dordrecht and Boston: D. Reidel, 1978, p. 232.

11   René Descartes, 'Le monde', in *Oeuvres*, ed. Charles Adam and Paul Tannery, vol. Xl, Paris, 1974, p. 31 [trans. Vesely].

12   Descartes, 'Correspondence', op. cit., vol. III, Paris, 1975, p. 722.

13   Heidegger, 'The Age of the World Picture', op. cit., p. 135.

14   Heidegger, 'Science and Reflection', op. cit., p. 165.

15 Karl Löwith, *Meaning in History*, Chicago, IL: The University of Chicago Press, 1957; Arthur O. Lovejoy, 'The Temporalising of the Chain of Being', in *The Great Chain of Being: A Study of the History of an Idea*, Cambridge, MA: Harvard University Press, 1974, pp. 242–87; Eric Voegelin, *From Enlightenment to Revolution*, Durham, NC: Duke University Press, 1975, pp. 83–109; Reinhart Koselleck, *Futures Past: On the Semantics of Historical Time*, Cambridge, MA: MIT Press, 1986.

16 Nikolaus Pevsner, *Academies of Art, Past and Present*, New York: Da Capo Press, 1973; Alberto Pérez-Gómez, *Architecture and the Crisis of Modern Science*, Cambridge, MA: MIT Press, 1983; Antoine Picon, *French Architects and Engineers in the Age of Enlightenment*, Cambridge: Cambridge University Press, 1992.

17 Hans-Georg Gadamer, 'Hermeneutics and Historicism', in *Truth and Method*, trans. William Glen-Doepel, ed. John Cumming and Garret Barden, London, 1975, pp. 460–91.

18 The belief in the universal intelligence to which humanity found access, an experience so characteristic of the period of the French Revolution, was articulated succinctly by Laplace who wrote in his *Essai philosophique sur les probabilités* in 1814: 'Given for one instant an intelligence which could comprehend all the forces by which nature is animated and the respective situation of the beings who compose it - an intelligence sufficiently vast to submit these data to analysis - it would embrace in the same formula the movement of the greatest bodies of the universe and those of the lightest atom; for it, nothing would be uncertain, and the future, as the past, would be present to its eyes. The human mind offers, in the perfection which it has been able to give to astronomy, a feeble idea of this intelligence. [...] Applying the same method to some other objects of its knowledge, it has succeeded in referring to general laws observed phenomena and in foreseeing those which given circumstances ought to produce. All these efforts in the search for truth tend to lead it back continually to the vast intelligence which we have just mentioned.' Marquis Pierre Simon de Laplace, *A Philosophical Essay on Probabilities*, trans. Frederick W. Truscott and F.L. Emory, London: John Wiley & Sons, 1902, p. 4.

19 Sergio Vigari, *J.N.L. Durand (1760–1834): Art and Science of Architecture*, New York, 1990, p. 33; Jean-Nicolas-Louis Durand, *Recueil et parallèle des édifices de tout genre, anciens et modernes, remarquables par leur beauté par leur grandeur ou par leur singularité, dessinés sur une même échelle*, Paris, 1800.

20 Jean-Nicolas-Louis Durand, *Précis des leçons d'architecture données a l'École Polytechnique*, Paris, 1802.

21 Ibid., Préface, p. III [trans. Vesely].

22 Gottfried Semper, *Kleine Schriften*, ed. Hans and Manfred Semper, Berlin and Stuttgart: Spemann Verlag, 1884, p. 262 [trans. Vesely].

23 Hans Semper, *Gottfried Semper: Ein Bild seines Lebens und Wirkens*, Berlin: S. Calvary, 1880, pp. 3–4 [trans. Vesely].

24 Gottfried Semper, 'The Four Elements of Architecture', in *The Four elements of Architecture and Other Writings*, trans. Harry Francis Mallgrave and Wolfgang Hermann, Cambridge: Cambridge University Press, 1989, pp. 74–129.

25   Semper, *Kleine Schriften*, op. cit., p. 402.
26   A detailed discussion of such a possibility appeared in Semper's 'Entwurf eines Systems der vergleichenden Stillehre'. The problem of style is discussed there in direct analogy with the mathematical formula Y = F (x, y, z, etc.), where x, y. z, etc. are external variable conditions, F stands for the internal and stable conditions, and Y is the work of art (architecture). The formula is meant to be read analogically and not literally, of course. The discussion can be found in: Semper, *Kleine Schriften*, op. cit., p. 259ff.
27   Mari Hvattum, 'Towards a Method of Inventing', in *Gottfried Semper and the Problem of Historicism*, Cambridge: Cambridge University Press, 2004, pp. 137–49.
28   Leszek Kolakowski, 'Positivism of the Neo-Romantic or Modernist Age', in *Positivist Philosophy from Hume to the Vienna Circle*, Harmondsworth: Penguin, 1972, pp. 125–97; Jürgen Habermas, 'Comte and Mach: The Intention of Early Positivism', in *Knowledge and Human Interests*, trans. J. J. Shapiro, Boston, MA: Beacon Press, 1972, pp. 71–90.
29   Hvattum, op. cit., p. 176.
30   Gadamer, 'Dilthey's Entanglement in the Impasses of Historicism', op. cit., pp. 192–204.
31   Ibid., pp. 204–25.
32   Jean Grondin, *Sources of Hermeneutics*, Albany, NY: SUNY Press, 1995; Jean Grondin and Joel Weisheimer, *Introduction to Philosophical Hermeneutics*, New Haven, CT: Yale University Press, 1994.
33   Hans-Georg Gadamer, 'Citizens of Two Worlds', in *Hans-Georg Gadamer on Education, Poetry, and History: Applied Hermeneutics*, ed. Dieter Misgeld and Graeme Nicholson, Albany, NY: SUNY Press, 1992, pp. 209–21, particularly p. 216. In his comment on the relation between modern theory, its application and *praxis*, Gadamer has this to say: 'As far as hermeneutics is concerned it is quite to the point to confront the separation of theory from practice entailed in the modern notion of theoretical science and practical-technical application with an idea of knowledge that has taken the opposite path leading from praxis toward making it aware of itself theoretically.' (Hans-Georg Gadamer, 'Hermeneutics as a Theoretical and Practical Task', *Reason in the Age of Science*, trans. Frederick G. Lawrence, Cambridge, MA: MIT Press, 1981, p. 131).

2   Architecture and the Question of Technology

There is a strong feeling that the multitudinous traditional ways of making and creativity are slowly being absorbed into one dominant way of making and thinking. This process of homogenisation is not new, but it has reached unprecedented levels today. To see the difference, it is enough to recall the nature and the depth of discussions, in the early decades of the present century, about creativity in different domains of culture, about the relation between art and science or technology, about the nature and status of the applied arts, industrial design and so on—in such movements, for example, as the *Werkbund*, *L'Esprit Nouveau*, *L'Architecture Vivante*, Futurism, Constructivism, etc. While some awareness of the distinction between invention, creativity and pure production remains, it is no longer clear how this distinction should be established; that may be one of the reasons why the current debate is mostly confusing, unsatisfactory and frustrating.

The topic of this debate, to which most other questions are usually reduced, is the merit of technical efficiency versus that of aesthetics. Even issues of cultural meaning or social and political relevance, or issues that directly affect the long-term well-being of our society, are often discussed in such simplistic terms. It is not too difficult to discover that this oversimplification has its roots in the dogmatically accepted belief in the universality of technical (instrumental) thinking. As a result, not only technical thinking itself but also a technical way of making has become the standard against which any kind of making is measured. This tendency is usually referred to as the technical or technological imperative. We hear often about the inevitability of technological development and progress, about the historical destiny—the 'mission'—of technology. Despite the growing number of sceptical voices and despite the amount of

DOI: 10.4324/9781003272090-3

literature devoted to the question of the technological transformation of modern culture, our understanding of the nature of technology remains surprisingly limited. One of the main obstacles to a better understanding is our inability to discuss technological problems from a non-instrumental point of view. In the current scientific parlance, this is often considered to be non-scientific—a verdict that seals the issue and encloses it hermetically in a vicious circle of understanding/non-understanding. A typical example is found in the recent attempts to study the problems of the natural environment by extending the existing technological knowledge into wider fields without changing the primary criteria, conditions and goals of research. The illusory nature of such studies and their inevitable limits have been very clearly summarised in the following analogy: 'With its seemingly unlimited growth of material power, mankind finds itself in the situation of a skipper who has this boat built of such a heavy concentration of iron and steel, that the boat's compass points constantly at herself and not north. With a boat of that kind, no destination can be reached, she will go around in a circle, exposed to the hazards of the winds and the waves.'[1]

Instrumental thinking tends to impose its hegemony by creating a world that it can fully control. Control of that nature requires not only a special kind of knowledge but also a particular kind of will. And the knowledge that meets the conditions of the will to control is 'knowledge as power.'[2] Because this kind of knowledge must be subordinated to the will, we can speak here simply of a 'will to power', which, as a consequence, becomes a 'will to will'. It is well known that knowledge as power represents the essence of modern science—its metaphysical foundation—but it is also the essence of modern technology.[3] This leads to a deeper insight into the hegemony of technical reason and into the nature of the vicious circle of our 'understanding' of technology. The difficulty in breaking that hegemony—and in understanding that technology as the fulfilment of the will to power is not unconditional—is well summarised by Heidegger:

> Because the will to will absolutely denies every goal and only admits goals as means to outwit itself wilfully and to make room for its game, the will to will may not appear as the anarchy of catastrophes that it really is. However, if it wants to assert itself in beings, it must legitimate itself. The will to will invents here the talk about 'mission'. Mission is not sought with regard to anything original and its preservation, but rather as the goal

assigned from the standpoint of fate, thus justifying the will
to will.[4]

The need of the will to justify its role and its fulfilment reveals that
the will itself is not absolute, that it is always situated and cannot completely disguise its own 'situatedness'.[5] References to mission and fate
are a clear manifestation of a deeper intentionality and deeper historical circumstances, in which the will appears as a historical possibility,
but always in contrast with other possibilities. If the will represents a
movement towards the appropriation of power, culminating in modern technology, the other possibilities represent a movement towards
participation that has most consistently been preserved in the domain
of the arts. The existence of other possibilities—and their replacement
by simple will—must be taken as a point of departure for any understanding of the apparent fatality of technological progress and of the
belief that this kind of progress is our historical destiny. It is true, as
we have seen, that such a belief belongs to the essence of modern technology; but it is also true that, in itself, this kind of belief is nothing
technological: 'Because the essence of technology is nothing technological, essential refection upon technology and decisive coming to
terms with it must happen in a realm that is, on the one hand, akin to
the essence of technology, and on the other, fundamentally different
from it. That art is akin to, but at the same time fundamentally different from it. Such a realm is art.'[6]

That art is akin to, but at the same time fundamentally different
from, technology is a result of historical development, in which the
two domains originally shared a common ground but became differentiated later into the arts and technology as we know them today. Art
originates in *techne*, which in its Greek sense is a knowledge related
to making and is always known in its final sense as *techne poietike*.
Techne, as a relatively new kind of knowledge, superseded spontaneous
knowledge and intuitive skills, which demanded a close contact with
objects and tasks but could lead to the discovery of what is common
and permanent in all of them. This emancipated knowledge teaches us
a general lesson about things and can be used *a priori*, without direct
reference to the things themselves. As a project of possible knowledge,
techne receives most of its knowledge from accumulated experience but
elevates it to *a priori* knowledge that can be taught.

What exists *a priori* and can be taught was for the Greeks a *mathema*—hence mathematics as a special form of such knowledge.
Mathema/mathematics is the true origin of the transformation of *techne*

into technique and finally into modern technology. In the Greek experience, however, *techne* was still far from becoming such a project. It was a drama situated between the new possibilities of knowledge and the intimate understanding of the inner possibilities of nature (*physis*). *Techne* was not yet seen as a human possession but as a power of nature, which humans could possess only to a limited extent. This may explain why 'the first man who invented art [*techne*] beyond common sense was looked upon by his fellow man as a wonder, not only because there was something useful in this discovery, but also because he was thought wise and superior to others.'[7]

The fact that *techne* is only a transition to technique is reflected in its relation to making (*poiesis*). Broadly speaking, making means to bring into being something that did not previously exist. *Poiesis* takes place not only in human effort but also in nature: 'All things that come into being are generated, some by nature (*physis*), others by art (*techne*).'[8] Art originally received its legitimacy and meaning from the universal divine order, which was seen as the product of an ultimate craftsmanship. 'When a thing is produced by nature, the earlier stages in every case lead up to the final development in the same way as in the operation of art, and vice-versa.'[9] In this rather dense formulation are already present all the future definitions of art as a reality that complements nature, as a completion and fulfilment of nature's inner possibilities, or as imitation of nature. The imitation of nature in particular is a creative process that contains a large residuum of mystery. The Greeks were very much aware of it and referred to it as chance (*tyche*). Aristotle made this very clear in a well-known passage: 'Art dwells with the same objects as chance [...] chance is beloved of art and art of chance.'[10] And he wrote elsewhere: 'Some hold that chance is the genuine cause of things, but one that has something divine and mysterious about it that makes it inscrutable to the human intelligence.'[11]

It should be emphasised here that making is based on productive knowledge but that such knowledge is never complete. It always depends on a prior understanding that has its origin in the spontaneity of making. The inscrutable element in making to which chance refers has its main source in *mimesis*. Because *tyche* is inscrutable to our intelligence, *mimesis* is equally so. In principle, it is possible to say that *mimesis* is a creative imitation where something that exists potentially is recognised and re-enacted as something actual. For example, movement can be recognised and re-enacted as a significant gesture; sound, as song or music; visible reality, as image or picture; and ideas, as an articulated and structured experience. In its most original sense, *mimesis* is a re-enactment of elementary order: 'Testifying to order, *mimesis* seems as valid now as it was in the past, insofar as every work of art, even in our own increasingly standard-ised world of mass production, still testifies to that deep ordering energy that makes our life what it is. The work of art provides a perfect example of that universal characteristic of human existence - the never-ending process of building a world.'[12] The role of *mimesis* in the process of making reveals the mystery of order as a tension between the potential and actual existence of order, which in its ulti-mate form always points towards the ultimate order—the cosmos. It is in that sense that the re-enactment of cosmic order can be seen as the most primordial form of making.[13]

The mimetic mode of making, which precedes the formation of *techne*, takes place most often in the domain of ritual. This is appar-ent not only in such rituals as dance or music but also in the rhythm and movement of the process of making itself, thus showing that the making of order and the making of things belong together. In both cases, the result of the mimetic action becomes a vehicle for partic-ipation in the overall order of things. The participatory meaning of *mimesis* and ritual—the need to come to terms with the universal order of reality—is challenged and, to a great extent, upset by the tendency to replace participation by the appropriation and manipu-lation of the order-creating powers. This tendency has its origin in the efficacy of traditional ritual, often wrongly identified as magic. It is obviously a great mistake to see magic where we are dealing only with the efficacy or instrumental aspect of traditional rituals.[14] It is well known that certain gestures or objects used in rituals may have the power to produce certain desirable results, but this does not mean that they can be described as magic or as primitive techniques. The power to influence the order of things in a culture that does not yet see a difference between the natural and the supernatural always depends on the reference to reality as a whole, which cannot become a domain of manipulation: 'There is an important difference between two kinds of actions, actions done by man and actions done by man in the belief that their efficacy is not human in any reducible sense, but proceeds from elsewhere. Only the second kind of action can be called any sort of a religious rite.'[15] The difference between the efficacy of ritual and magic is manifested in the nature of magic itself. Magic differs from all other forms of religion in that the desire to dominate the world belongs to its essential nature.

The emancipatory, appropriative tendency of magic, in contrast to the participatory nature of ritual, could become an important phenomenon only under certain historical conditions because 'the domination by will has one essential condition: before the world can be thus controlled it must. be transferred inwards and man must take it into himself. He can actually dominate it only when it has in this way become an inner realm. For this reason, all magic is [...] living within oneself.'[16] Historically, this became possible for the first time and in any real sense during the Hellenistic period, when the disintegration of the cultural and political institutions of the *polis* led to the disintegration of traditional corporate rituals and left people to their own resources and in relative isolation. 'Magic is commonly the last resort of the personally desperate, of those whom man and God have alike failed.'[17] The emancipation of magic was closely linked to the growing interest in other esoteric disciplines (such as astrology, alchemy or theurgy), as well as to the new interest in mechanics and technicity in general.

In the introduction to his book on mechanics, Pappus of Alexandria recognised the link between mechanics and magic quite explicitly: 'The ancients also describe as engineers (*mechanikos*) the won-der-workers, that is the magicians (*thaumasiourgos*) of whom some work with air as Heron in his *Pneumatica*.'[18] It was under such cir-cumstances that *techne* came to exist as technique in its most elemen-tary form. This is confirmed by, among others, Jean-Pierre Vernant, who, at the end of a long study on the possibilities and limits of tech-nical thinking in ancient Greece, came to the same conclusion: 'Only in the work of the Alexandrian engineers, especially Heron, is there any evidence of interest in the instruments and machines as such, and only here was their construction undertaken with an attitude that we can describe as truly technical.'[19] What makes this attitude truly technical is not only a new type of knowledge, but rather a new interest and will. In a typical Hellenistic definition of a machine, we can see that 'machine is a continuous material system [...] moved by appropriate revolutions of circles which by the Greeks is called *kiklike kinesis*.'[20] That circular movement is not a purely mechanical phenomenon, however; the text points to its origin in the regularity of the celestial movement, which is also imitated in ritual and dance but is represented here in a more tangible form by the body of the machine (Fig. 2.1).

The incomprehensibility of the movement of nature, mani-fest most explicitly in the movement of the celestial bodies, has been identified by modern anthropology as the deepest motif of

2.1 Cesare Cesariano, translation and commentary on Vitruvius's
De architectura, 1521. Illustration of the regularity of the supralunar world.

technicity and described as a 'fascination with automatism.'[21] The
nature of this fascination is a continuous attempt to grasp what
is most incomprehensible through something that we understand
and can construct and manipulate. One can also describe these
attempts as a technicisation of the original mimetic re-enactment

and participation. The machine is a tangible model of such a process and, as a consequence, is also a model of the inscrutable cosmic order. A model is comprehensible because we have made it. It is surprising to see how close the Hellenistic authors themselves came to such an understanding:

> All machinery is generated by nature and the revolution of the universe guides and controls it. For first indeed, unless we could observe and contemplate the continuous motion of the sun, moon and the five planets; unless these revolved by the device of nature, we should not have known their light in due season nor the ripening of the harvest. Since then our fathers have observed this to be so, they took precedence from nature, imitating them and led on by what is divine, they developed the necessities of life by their inventions.[22]

It is at this historical stage that technique becomes, at least potentially, a methodical operation that can be carried out in such a way that it can accomplish a particular predictable end. Unlike *techne*, which is always rooted in the concrete life of the *polis*, magic and technique are, to a great extent, emancipated from the political and cultural context. In the ethical sense, they represent individual or group egocentrism, based on the acquisition of power and on domination. The emancipation of magic and technique from the ethically oriented life of the *polis* creates a situation of new freedom in which there is no room for good or evil and for the sense of guilt or sin. It is in such a situation that the question of truth is replaced by the question of practical achievement. Because this is true for both magic and technique, it is very difficult to draw a clear line between them. On the other hand, it is possible to say that magic recedes into the background, leaving a certain residuum of its original power in the more rationalised forms of technique. It is for this reason that it would be more appropriate to speak of an element of magic than about magic itself in the development of modern technique. And it would also be more appropriate to speak about a technical tendency in the domain of the existing arts (*artes technai*) than about technique when we refer to the act of making or production. This would certainly simplify the confusing and very often misleading discussions about the role of magic in the formation of modern technology.[23] We have to keep in mind that the traditional understanding of art includes every kind of making—from the making of shoes or tools to arithmetic and geometry in the *quadrivium*. The difference between the arts was their involvement with matter and manual labour and with their theoretical status, which was most often expressed only through adjectives—the mechanical arts (*artes mechanicae*), usually situated at the bottom of the hierarchy because of the labour involved; the liberal arts (*artes liberales*), which included the *trivium* and the *quadrivium*; and, finally, the theoretical arts, sometimes known as *scientiae*, consisting of theology, mathematics and physics.[24] That the arts represented not only experience and skills but also an important mode of knowledge, is reflected in the ambiguity of their relation to science.[25]

The sciences that contributed to the formation of modern technique and eventually to technology were mainly astronomy, optics and mechanics, known as *scientiae mediae* (the 'middle sciences'). The reason for that designation was not their 'mixed' nature, as is sometimes thought, but their position halfway between metaphysics and physics.[26] The *scientiae mediae* should be seen as a branch of mathematics—physical mathematics— that prepares the way for the development of mathematical physics but is, in principle, radically different from it. It is important to bear this in mind, particularly in view of many current interpretations of Renaissance perspective and mechanics. These interpretations do not always seem to recognise the fundamental ontological difference between the indirect and direct 'mathematisation' of reality. In the domain of Renaissance art, mathematics plays a role of approximation, mediation and symbolisation. It still represents, on the one hand, the essential (i.e., intelligible) structure of reality (Being) and, on the other hand, the visible manifestation of such structures. It is the mediating and symbolic role of mathematics—and not only its precision—that gives it such a prestigious place in early modern thinking. The process of the indirect mathematisation of reality—the main characteristic and contribution of the middle sciences—can be seen particularly clearly in the role played by Medieval optics in the development of perspective as well as in the mechanical inventions of the sixteenth century. The attempts to bring the physical reality of vision and movement into the sphere of mathematical reasoning were, for a very long time, laced with a paradox of apparent success and real failure. Each successful step in mathematisation revealed a new area of reality that would resist completion of the process. This was expressed very often in the frustrations of sixteenth-century artisan-'engineers', who became only too aware of the gap that separates speculative mathematics from the concrete reality of the artisan. The concepts with which the mathematician works 'are not subject to those impediments, which by nature are always conjoined to the matter which is worked on by the artisan.'[27] It is for these reasons that Renaissance perspective and mechanics cannot be seen as true sciences in the modern sense. The middle sciences, like the arts, can be called sciences only by analogy. True sciences are concerned with universal reality and require absolute proof. Perspective and mechanics, on the other hand, are concerned with particular situations, with human works and operations, and with contingent things. If we take into account how perspective and mechanics were really practised, and not just how they are presented in textbooks or in projects, we may see them as arts, deeply influenced and informed by science (Fig. 2.2). But unlike the sciences or the emancipated techniques, the arts deal with direct experience and with the probable. They belong to the primary mode of embodiment—to the visible world, which is the ultimate criterion of their meaning, relevance and success. Indirect or partial mathematisation could not change these conditions.[28] This also shows the clear limits of the mathematisation and technicisation of the traditional arts. As long as the arts were situated in the life of nature and society, they could not become a subject of mathematical understanding and control, and to that extent their technicisation remained inevitably partial and limited. Only a total mathematisation of reality could remove these limits.

It was in the second half of the sixteenth century that such a project became, for the first time, a real possibility. The initial inspiration came from the middle sciences, where the old and jealously guarded boundaries between mathematics and physics were crossed.[29] However, the most decisive changes took place in the domain of mathematics itself, particularly in the sphere of algebra, which had developed into a 'universal mathematics'. This was complemented by similar changes in the domain of metaphysics, where the *prima philosophia* became a 'universal science'. Universal mathematics became the mathematical equivalent of traditional logic. Because universal mathematics operates with the pure essences of things, which are taken for simple magnitudes, the formal essence becomes identical with pure mathematical essence/magnitude.

It is under these conditions that universal mathematics can claim to cover the same area of knowledge as traditional logic—in other words, the area of all possible knowledge.[30] The new idea of all possible knowledge is very different from traditional dialectical or

2.2 Abraham Bosse, *Manière universelle de M. Desargues*, 1647.
Illustration of the effects of perspective on perception and the
transformation of the world into a picture.

demonstrative knowledge. It aims to explain things only in terms
of order and measure, regardless of their material and qualitative
determination. It was because of the universality of such a claim that
universal mathematics earned the title, as long ago as the sixteenth
century, of 'queen of sciences' (*regina scientiarum*), sometimes elevated to *scientia divina* or *ars divina*.[31] These lofty definitions would

obviously not be convincing without some supporting evidence that must come from the understanding of the physical world. In a similar way as in mathematics, the development of knowledge in sixteenth-century physics went through a radical change. The traditional distinction between divine and human knowledge was weakened to such an extent that it became possible to speak about physics and metaphysics in the same language and in terms of the same principles.[32] The affinity between the metaphysical interpretation of physics and universal mathematics was reflected in the new understanding and use of *scientiae mediae* and, in particular, of mechanics. It is very important to realise that contrary to a widely held opinion, the usefulness of mechanics was secondary to its primary meaning—the understanding and representation of movement in the created world.

The continuity of movement between the celestial and terrestrial domains played a critical role, first in Aristotelianism and later in scholastic metaphysics; as we know, it was the latter which played a decisive role in the formation of modern mechanics.[33] It is only with great effort that we can understand today the complexity and importance of movement (motion) in the seventeenth-century vision of reality. The enigma of creation, the manifestation of the divine order in the terrestrial world and the continuity of this order were all related to the phenomenon of movement. Movement was seen not only as a universal principle of reality but also as the efficient cause of everything that persists in life. The divine origin of movement was not yet in doubt, nor was the tradition in which divine reality manifested itself as an eternal truth that could eventually be grasped as mathematical truth. Descartes made this clear when he wrote: 'Mathematical truths which you call eternal were established by God and depend on him entirely like all other created beings. Do not hesitate to assert and proclaim it everywhere that it is God who set up these laws in nature as the king sets up laws in his kingdom.'[34] Attempts at understanding these laws were strongly influenced, if not determined, by the new idea of knowledge—knowing by doing or by construction. In other words, universal reality can be known by the art whereby it was made. In Descartes's own words, 'God's will, understanding and creation are one and the same thing; none is prior to another, even conceptually.'[35] The identity of understanding and creation was the last condition needed to open the door for mechanics to become the critical discipline in the formation of science and technology.

It is important to see that it was not utilitarian and purely technical interests but a metaphysical quest that gave mechanics such a privileged position. It was in the domain of mechanics that the mathematisation of physical movement could be investigated or explored and finally accomplished. The tendency to treat physical reality and movement as inevitable and potentially mathematical was most certainly motivated by the growing desire to discover more tangible links between human and divine reality—which, in Galileo's time, meant more tangible links between physical and mathematical reality. In Galileo's *Dialogues*, we find the following statement: 'I still say with Aristotle that in physical matters one need not always require a mathematical demonstration. Granted, where none is to be had, but when there is one at hand, why do you not wish to use it?'[36] What can possibly motivate such a wish? Galileo himself answers this question:

> As to heaven, it is in vain that you fear for that which you yourself hold to be inalterable and invariant. As for the earth, we seek rather to ennoble and perfect it when we strive to make it like the celestial bodies, and, as it were, place it in heaven, from which you philosophers have banished it. Philosophy itself cannot but benefit from our disputes, for if our conceptions prove true, new achievements will be made.[37]

It is well known that the key to Galileo's achievements is the mathematical demonstration performed in a domain that had traditionally been considered to be only contingent. This demonstration, which was radically new, can best be described as a dialogue between an a priori mathematical formula and idealised physical reality. In this dialogue, the mathematical formula, used as a hypothesis (as an argument *ex suppositione*), is followed by an approximation and anticipation of the physical results.[38] On the physical side of the experimental dialogue, phenomena are simplified through abstraction to the point that the approximate mathematical form is free of all difficult material impediments and circumstances. When Galileo speaks about the conditions of the free fall, he comes to the following conclusion: 'A more considerable disturbance arises from the impediment of the medium by reason of its multiple varieties, this is impossible [to subject] to firm rules, understood and made into science. No firm science can be given of such events [as] heaviness, speed and shape which are variable in infinitely many ways. Hence, to deal with such matters scientifically, it is necessary to abstract from them.'[39]

Galileo's experimental method and its potential rigour include a zone of deep ambiguity that can only be eliminated when physical impediments can be successfully abstracted. But this is not always possible—certainly not in the same degree. To that extent, Galileo's mechanics remains a promise and, even in its best moments, a rigorous hypothetical discipline rather than a rigorous science. It contains an enigmatic element that will never be completely eliminated. The enigma has much to do with the process of mathematisation and, in particular, with the nature of the experimental dialogue. Paradoxically, the main source of the enigma is the nature of experimental reasoning, which substitutes an implicit demonstration for an explicit one. In the implicit demonstration, it is not necessary to take into account or to know all the circumstances, conditions, and causes of a particular phenomenon or event (irregular movement, for instance). What is not necessary to know remains enigmatic because, when it comes to understanding, this negligence also remains unknown—and therefore enigmatic.

It is for these reasons that it would be more appropriate to see the experimental dialogue as the result of intellectual craftsmanship rather than a rigorous philosophy of science. As a consequence, the *topos* of the workshop or laboratory is a more appropriate vehicle for understanding the nature (essence) of modern technology than the *topos* of a study. The laboratory is a place where nature is systematically transformed into mathematically idealised models. In a world that has been transformed into a laboratory model, construction and making become the privileged form of knowing.

As ideal places for the conduct of experimental dialogue, the workshop and the laboratory represent a new, secondary mode of reality where new rules of knowledge can be developed and cultivated. Unlike traditional knowledge, which was cultivated in a dialogue with the primary conditions of reality, the new rules are articulated in the relatively closed world of the experimental dialogue. The imaginary nature of this new world is well described in Descartes's own words: 'For a short time, therefore, allow your thought to leave this world in order to come to see a wholly new one, which I shall cause to be born in the presence of your thought in imaginary spaces.'[40] As for the nature of knowledge or science that can be developed in the new 'imaginary spaces', Descartes again tells us what is possible and what is also seriously anticipated: 'By science I understand skill at resolving all questions and in inventing by one's own industry everything in that science that can be invented by human ingenuity (*ars inveniendi*).

Whoever has this science does not desire much else foreign to it, and indeed is quite properly called *autarches* – self-sufficient.'[41] The science invented by human ingenuity is a construct. It is a productive science, motivated by an ambition to be nothing less than *creatio ex nihilo*, traditionally linked only with divine creativity. However, what is traditionally true for the divine is now considered to be also true, or at least possible, for humanity. In other words, we know, and can create, at least in principle, exactly as God knows or can create.

This new, unusual confidence has its origin in the drastically simplified representation of reality, which became possible because of the deep metaphysical faith in the mathematical nature of reality sanctioned by divine presence. The result, most likely unintentional, was a method for the construction of productive knowledge, based on the unlimited possibilities of experimental dialogue. '"Idea" was the term I used because it was the familiar philosophical term for the forms of which the divine mind is aware (*formas perceptionem mentis divinae*).'[42] In terms of our own interpretation, however, the idea also represents a new type of knowledge—a primary force of production and the origin of modern technology. The unlimited possibilities of invention opened through experimental dialogue have their source in the infinity of will, which for Descartes is a single analogy of the human and the divine. The full meaning of the infinity of will is 'most visibly displayed in the programmatically anticipated infinity of artifices through which the new sciences are to prove their credentials.'[43] In the openness to future possibilities lay the foundations of the ideal of progress and, on a deeper level, the intra-mundane eschatology of modern technology.[44] The convergence of the infinity of will and the infinity of artifices completes the ambition to understand given reality as a priori and whole, and from a clearly defined position. 'Applying knowledge through construction to the whole world was as inevitable as it was dangerous. It was dangerous because it makes mankind be like God, knowing good and evil. Many seventeenth-century philosophers shunned its inevitable consequences, but only a few had the courage to deny categorically that this kind of knowledge reveals reality.'[45]

In a sense, that is still true today. We do not yet fully understand the real nature of the experimental knowledge on which modern technology is based because it is difficult to follow the transformation of reality and the nature of its representation in a picture (model) from which all but efficient causes have been eliminated and where the qualitative diversity of phenomena has been reduced to a mathematical interpretation of matter in motion. There is quite clearly a gap between the domain of situated knowledge and productive knowledge. This gap, which represents a radical discontinuity with the natural world, reduces the gnostic value of productive knowledge and makes it merely a technical tool. The fact that a technical tool can represent the most sophisticated achievements at the same time is demonstrated, for example, by nuclear research and its results or by the aspirations of current genetics or electronics. From the very beginning, however, the overwhelming success of productive knowledge was limited to phenomena susceptible to mathematical treatment. This has also determined the selective and uneven development of modern technology. Architecture itself can serve as a very good example here.

The area where technology had the greatest influence was in the calculation of structures; this, as a consequence, led to a more inventive use of certain materials and new types of construction. But as we know, extending the role of instrumental thinking in architecture was a very slow process. It is perhaps not surprising that it was only in certain, rather limited areas that technicisation had some success. Factories, railway stations, exhibition halls and generally structures that could be treated as an engineering problem can be seen as good examples. On the other hand, there were whole areas that proved extremely difficult to mechanise. These were mostly areas of greater complexity or areas dominated by values more deeply rooted in cultural tradition. Because of the particular development of modern European culture, the public domain became rather indifferent to private interests, could therefore be simplified, and as a consequence became rather anonymous. It was for these reasons that technology could be applied more easily in the public domain. As a result, the modern city shows more clearly the true impact of technological thinking than do private homes or residential areas.

In contrast to the earlier, rather slow and partial improvements, the transformations that took place during the nineteenth century were, for the first time, truly systematic and comprehensive. What made these transformations fundamentally different was the possibility of interpreting whole segments of reality in terms of self-referential models and systems. 'System' was not a new term, but it had already received a new and very different meaning during the seventeenth century. It was at that time that a system ceased to be a representation of the essential structure of the given reality and instead became a simulated equivalent—an a priori instrumental representation with the ambition to become a universal matrix. That ambition could not be fulfilled everywhere but only in those situations where it was possible to represent the given reality through a model and its purely formal language. Because the formation of systems followed the paradigm of the laboratory experiment, the principles of non-contradiction and sufficient reason—the only criteria of experimental reality—also apply to the instrumental representation of any reality that might eventually be represented in that manner (i.e., as a system). The intrinsic conditions of a particular system cannot determine how far it can be extended and what kind of reality can be incorporated into the instrumental representation. This always remains an open question that can only be decided in light of the actual conditions of specific cases.

An example may show this more clearly. The development of railways in the last century—and, in particular, their extension into the cities—stands in sharp contrast not only to the surrounding landscape or urban fabric but also to the earlier forms of transport, such as roads or canals. Unlike roads or canals, built in an open dialogue with the situational conditions of the given world, railways were designed as comprehensive systems from the very beginning. Designing a comprehensive system requires an a priori plan in which everything is designed beforehand, and in the language and logic of the system chosen. This must be done in such a way that nothing outside the system can interfere with its coherence and its working. In the case of railways, this amounted to nothing less than creating a relatively complete and autonomous reality within the given world. As a result, the movement of trains, the functioning of stations and signals, etc. must be predictable and reliable.

The relative perfection of a system is not unconditional, however. A whole set of conditions must be met if the system is to exist and work. The first is the spatial environment in which everything that we make must be situated. The second, closely linked with the first, is the cultural environment in which every system must be absorbed, incorporated and reconciled with everything that is already there. Only under such conditions can technological production be creative in any way. However, the distance or gap that, in most cases, separates the systems produced from the given world illustrates how limited is our understanding of their conditional nature, how strong is the faith in their autonomy, and how difficult it is, therefore, to bridge the gap. The gap is very often discussed as a problem of adaptation. But what should adapt to what? Today, it is rather taken for granted that the given world should adapt to the imperative of technological possibilities. This shows the limit of our understanding of what is really taking place, what is the nature of the given reality, and what technological interference and manipulation really mean. It is this lack of understanding that is the source of the confused belief that we live in a 'technological world'. And yet, to understand what is the true nature of the world in which we live is probably the most difficult task. We certainly live in a world that is profoundly influenced and shaped by technology. But this is very different from living in a technological world, if we understand by 'technology' what has been established in this essay. What is at stake here is not a semantic difference but the very nature of our current civilisation, which we may or may not understand. If we do not understand it, we will never be able to see the ambiguity, tension and very often deep conflict that exist between the being of technology and the being of the world. In that case, we will also be unable to recognise that ambiguity, tension and conflict are, in fact, essential characteristics of the world in which we really live.

Only when we take into account the reality that is not directly affected by technology—the primary conditions of our embodiment, the finitude of our life and so on—can we understand the true nature of the so-called 'technological world'.

Notes

1 Werner Heisenberg, 'Rationality in Science and Society', in *Can We Survive our Future?*, ed. George R. Urban with Michael Glenny, London: Bodley Head, 1971, p. 84.
2 This was programmatically formulated for the first time in the well-known passage of Francis Bacon's *Instauratio magna* (Sp. I; 132 [V, 21]): 'I am labouring to lay the foundation not of any school of thought, but of human utility and power.' [trans. Vesey].
3 'The basic form of appearance in which the will to will arranges and calculates itself in the unhistorical element of the world of completed metaphysics can be stringently called technology'; Martin Heidegger, *The End of Philosophy*, trans. Joan Stambaugh, London: Souvenir Press, 1975, p. 93.
4 Ibid., p. 101.
5 This is particularly apparent in the situatedness of will in the context of time, formulated for instance by Nietzsche as the attempt to overcome time through the 'eternal return'.
6 Martin Heidegger, *The Question Concerning Technology and other Essays*, trans. William Lovitt, New York: Harper Colophon Books, 1977, p. 35.

7 Aristotle, *Metaphysics*, Loeb Classical Library, trans. Hugh Tredennick, Cambridge, MA: Harvard University Press, 1933, 981b14.
8 Aristotle, *Physics*, trans. Philip H. Wicksteed and Francis M. Cornford, Loeb Classical Library, Cambridge, MA: Harvard University Press, 1937, 199a7.
9 Ibid. 199a9.
10 Aristotle, *Nichomachean Ethics*, trans. Harris Rackham, Loeb Classical Library, Cambridge, MA: Harvard University Press, 1968, 1140a20.
11 Aristotle, *Physics*, op. cit., 196b5.
12 Hans-Georg Gadamer, *The Relevance of the Beautiful*, trans. Nicholas Walker, ed. Robert Bernasconi, Cambridge: Cambridge University Press, 1986, p. 104.
13 Examples that may illustrate this point can be found in ancient Near Eastern cosmogonies and in the Greek understanding of creation, as well as in the articulated cosmologies and in the role of the craftsman as *demiourgos*, which also correspond to Heidegger's understanding of metaphysics.
14 'For a science of religion which regards only instrumental action as meaningful, magic is the essence and origin of religion'; Walter Burkert, *Greek Religion*, trans. John Raffan, Oxford: Blackwell, 1985, p. 33. 'Science views religion and its manifestations according to its own image and regards everything which refuses to succumb to its techniques as 'magical' and primitive'; Roger Granger, *The Language of the Rite*, London: Darton, Longman & Todd, 1974, p. 90.
15 Granger, *Language*, p. 78.
16 Gerardus Van der Leeuw, *Religion in Essence and Manifestation*, trans. John E. Turner, Gloucester, MA: Peter Smith, 1967, p. 548.
17 Eric R. Dodds, *The Greeks and the Irrational*, Los Angeles, CA: University of California Press, 1968, p. 288.
18 Pappus, *Greek Mathematical Texts*, Loeb edition, v. 2, trans. Ivor Thomas, Cambridge, MA: Harvard University Press, 1939, p. 61.
19 Jean-Pierre Vernant, *Myth and Thought Among the Greeks*, London: Routledge & Kegan Paul, 1983, p. 295.
20 Vitruvius, *On Architecture*, vol. II, book X.I.1, trans. Frank Granger, Loeb Classical Library, Cambridge, MA: Harvard University Press, 1931, p. 275.
21 Arnold Gehlen, *Die Seele im technischen Zeitalter*, Hamburg: Rowohlt Verlag, 1957, p. 15.
22 Vitruvius, op. cit., Book X.I.4, p. 277.
23 See, for example, the discussions that followed the explicitly formulated opinion about the role of magic in the development of modern science and technology by Frances Yates, recently summarised by Brian P. Copenhaver in *Reappraisals of the Scientific Revolution*, ed. David C. Lindberg and Robert S. Westman, Cambridge: Cambridge University Press, 1990, pp. 261–303. A similar difficulty seems to arise in discussions about the relationship of art and technique before the seventeenth century, particularly during the late Renaissance. The most interesting here are the discussions about the contribution of such personalities as Leonardo da Vinci and his role as artist, engineer or scientist.

24 For a more detailed discussion of the nature of the arts and their status in the Middle Ages and in the early modern era, see Paul O. Kristeller, *Renaissance Thought and the Arts*, Princeton, NJ: Princeton University Press, 1980, p. 163ff; and *The Seven Liberal Arts in the Middle Ages*, ed. David L. Wagner, Bloomington, IN: Indiana University Press, 1986.

25 It is characteristic that the arts have been very often referred to as science (*espiteme*), not only in Classical but also in Medieval scholarship. This is illustrated in the well-known debate, at the end of the fourteenth century, on the completion of Milan's cathedral, where the main question raised is known as *ars sine scientia nihil est*. For details, see James S. Ackerman, '"Ars Sine Scientia Nihil Est": Gothic Theory of Architecture and the Cathedral of Milan', *The Art Bulletin* 31, 1949, pp. 84–111.

26 In the Classical ontology, mathematics, and geometry in particular, are seen as a mediating link between metaphysics (theology) and physics, just as the soul (*psyche*) is a mediating link between the intelligible and sensible realities.

27 Buonaiuto Lorini, *Delle fortificazioni*, book V, Venice, 1575 [trans. Vesey].

28 Further illustrations of the limits of mathematical mechanisation and the discussion of the achievements of Leonardo da Vinci can be found in Eduard J. Dijksterhuis, *Mathematisation of the World Picture*, Oxford: Oxford University Press, 1961, pp. 35–50.

29 Robert E. Butts and Joseph C. Pitt, eds, *New Perspectives on Galileo*, Boston, MA: D. Reidel, 1978, p. 187; William A. Wallace, *Galileo and his Sources*, Princeton, NJ: Princeton University Press, 1984, pp. 126–49.

30 François Viète, 'Introduction to the Analytical Art', in Jacob Klein, *Greek Mathematical Thought and the Origin of Algebra*, Cambridge, MA: MIT Press, 1968, Appendix.

31 Ibid., p. 181.

32 Like universal mathematics, *prima philosophia* refers ultimately to the principle of non-contradiction and sufficient reason. The new algebra of a meta-mathematical kind and physics of a metaphysical kind have the same characteristics.

33 Étienne Gibson, *Études sur le role de la pensée médiévale dans la formation du système cartésien*, Paris: J. Vrin, 1967; and Wallace, *Galileo*, op. cit.

34 René Descartes, letter to Mersenne, 15 April 1630, in *Philosophical Writings*, ed. and trans. Elizabeth M. Anscombe and Peter T. Geach, Edinburgh: Nelson's University Paperbacks, 1954, p. 259.

35 Descartes, letter to Mersenne, 27 May 1631, in ibid., p. 261.

36 Galileo Galilei, *Dialogues Concerning the Two Chief World Systems*, trans. Stillman Drake, Los Angeles, CA: University of California Press, 1967, p. 14.

37 Ibid., p. 38.

38 'I argue *ex suppositione* about motion, so even though the consequences should not correspond to the events of naturally falling heavy bodies, it would little matter to me, just as it derogates nothing from the

demonstrations of Archimedes that no moveable is found in nature that moves along spiral lines. But in this I have been, as I shall say, lucky: for the motion of heavy bodies and its events correspond punctually to the events demonstrated by me from the motion I defined'; cited in Butts and Pitt, *New Perspectives*, op. cit., p. 234.

39 Ibid., p. 232.

40 René Descartes, 'Le monde', in *Oeuvres*, ed. Charles Adam and Paul Tannery, vol. XI, Paris, 1974, p. 31 [trans. Vesey].

41 Ibid., tome III, p. 722.

42 Descartes, *Philosophical Writings*, op. cit., Objections V, p. 136.

43 David R. Lachterman, *The Ethics of Geometry*, London: Routledge & Kegan Paul, 1989, p. 140.

44 Jean Ladrière, 'Technique et eschatologie terrestre', in *Civilisation, technique et humanisme*, Paris: Aubier-Montaigne, 1968.

45 Amos Funkenstein, *Theology and Scientific Imagination*, Princeton, NJ: Princeton University Press, 1986, p. 327. Among those who had this courage are Malebranche and the *occasionalistes* (Geulincx, for example) and, most explicitly, Leibniz.

3 The Architectonics of Embodiment

The relation of body to architecture and the complex phenomenon of corporeality have always had a privileged position within the history of European culture. This is particularly true of the tradition springing from Vitruvius, who compares the human body directly to the body of a building (in book III, chapter 1 of *De architectura*), and then makes a sequence of claims for this analogy that far transcend the need to explain the meaning of proportion, symmetry and harmony in architecture. Although this highly provocative subject has been treated with great attention and subtlety by critics, it remains nonetheless poorly understood.

The notion of body

The most critical aspect of the role of the body in understanding reality is the relation between the body and that which truly exists. It was raised originally by the Eleatics (Parmenides and Melissos), who sought to define that which must be homogenous, and therefore exist without a body. Their definitions led to a reaction by such fifth-century thinkers as Gorgias of Leontini,[1] the Atomists (Leukippos and Demokritos),[2] and the Pythagoreans (such as Ekphantus).[3] Thereafter, the body is used to designate not only conceptual, but also material reality. Plato, followed by Aristotle, took the decisive step towards a coherent understanding of corporeality. The body for Plato is not a given or something that can be isolated or defined as an entity; rather, it is part of a process of ordering within the domain of necessity. This process is never complete and is always open to further improvement through the continuous reciprocity of necessity and reason.[4] As a result, the body appears as a relatively stable structure ordered in the context of reality as a whole (*cosmos*). The openness of the ordering

DOI: 10.4324/9781003272090-4

process speaks not only about the contingency of the world but also about the contingent nature of the body. Contingency, in this case, stems from the tension between the conditions and possibilities of what is perceived as the cosmological process itself.[5]

Aristotle's contribution to the understanding of corporeality has much to do with his emphasis on the individualisation of *eidos*, on the particularity of the essential structure of things or bodies and their substance, *ousia*. That only particular substances are self-subsistent does not mean, of course, that they are the only substances that exist. Aristotle insists that there can be no action without contact, and from that he deduced the importance of contact, not only contact but also position, existence in place, lightness and weight.[6] This brought his vision of corporeality dangerously close to the later Stoic doctrine in which everything that either acts or is acted upon is a body; in other words, the only things that truly exist are material bodies. Aristotle himself had feared that if the existence of immaterial substances ever came to be doubted, physics and not metaphysics would be considered the first science. In the Stoic manner of thought, this is exactly what has happened: the notion of material body extended not only to the human body but also to the human soul—*pneuma*. The Stoics believed that 'nothing can act or be acted upon without body nor can anything create space except the void and emptiness. Therefore, beside void and bodies there can be no third nature of itself in the sum of things.'[7] This led inevitably to the conclusion that even the soul and the divine are corporeal.[8] On this basis, it became possible to read the meanings traditionally associated with the incorporeal nature of the soul directly into the visible manifestation of the body. It was under the influence of this radicalised and, in a certain sense distorted, Aristotelian understanding of corporeality that the Vitruvian doctrine of the body came into existence. In the Vitruvian understanding of corporeality, which was very strongly influenced by Stoic philosophy (Posidonios), the relation of body and soul was no longer clear.

The Vitruvian tradition was strongly influenced by the general reification of the inherited Classical culture as manifested in eclectic commentaries and encyclopaedic treatises during the first century BCE. The consequences of this influence are later evident in the need for elaborate commentaries on Vitruvius after he was 'rediscovered' in the fifteenth century and in the inconclusive attempts to understand areas of implied or potential meaning that nonetheless remained enigmatic. It was difficult to understand the meaning of the text as long as its reading followed the same assumptions on which the original text itself was based. An additional reason for the difficulty in seeing the problematic and derivative nature of Vitruvianism was the uncritical acceptance of the ancient authority of the text, combined with a concern to support the new author's own position.[9]

There is good reason to believe that creative architectural thinking is possible only in collaboration with other disciplines such as philosophy, astronomy, music, geometry and rhetoric. Otherwise, the difficult formulations that we find so often in architectural treatises remain enigmatic and often controversial. The exceptions are those commentaries that broke the orthodoxy of dogmatic thinking by moving into more distant areas of culture. A good example is Guarino Guarini's *Architettura civile* (1737), which, without his *Placita philosophica* (1665) and other philosophical and scientific writings, would be regarded as no more than a dogmatic technical treatise that is difficult to comprehend. It seems appropriate, therefore, to view Vitruvianism as a secondary tradition—one that is not only derivative but also has a tendency to dogmatism that obscures the 'primary tradition', alive until recently in a more or less uninterrupted continuity.

Body and microcosm

In the primary tradition that goes back to Plato and Aristotle, and remained alive until recent times, the body is always seen as linked with the soul, which in turn is related to the animated structure of reality as a whole. In a discussion of the 'generation of bodies' in *Timaeus*, Plato explains:

> The revolutions which are two and are bound within a sphere, shaping body in imitation of the spherical form of the all, which body we now call head, it being the most divine part and reigning over all the parts within us. To it the gods delivered over the whole of the body, which they had assembled to be its servant, having formed the notion that it should partake in all the motions which were to be.[10]

In his interpretation of a living body and its relation to cosmic movement, Aristotle argues:

> If a living body or thing is ever absolutely at rest, we shall have a motionless thing in which motion is originated by the thing

itself and not from without. If this can happen to a living thing, why not to the universe? And if in a smaller cosmos [*microcosmos*], why not with the larger cosmos [*megalocosmos*].[11]

This is probably the first consistent formulation of a relationship between the human body and the rest of reality, which is better known as microcosm, and later, in the Middle Ages, is referred to as *minor mundus*. This issue dominated the nature of European cosmology and anthropology until the eighteenth century. In fact, the shadow of this tradition still appears in Wilhelm Humboldt, Hermann Lotze and Gustav Fechner, in the nineteenth century. In this, the primary tradition, the problem of human existence is seen as a drama played out on a cosmic stage and the vision of human existence is more often than not identified with the human body, where there is a close affinity between human, corporeal and sensible realities (Fig. 3.1). Under these conditions the human body becomes a manifestation or *exemplum* of reality as a whole, encapsulated in the Middle Ages in the formula *mundus minor exemplum est—maiores mundi ordine*.[12] In his *Hexaemeron*, St. Ambrose speaks about the nature of the world (*mundus*) as being 'framed like man's body and as in man the head, so in the world the sky is the most excellent member, and as the eyes in man so are the sun and moon in the world.'[13] In his influential commentary on Plato's *Timaeus*, Chalcidius speaks summarily about man as *mundus brevis*—man as the abbreviation of the world.[14]

There is little doubt that the phenomenon of microcosm poses serious difficulties to modern thinking. Yet if we ignore the problematic speculations, the excessive level of mysticism and the excessive physical or naturalistic analogies (such as 'man's hair is like a grass, his veins and arteries like rivers and canals and his bones like mountains'[15]), then we are likely to be rewarded by a surprising richness and depth of understanding of the relation between the human body and the world—their common corporeality and meaning. This coincides, to a great extent, with current views of philosophical anthropology, the phenomenological understanding of corporeality, the world structure of human existence and the communicative nature of the world as understood in current hermeneutics. Together they suggest a fusion of horizons in which the nature of the human body and its relation to architecture and the rest of reality changes into one of embodiment. This is inevitable because the reality of the world is not structured around identifiable independent entities such

3.1 Hildegard von Bingen, *Liber divinorum operum*, 1163–73. The cosmic
spheres and human being.

as isolated human bodies or isolated architectural elements and their
corresponding meanings. Rather, it is structured through degrees of
embodiment, which represent a continuum of mediation between
the human and divine, terrestrial and celestial, sensible and intelligible levels of reality.

To appreciate the real meaning of microcosm and its contemporary relevance, we should look more closely at the deep reciprocity that exists between the human body and the world and, by implication, between the human body and architecture (Fig. 3.2). In the Aristotelian tradition, the body is always seen as engaged with its place and ultimately with the hierarchy of places (topology) within a unified cosmic framework. Aristotle explains: 'If a thing [body] is not separated from its embracing environment, but is undifferentiated from it, it is indeed "included in" it – not however as in its

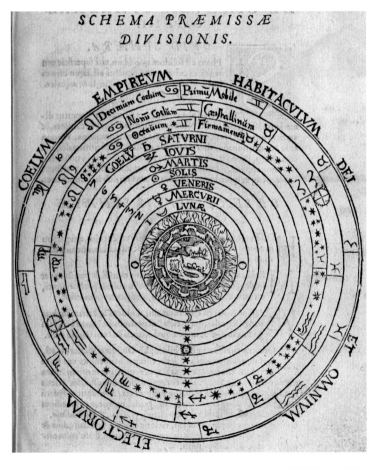

3.2 Peter Apian, *Cosmographia*, 1550. Macrocosmos.

place, but only in the sense in which a part is said to be "included in" its whole.'[16]

If the notion of reciprocity between places and bodies is taken one step further, then it is clear that places must be contained and situated in the same way as things or bodies are. Moreover, they constitute the same hierarchy, culminating in the same unifying cosmic place. Aristotle explains the nature of the hierarchy in the following statement: 'The earth as the centre of the universe and the inner surface of the revolving heavens constitute the supreme "below" and the supreme "above"; the former being absolutely stable and the latter constant in its position as a whole.'[17] When considering the human body, the hierarchically structured space in which all bodies have their place (*topos*) must be further qualified with respect to its animation by the soul.[18]

It is a serious mistake to see the human body as isolated from the soul and to discuss the problem of order and harmony as a direct manifestation of the invisible principles in the visible appearance of bodies. Such a simplified and distorted understanding can be found in many Renaissance architectural treatises and modern commentaries (Fig. 3.3). The following statement illustrates my point very well: 'The man-created forms in the corporeal world were the visible materialisations of the intelligible mathematical symbols, and the relationship between the pure forms of absolute mathematics and the visible forms of applied mathematics were immediately and intuitively perceptible.'[19]

It is appropriate to speak here about a general tendency that coincides with the development of modern perspective. Its main characteristic is the confusion of the distinction between sense and intellect, and a naive belief in the ability of sight to see intelligible reality directly, without any mediation with sensible reality. In his *Questiones Perspectivae*, Biagio Pelacani da Parma speaks about the judgement of sense (*Iudicium sensus*) and about the ability of sight to grasp things in the same manner as intellect does or can.[20] This immanentisation of the soul, the reduction of its higher capacities to corporeal form, makes it almost identical with the body. The body is still animated, but, in our modern way of thinking, the cryptic presence of the soul cannot be easily detected. For evidence of the presence of the soul we have to turn to more explicit examples. In his *Idea del tempio della pittura*, Lomazzo describes the axis of a figure as its *anima* or soul: 'It is necessary that painters and sculptors know what the soul is, that which descends from the head to

3.3 Cesare Cesariano, translation and commentary on Vitruvius's *De archi-tectura*, 1521. The Persian portico.

the bottom of the foot through the middle and equally from one extended hand to the other. See the figures drawn in the *Simmetria* of Dürer which have a line which passes through the centre of the figure which is its soul.'[21]

The identification of the soul with the axis of the body or with the body's centre of gravity (for example in Alberti's *De statua*, 1464, or Francesco di Giorgio's *Trattati di architettura ingegnieria e arte militare*, 1482, has its origin in the Aristotelian tradition where the notion of animation is seen as a dialectic of movement and its source (Fig. 3.4). Speaking about the place of the soul in the human organism, Aristotle says: 'Since the left and the right sides are symmetrical and these opposites are moved simultaneously, it cannot be that the left is moved by the right when it remains stationary, nor vice versa; the origin of movement must always be in what lies above both. Therefore, the original seat of the moving soul must be in that which lies in the middle.'[22]

In a complementary statement, critical to my subsequent argument, Aristotle describes the role of the soul in the following manner: 'The soul does not have to be in each part of the body, but she resides in a kind of central governing place of the body and the remaining parts live by continuity of natural structure, and play the parts nature would have them play.'[23] The notion of 'the continuity of natural structure', which gives life to the remaining parts of the human body, is very close to the contemporary phenomenological understanding of the same problem, most notably to the position of Maurice Merleau-Ponty when he says that 'there are several ways

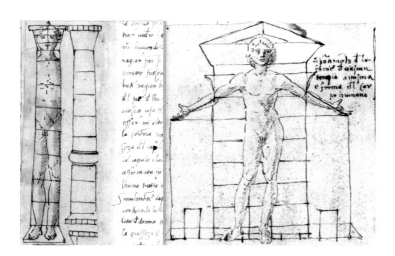

3.4 Francesco di Giorgio Martini, *Trattati di architettura ingegneria e arte militare*, 1476–77. Details from marginal drawings.

for the body to be a body, several ways for consciousness to be consciousness.'[24] In both cases the conventional vision of the body—distinct from the soul—appears as an abstraction that obscures the traditional notion of corporeality manifested as embodiment and animation.

The analogy of body and architecture, or body and cosmos, would be incomprehensible without a mediating link or structure between such ontologically different realities. It is all too easy to say that cosmic order is reflected in the human body, or that the proportions and configuration of architectural elements can be derived from the human body. How is it possible, then, and what are the conditions under which such claims can be turned into a meaningful and convincing understanding? These questions are usually left unanswered. The role of the human body in the process of embodiment in which architectural and cosmic order become apparent is comprehensible only in the context of the primary reality. This is a reality of our natural world where all relationships and references are constituted in the spontaneity of our continuous encounter with the conditions of our existence. In the context of the natural world, it is as futile to speak about anthropomorphism as it would be to speak about cosmomorphism. Both represent given conditions that we cannot escape. We can only isolate ourselves from them, or suppress them, and pretend that our own vision of reality is neutral and self-sufficient. It is quite obvious that upholding such a vision requires a considerable effort and a high integrity of representation, which is by definition derivative and secondary. And yet it is the secondary representation that we usually encounter first. The analogy on which secondary representations are based is a symbolic structure that links together similar yet heterogeneous phenomena through participation in the articulated continuum of our natural world.

Most decisive for the nature of analogy and its historical development is the breakdown of the symbolic structure that had sustained its meaning and authenticity. Its dissolution led to the transformation of direct symbolic relations into distant abstract concepts, or into a continuous metaphor, culminating in speculative and far-fetched allegory. Abstraction is characteristic of the transformation that led to determinism and the calculated appropriation of reality. Metaphor, conversely, leads to numerology and the comparative 'anatomy' of the human body to elements of architecture and to certain themes in astrology. The attempt to establish a precise relation between zodiacal phenomena and zones of the human body, for example, is frequently discussed and illustrated in the naturalistic microcosmic texts.[25] To assess the plausibility of a particular text requires a certain level of historical imagination and interpretative skill, but in many cases certain analogies remain problematic and unproductive, as they may have been already in their own time.

The tendency to reduce the continuum of transcendental relationships to purely corporeal analogies undermines not only the relevance of microcosmic speculations but also the relevance of analogy itself. Already in the fifteenth and sixteenth centuries, many intelligent minds struggled with the question of whether the body is a literal or figurative microcosm. The following text is a good illustration of the dilemma:

> The body also, as far as it was possible, carries the image of God not in figure as Audius and his followers the Anthropomorphites have foolishly dreamed [...] but because the admirable structure and accomplished perfection of the body carries in it a representation of all the most glorious and perfect works of God as being an epitome or compendium of the whole creation, by which he is rather signified than expressed. And hence it is that man is called a Microcosm or little world [...] The Divines call him *Omnem Creaturam*, every creature, because he is (in a manner) *All Things*; not for matter and substance as Empedocles would have it but analogically by participation or reception of the several species or kinds of things.[26]

Participation and reception refer to the most important aspect of analogy: its symbolic nature. In the process of symbolisation, analogy articulates the relationship between soul and body, between the intelligible order of reality and its visible corporeal manifestations. The process of symbolisation belongs to the vertical organisation of our culture, where the high and low, divine and human, were related and mediated by a sequence of stages, better known as the 'Chain of Being' (*catena rerum*). It is against this background that the meaning of the relationship between the individual parts of the body or a building may be understood. The relationship would be empty and meaningless without such a background.

The same is true for some of the more significant concepts that shaped the history of European architecture, such as order,

proportion and harmony (Fig. 3.4). Proportion, the most important in this sequence, is a key to the process of mediation mentioned
above. Before it is a relationship that can be represented numerically, proportion is, as the original Greek term *analogia* indicates,
an analogy.

Metaphor, analogy and proportion

In the primary tradition *analogia* is a symbolic structure that has
nothing directly to do with numbers. It depends on resemblances,
similarities and eventually on a balanced tension of sameness and difference when related to various phenomena. This confirms that the
origin of proportion is not in mathematics, understood in the conventional sense, but in language, and even when expressed numerically,
it still depends for its meaning on language.[27] In order to appreciate
the close link that exists between language and mathematics we need
only remember the role which geometrical demonstration played in
the formation of syllogistic reasoning.[28] The representation of proportion as number derives from the original form of analogy, and
more specifically the tension between 'the one and many' (identity
and difference), which is the essence of metaphor.[29] It is perhaps no
coincidence that geometrical proportion, which is a paradigm of all
other proportions, reflects the structure of metaphorical analogy
(A is to B, as C is to D).[30] The principle of 'the one and many' is
preserved in the original understanding of number as 'how many',
whereas modern number is a pure concept.

The system of proportions that dominated architectural thinking
for almost two millennia has its origin in the Pythagorean-Platonic
tradition, in which number was known as *arithmos*. Apart from its
prosaic meaning as a sum of numbers for counting, *arithmos* has a
more elevated meaning as a paradigm of unity in multiplicity. Each
sum contains 'many' units and yet it is always 'one'. This rather
mysterious character of *arithmos* is well described as the '*arithmos*
structure of logos'.[31] It reveals the deep structure of our experience,
the metaphorical articulation of analogies, and dialectical reasoning:
'Precisely for that reason the sum number (*arithmos*) proffers itself as
a prototype of the order of Being and the ideas. And it claims nothing more for itself than to be such a prototype.'[32] The metaphorical
nature of analogy, represented numerically as a form of proportion
(similar to the nature of syntax or grammar in language), suggests
that underlying proportion (and other summary notions such as

universal beauty, order and harmony) there is always a deeper level of articulation, coextensive with the articulation of the world as a whole.

Scrutinising the ontological foundations of proportion reveals its equivalence to embodiment: that which manifests itself as a proportionality or analogy of the visible and invisible, sensible and intelligible levels of reality. This revelation challenges the conventional understanding of proportion as a static harmony of different elements and supplies a more authentic understanding, where proportion is an open and dynamic paradigm of mediation and participation of the visible phenomena in the unity of the world, in the one (*hen*) and the good (*agathon*). Proportion tends towards mediation, but this can never be fully achieved. None the less, proportion remains a tool with which it is possible to approximate the process and its goal. Plato speaks in this context about *hypothesis*, as something we humans can achieve in order to anticipate the essential nature of reality.[33] Through *hypothesis* numbers and proportions serve as a model, or *propaedeutics*, to a full representation of reality through dialectics. In that role they 'facilitate the apprehension of the idea of good [...] and force the soul to turn its vision round to the region where dwells the most blessed part of reality.'[34] Numerical proportions share the advantages but also the limits of mathematical disciplines, which, like 'geometry and the studies which accompany it, are, as we see, dreaming about being, but the clear, waking vision of it is not possible for them as long as they leave the assumptions which they employ undisturbed and cannot give any account of them.'[35]

Returning to the problem of proportion in architecture, there is very little dialectical thinking in Renaissance architectural treatises and, regrettably, even less in modern commentaries. We hear about basic harmonies of the universe, universally valid ratios and proportions, about the parallelism of musical and visual harmonies, but it is far from clear how these ambitious statements relate to reality or under what conditions they can be sustained or justified. In a memorandum written in 1567, Andrea Palladio goes one step further than most other architect-theorists do when he writes: 'The proportions of the voices are harmonies for the ears; those of the measurements are harmonies for the eyes. Such harmonies usually please very much without anyone knowing why, excepting the student of the causality of things.'[36]

The knowledge of the 'causality of things' is not a reference to musical theory or to the study of analogies but to demonstrative thinking. There is no evidence that Palladio himself was at home in this field.

But some of his friends were, particularly Daniele Barbaro, whose knowledge of philosophy, mathematics and music was exceptional, and who was in close contact with scholars such as Francesco Barozzi, the translator of Proclus' commentary on Euclid, an exemplary introductory text to Platonic dialectics. In his commentary on Vitruvius, Barbaro speaks about 'certain knowledge', 'true architecture' and the knowledge of how to 'conclude many things from the right principles (*scire per causas*)'. Early in his introduction he states that 'truly divine is the desire of those, who raising their minds to consider things, search for the reasons behind them.'[37] (Fig. 3.5). In the musical section of the commentary, Barbaro raises questions about too simplistic a reliance on musical analogies: 'Many think that with the diatonic genus they can satisfy every quality of things [...] I wish this were the place to explain the ideas and colours suitable to every quality of thing according to their genera, because with the living experience of their ears confirmed by invincible reasoning - I would make them confess their errors.'[38]

The example of Barbaro illustrates the extent to which the meaning of architectural proportions depends on a broader milieu of discourse. Moreover, it demonstrates the necessity of being situated in a culture where communication between the different arts and disciplines still play an important role. This was openly recognised by a number of authors, including Leon Battista Alberti, who referred to philosophers and mathematicians to substantiate his statements. We know that among those very close to him were Nicolas Cusanus and possibly Paolo Toscanelli and Marsilio Ficino, scholars with a deep understanding of Platonic dialectics and of the ontology of proportions. In view of the presentation of the same issues in architectural discourse, however, it is not easy to see how their position influenced contemporary architectural thinking. The difference between philosophical and artistic interpretations can be explained as a tendency in art to treat the tradition of transcendental dialectical understanding of proportion and harmony as an immanent problem. This is clearly illustrated in Alberti's own words: 'The very same numbers that cause sounds to have that *concinnitas*, pleasing to the ears, can also fill the ideas and mind with wondrous delight.' As a result, 'we define harmony as that consonance of sounds which is pleasant to the ears'.[39]

The audible musical consonants accepted as a paradigm of universal harmony became a foundation of architectural thinking in the early fifteenth century, the role of which was not seriously questioned for almost three hundred years. The primary consonances and

3.5 Robert Fludd, *Utriusque cosmi…historia*, 1617–24. The temple of music.

their legitimacy were derived from the description of the structure of the soul in Plato's *Timaeus*, which has nothing to do directly with music. It is surprising that Renaissance authors and most modern commentators appear not to recognise this. The *tetractys*, which Plato chose as a point of departure, includes musical ratios, but its primary meaning is elsewhere. It is a progression of the first four numbers generating the perfect number ten (*decad*), which 'completes the series of numbers, containing in itself the nature of both even and odd and of that which is in motion and that which is still'.[40] The *tetractys* is used primarily as a key to dialectical reasoning. In the creation of the body of the world that the soul is supposed to animate, the process described by Plato begins with the making of fire and earth, representing the visible and tangible characteristics of corporeality, and also the highest and lowest elements in the vertical structure of the world. They are linked together by two means, air and water, in 'a continued geometrical proportion to effect this most perfectly'.[41] Continuous proportion is used for reasons of mediation and unity, as a vehicle in the formation of the soul. The progression from one to whole numbers represents the process of participation (*methexis*) in which the corporeal phenomena are related through a continuous sequence with the source of their potential unity (one).[42]

The meaning of the process of participation is ontological and not musical.[43] Music plays only an intermediate role in the generation of proportional ratios, as is illustrated in the following commentary:

> Seeing, then, that the Tetraktys supplies the proportion of the symphonies mentioned, and the symphonies serve to make up the perfect harmony, and according to the perfect harmony all things are arranged, on this account they have described it as 'the fount containing the roots of Nature ever-enduring'. Again, they argue that it is according to the ratios of these four numbers that both body and the incorporeal, from which come all things, are conceived – for it is by the flow of a point that we form a notion of a line, which is length without breadth, and by the flow of a line we construct breadth, which is surface without depth, and by the flow of surface solid body is produced. [...] Thus, it is reasonable to hold that the Tetraktys is the fount of universal Nature.[44] (Fig. 3.6)

The ontological meaning of embodiment is closely linked with the phenomena of proportion, in the sense that one speaks for the other. In the primary tradition in which proportion is understood dialectically, the relationship between different levels of reality coincides with the degree of their embodiment. This was most clearly expressed in the late Medieval philosophy of light: 'It is clear that light through the infinite multiplication of itself extends matter into finite dimensions that are smaller and larger according to certain

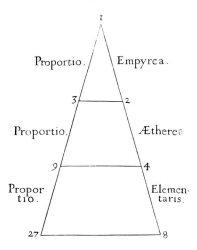

3.6 Robert Fludd, *Utriusque cosmi...historia*, 1617–24. The Platonic
  lambda (*tetractys*) as structure for the three levels of creation.

proportions that they have to one another and thus light proceeds
according to numerical and non-numerical proportions.'[45]
   The philosophy of light was incorporated into architectural thinking and found its expression in the overall vertical organisation of
the architectural body. The paradigm of such an organisation was
the structure of the spire or pinnacle that can be seen as a pyramid of
light articulated by a continuous proportion. In Albertus Magnus's
interpretation the creator is a source and point of light (*punctus lucis*)
that radiates layers of light in the form of an infinite pyramid towards
its base, which becomes increasingly dark in the shadowy domain
of the material region. All the strata of the cosmos have their origin
in this first principle of light, which radiates light as a form (species)
of all created things in a pyramid, that is, in accordance with the
laws of light geometry. The pyramidal shape of the spire or pinnacle is the symbolic representation of the process of creation and, in
another sense, of a participation in the unity of Being and in the
good. Things are beautiful only to the degree to which they participate in the good.[46] In the introductory section of his *Fialenbüchlein*,
Mathes Roriczer speaks about the correct proportion of the pinnacle:
'Since each art has its own matter, form and measure I have tried with
the help of God to make clear this aforesaid art of geometry and for
the first time to explain the beginning of drawn-out stonework, how

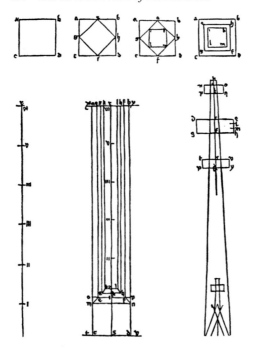

3.7 Drawing after Mathes Roriczer, *Das Büchlein von der Fialen*, 1486.
Generational square and elevation of a pinnacle.

and in what measure it rises out of the fundamentals of geometry
through manipulation of the dividers and how it should be brought
into the correct proportions (*rechten Masse*)'[47] (Fig. 3.7).

If we accept that the hierarchy of reality is articulated in a precise
proportional manner as a world, then we may be able to describe the
process as the architectonics of embodiment in which architecture
itself plays a very important role. Architecture represents the most elementary mode of embodiment that enables the more articulated levels
of culture, including numbers and ideas, to be situated in reality as a
whole. The distance that separates architecture from ideas or numbers
cannot be bridged directly and in a simple way. The task is open to mediation, but this is never a perfect or complete process because human
understanding and modes of representation limit it. Representation
is mediated through culture, and thus primarily through philosophy, science, literature, music, painting, sculpture and architecture.
In a hierarchically differentiated way, each area represents a particular

mode of articulation with a corresponding mode of embodiment. The continuity of embodiment that penetrates and unites them all is only a different term for the architectonics of embodiment mentioned earlier. The way in which the primary structure of architecture (architectonics) determines the structure of sculpture, painting, language and eventually the structure of ideas cannot be discussed here in further detail. Suffice it to say that what a book is to literacy, architecture is to culture as a whole.

It can be concluded that the architectonics of embodiment reveals the most essential characteristics of proportion as they were understood in the primary tradition. In that tradition, as we have seen, things are proportioned with respect to a unifying whole, as an open dialectical structure, and not for themselves as a visible unity or closed system of proportions. This difference is a sure guide to a better understanding of the much quoted commonplace about the nature of the cosmos—that it is arranged 'by measure and number and weight'.[48] It is the credo of so many discussions about proportion, yet this phrase is interpreted, almost without exception, as a confirmation of the mathematical (numerical) structure of reality, while the original meaning, clearly grasped until modern times, was fundamentally different. In many earlier texts, for example, we find a definition like that of Bonaventura:

> In the first way of seeing the observer considers things in themselves and sees in them weight, number and measure; weighted with respect to the place towards which things incline; numbers by which things are distinguished and measure by which things are determined. Hence, he sees in them their mode, species and order, as well as substance, power and activity. From all these considerations the observer can rise, as from a vestige to the knowledge of the immense power, wisdom and goodness of the creator.[49]

Modus, species and order 'are in fact various modalities of proportion'.[50] Together they represent the qualitative criteria of harmony, the beautiful and the good.[51]

This brings us to the last point, the nature and use of a module by which the nature of proportion is probably most clearly revealed. In conventional interpretations the module is seen as a vehicle for a clearer and more efficient execution of a building, or simply as a unit of commensurability (Fig. 3.8). If, however, we take into account the importance of the concept of identity and the good or the unity of

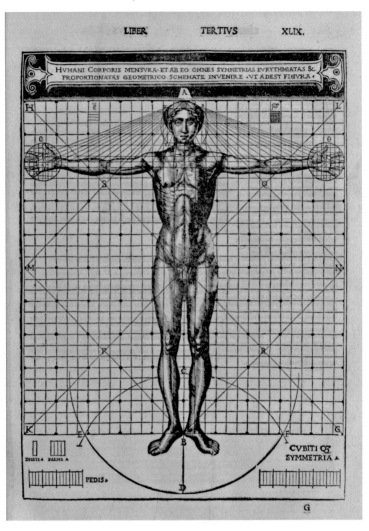

3.8 Cesare Cesariano, translation and commentary on Vitruvius's *De architectura*, 1521. Vitruvian man within a square.

being in the understanding of harmony, then the module is something quite different. It appears as a visible manifestation of identity and as an embodiment of our efforts to grasp the moments of sameness in the hierarchical order of things.[52] The numerical representation of the module is a visible entry into a world structured by analogy and proportion. In relation to that world, it is the most tangible embodiment and paradigm of proportion in the primary tradition. The meaning of the module and its role in proportioning architectural elements or the human body depends entirely on the presence of an articulated world in which the body is connected with embodiment and proportion with architectonics. The presence of an articulated world and 'primary tradition' determined architectural thinking and practice in the past. I believe it should continue to determine the relevance of our interpretations today.

Notes

1 Hermann Diels and Walter Kranz, *Fragmente der Vorsokratiker*, 5th ed., Berlin: Weidmann, 1934–37, DK 82 B3 73.
2 Ibid. DK 68 B156.
3 Ibid. DK 51.2 and 51.4.
4 Plato, Timaeus, 51a–53d. For a more detailed discussion see Hans-Georg Gadamer, *Dialogue and Dialectics*, trans. P. Christopher Smith, New Haven, CT: Yale University Press, 1980, pp. 172–93.
5 The elementary conditions of the process are discussed in Plato, *Philebus*, 16d, and also in Gadamer, op. cit., p. 205.
6 Aristotle, *De generatione et corruptione*, 322b26–323a9.
7 Lucretius, *De rerum natura*, I, II, 440–46 [trans. Vesely].
8 David E. Hahm, *The Origins of Stoic Cosmology*, Newark, OH: Ohio State University Press, 1977, pp. 3–29.
9 There is a close affinity between 'primary tradition' and 'effective history' (*Wirkungsgeschichte*), a term used in current hermeneutics: see Hans-Georg Gadamer, *Truth and Method*, trans. William Glen-Doepel, ed. John Cumming and Garret Barden, London: Sheed & Ward, 1975, pp. 245–58 and pp. 267–74. In the domain of architecture, 'primary tradition' refers to the concrete historical situation in which architecture is created. This includes studio and workshop practice, oral tradition, and the communicative space of culture as a whole. At a deeper level, the 'primary tradition' coincides with the tradition of Classical and Christian humanism. We are only beginning to understand its presence and role, and the following text is therefore no more than a small contribution to such an understanding.
10 Plato, *Timaeus*, trans. W.R.M. Lamb, Loeb Classical Library, Cambridge, MA: Harvard University Press, 1925, 44d [modified Vesely].
11 Aristotle, *Physics*, Books V–VIII, trans. Philip H. Wicksteed and Francis M. Cornford, Loeb Classical Library, Cambridge, MA: Harvard University Press, 1934, 252b26.
12 Gabirol ibn Solomon, Latin trans. I. Hispanus and D. Gundissalinus, ed. Clemens Baeumker, in *Beiträge zur Geschichte der Philosophie des Mittelalters*, I. II, Munster, 1892.

13 St. Ambrose, *Hexaemeron*, 4th c., in Jacques Paul Migne, *Patrologia Latina*, 55, vol. XIV, col. 265, as translated in George Perrigo Conger, *Theories of Macrocosms and Microcosms in the History of Philosophy*, New York: Columbia University Press, 1922, p. 34.

14 Chalcidius, *In Platonis Timaeum commentarius*, in Friedrich W.A. Mullach, *Fragmenta philosophorum graecorum*, Paris, 1881, vol. II, CC cf. CCXXX, as cited in Conger, op. cit., p. 23.

15 Josef ibn Zaddik, German trans. Max Doctor, *Die Philosophie des Josef (Ibn) Zaddik* in *Beiträge zur Geschichte der Philosophie des Mittelalters*, II. II, Munster, 1895, p. 20 [trans. Vesely].

16 Aristotle, *Physics*, Books I–IV, op. cit., 211a30.

17 Ibid., 212a20.

18 I am not using here the term *human soul*, leaving the meaning of the soul open for a more general reading, which includes the notion of world soul as well as the contemporary understanding of the soul as an ontological movement of human existence. See Jan Patočka, 'Reflection as the Practice of Self-Discovery', in *Body, Community, Movement, World*, trans. Erazim Kohák, Chicago and La Salle, IL: Open Court, 1998, pp. 109–18.

19 Rudolf Wittkower, *Architectural Principles in the Age of Humanism*, London: A. Tiranti, 1967, p. 29.

20 Graziella Federici-Vescovini, *Studi sulla prospettiva medievale*, Turin: G. Giappichelli, 1965, pp. 158–75.

21 Roberto P. Ciardi, ed., *Gian Paolo Lomazzo: Scritti sulle arti*, Florence: Marchi & Bertolli, 1973, cap. 35, p. 351 [trans. Vesely].

22 Aristotle, *De partibus animalium*, trans. A.S.L. Farquharson, Oxford: Clarendon Press, 1913, 669b.

23 Ibid., 703a.

24 Maurice Merleau-Ponty, *The Phenomenology of Perception*, trans. Colin Smith, London: Routledge & Kegan Paul, 1962, p. 143.

25 The period of Mannerism is particularly rich in the production of such texts (Paracelsus, Böhme, Cardanus, Campanella). In Jakob Böhme's *Aurora*, we find the following analogies: 'The body cavity signifies the space between the stars, the arteries signify the courses of stars.' In Karl W. Schiebler, ed., *Jakob Böhme*, Leipzig, 1832, vol. II, p. 28 [trans. Vesely].

26 Helkiah Crooke, *Microcosmographia*, London, 1615, pp. 2–3.

27 The role of language in the understanding of proportion is well illustrated by the role that *trivium* (grammar, rhetoric, dialectics) played as a propaedeutics for the *quadrivium* (arithmetic, geometry, music, astronomy). See David L. Wagner, ed., *The Seven Liberal Arts in the Middle Ages*, Bloomington, IN: Indiana University Press, 1986.

28 Aristotle, *Analytica posteriora*, 78a.

29 Paul Ricoeur, *The Rule of* Metaphor, trans. Robert Czerny et al., London: Routledge & Kegan Paul, 1978, p. 199.

30 The relation between geometrical proportion and metaphorical analogy is well illustrated in Plato, *Gorgias*, 508a.

31 Jacob Klein, *Greek Mathematical Thought and the Origin of Algebra*, Cambridge, MA: MIT Press, 1968, p. 79ff.

32 Gadamer, *Dialogue and Dialectics*, op. cit. p. 151.
33 Plato, *Phaedo*, 100a; *Meno*, 86c; *Parmenides*, 137b.
34 Plato, *Republic*, trans. Paul Shorey, Loeb Classical Library, Cambridge, MA: Harvard University Press, V. II, 1935, 526e.
35 Ibid., 533c.
36 Antonio Magrini, *Memorie intorno A. Palladio*, Padova, 1845, Appendix, 12, in, Wittkower, op.cit., p.113.
37 Daniele Barbaro, *Vitruvio, I dieci libri dell'architettura*, Venice, 1567, Milano, Edizioni il Polifilo, 1987, Book I, Proemio, p. 8 [trans. Vesely].
38 Ibid., Book V, p. 230.
39 Leon Battista Alberti, *On the Art of Building in Ten Books*, trans. Joseph Rykwert et al., Cambridge, MA: MIT Press, 1988, p. 305.
40 Theon of Smyrna, *Mathematics Useful for Understanding Plato*, trans. Robert and Deborah Lawlor from the 1892 Greek/French edition of Jean Dupuis, San Diego, CA: Wizard's Bookshelf, 1979, p. 70.
41 Plato, *Timaeus*, op. cit., 31c.
42 The importance of mediation towards unity and of the continuity of proportion is demonstrated by the insertion of arithmetic and harmonic means in the intervals of the primary structure of the soul articulated by geometrical proportion. The insertion of the harmonic (musical fourth) and arithmetic (musical fifth) means the scale was completed in terms of perfect harmonic continuity.
43 In the articulation of the structure of the soul, Plato has taken into account all that is necessary for the dialectical understanding of reality—Being, sameness, difference and participation (*methexis*)—and 'constructed a section of the diatonic scale whose range is fixed by considerations extraneous to music.' (Francis M. Cornford, *Plato's Cosmology*, Indianapolis: Hackett Publishing, 1975, p. 72). One of the extraneous reasons was to attune the scale down to whole numbers. 'Modern commentators seem not to have taken sufficient notice of the fact that this decision has nothing whatever to do with the theory of musical harmony.' (Ibid., p. 67).
44 Sextus Empiricus, *Against the Logicians*, trans. Robert G. Bury, Loeb Classical Library, Cambridge, MA: Harvard University Press, 1932, l. 98–101.
45 Robert Grosseteste, *On Light*, trans. Clare C. Riedel, Milwaukee, WI: Marquette University Press, 1978, p. 12.
46 Klaus Hedwig, *Sphaera Lucis: Studien zur Intelligibilität des Seidenden im Kontext der Mittelalterlichen Lichtspekulation*, Münster: Aschendorff, 1980, p. 177.
47 Lon R. Shelby, *Gothic Design Techniques*, Carbondale, IL: Southern Illinois University Press, 1977, p. 83.
48 Wisdom of Solomon, 11.20, in Robert H. Charles, *The Apocrypha and Pseudepigrapha of the Old Testament in English*, Vol. I, Oxford: Oxford University Press, 1913, p. 553.
49 St. Bonaventure, *The Soul's Journey into God*, trans. Ewert H. Cousins, New York: Paulist Press, 1978, I.11, p. 8.
50 Umberto Eco, *The Aesthetics of Thomas Aquinas*, trans. Hugh Bredin, Cambridge, MA: Harvard University Press, 1988, p. 67.

51   Alberti's criteria for *concinnitas* are rather revealing. Alberti's number, outline (*finitio*) and position (*collocatio*) seem to correspond very closely with number, measure and weight. Number has the same meaning in both cases: 'Finitio of the building is the building's measure'. *Collocatio* refers to the place of individual parts in the building as a whole (Joan Gadol, *Leon Battista Alberti: Universal Man of the Renaissance*, Chicago, IL: University of Chicago Press, 1973, p. 110).

52   Coming to terms with the problem of identity, the equivalent of participation in the ultimate good, the unity of Being and the presence of the divine in the human world dominated European history until the end of the seventeenth century. The problem of identity found its most explicit and most influential articulation in Proclus' *Elements of Theology* based on the hierarchy of ones (*henads*) and in the metaphysics of light culminating in the multiplication of species (see R. Bacon *De multiplicatione specierum*, in *Roger Bacon's Philosophy of Nature*, ed. & trans. David C. Lindberg, Oxford: Clarendon Press, 1983).

4 The Relation of Religion and Science

The distance that separates religion and science today is a result of a relatively recent development. Its emergence coincides with the foundation of a new kind of knowledge in the seventeenth century, named later as modern natural science. The traditional equivalent in Christian Europe was a general knowledge or philosophy of nature, known as *episteme* or later as *scientia*, but both terms referred to a general philosophy of nature and not to a specialised discipline. The general character of the knowledge of nature was present in its hierarchical organisation, linking together the sensible, material levels of reality with the intelligible ones, culminating in theology. This can be illustrated by many contemporary statements, among which would be this from Roger Bacon in the thirteenth century: in Bacon's view there is only one wisdom that unfolds through the different disciplines (sciences). It unfolds, as it were, 'in the palm with these disciplines (sciences) as fingers and yet it gathers within its own grasp all wisdom, since all wisdom has been given by one god to one world for one purpose.' Following the same line of thought, Bacon writes, 'One science is the mistress of the others, namely theology, to which the remaining sciences are vitally necessary and without which it cannot reach its end.'[1]

The unity of knowledge, understood to be the condition of salvation, was seen by Bacon and his contemporaries as a goal that could be reached only through a series of steps, beginning with sensible experience and ending with the intelligible understanding of the divine. The typical sequence was a movement, expressed in the progression of knowledge, from physics through mathematics to metaphysics (theology). This understanding of the relation between religion (theology) and the philosophy of nature dominated European history until the beginning of the eighteenth century. It is interesting and

DOI: 10.4324/9781003272090-5

rather characteristic that Newton, one of the founders of modern natural science, saw himself as theologian and that his *opus magnum* was still called *Philosophy of Nature* (*Philosophiae naturalis principia mathematica*).[2]

It is a deep paradox, not yet fully understood and appreciated, that modern science, including the ensuing collisions with theology, had its origins not in some independent body of new knowledge, but in the development of theology itself. This is a long story, but a short version may suffice. The science of what may be described as the transitional period (between the end of the sixteenth century and the beginning of the eighteenth) is closely linked not only with philosophy, metaphysics and theology, but still with the culture as a whole. The culture of that period was haunted by religious conflicts and a profound relativism of values but, at the same time, by a search for a new unity and universality of political and cultural order. Under such conditions it is not surprising that the possible unity was found in the universality of mathematics, closely associated with the ultimate principles of non-contradiction and sufficient reason of metaphysics and with the new principles of theology, identified at that time with the primary principles of metaphysics. The possibility to see the divine in these most abstract terms was anticipated by the earlier development, exemplified already in Roger Bacon's appraisal of geometry: 'From the ineffable beauty of the divine wisdom would shine and infinite benefit would overflow if these matters relating to geometry which are contained in scripture should be placed before our eyes in their physical forms. Therefore, I count nothing more fitting for a man diligent in the study of God's wisdom than the exhibition of geometrical forms of this kind before his eyes.'[3] Theology, elevated to this level of abstraction and intelligibility, can be rightly described as *theologia more geometrico*, following the tradition of the *Deus Geometra*.[4]

The decisive step in the genesis of modern science was the development of the theological-mathematical studies in the Jesuit College in Rome (Collegio Romano), which became the main source of inspiration and justification of the mathematical treatment of reality for Galileo and his contemporaries.[5] Galileo argued:

> [T]aking man's understanding intensively, in so far as this term denotes understanding some propositions perfectly, I say that the human intellect does understand some of them perfectly, and thus in these it has as much absolute certainty as Nature has. Of such are the mathematical sciences alone;

that is geometry and arithmetic, in which the Divine intellect indeed knows infinitely more propositions, since it knows all. But with regard to those few which the human intellect does understand, I believe that its knowledge equals the Divine in objective certainty, for here it succeeds in understanding necessity, beyond which there can be no greater sureness.[6]

The nature of modern science

The main characteristic of modern science was its experimental nature, based on the dialogue between *a priori* mathematical formulae and idealised physical reality. In this dialogue, the mathematical formula, used as a hypothesis, is *followed* by an approximation and anticipation of the physical result. On the physical side of the experimental dialogue, phenomena are simplified through abstraction to the point where the approximate mathematical form is free of all difficult material impediments and circumstances. It is for these reasons that it would be more appropriate to regard the experimental dialogue as the result of intellectual craftsmanship rather than a rigorous science. As a consequence, the *topos* of the workshop or laboratory is a more appropriate vehicle for understanding the nature of modern science than the *topos* of the study or the given phenomenal world. The result of this new development is a science emancipated from the context of the natural world and free to create through technical application its own independent reality. The possibility of an action emancipated from the given conditions of reality, tradition, ethical principles and values, is the main source of the modern environmental crisis. It is interesting to see to what extent even this stage of development is shadowed by religious thinking. This is illustrated by the fact that, in Newton's circle, what came to be known as *physica sacra* evolved. The history of creation in Genesis could be shown, line by line, to be in perfect harmony with the works of Newton. Later, Herder could still refer to fifty systems of physical theology (*Physik-theologie*), in all of which God's actions followed mathematical laws.[7]

The different criteria of truth and growing authority of the new science challenged not only the traditional philosophy of nature, but also the role of religion and theology. This was assessed by a modern thinker in a critical summary:

Yet there is something for which Newton - or better to say not Newton alone, but modern science in general - can still be made responsible: it is the splitting of our world in two [...] It did this by substituting for our world of quality and sense perception, the world in which we live, and love, and die, another world - the world of quantity, of reified geometry, a world in which, though there is a place for everything, there is no place for man. This, the world of science - the real world - became estranged and utterly divorced from the world of life, which science has been unable to explain - not even to explain away by calling it 'subjective'. True, these worlds are every day - and even more and more - connected by the *praxis.* Yet for *theory* they are divided by an abyss. Two worlds, this means two truths. Or no truth at all. This is a tragedy of modern mind which 'solved the riddle of the universe' but only to replace it by another riddle, the riddle of itself.[8]

The reference to the 'splitting of our world in two' is only part of the story. The use of the term 'science' is based on the assumption that there is such a thing as one science, while in reality there are only individual sciences. The differentiation of knowledge is a natural outcome of the application of the experimental method. In the experimental situation each science creates its own domain of competence (expertise), its own concepts and modes of interpretation. The result is a mosaic of sciences, each studying a chosen segment of reality (topic), leaving behind areas that are not easy or even possible to study with their methods. There are understandable attempts to overcome the mosaic-like nature of knowledge by developing theories of unified science, unified theory of matter or reality, etc. So far, none of them have been successful. The creation of a unified knowledge of reality is hampered not only by the fragmented results of individual sciences, but also by the highly abstract nature of knowledge of some of them. This is a problem addressed by philosophically oriented modern scientists. One such scientist is Werner Heisenberg, who questions the relation between abstract mathematical language and phenomenal reality. There are situations, he writes, when 'we don't know how far the mathematical language can be applied to the phenomena. In the last resort, even science must rely upon ordinary language, since it is the only language in which we can be sure of really grasping the phenomena.'[9] Behind Heisenberg's reference to ordinary language are two intentions: one is to resolve the tension between scientific method and everyday reality, the second is to understand the conditions of the unity of society and culture (including religion) in their relation to the traditional notion of 'One'. In order to develop the unified knowledge of reality, he says further,

> [...] having pointed out with the outmost clarity the possibilities and limitations of precise language, we must switch to the language of poetry, which evokes in the hearer images conveying understanding of an altogether different kind .... The language of images and likenesses is probably the only way of approaching the 'one' from more general domains. If the harmony in the society rests on a common interpretation of the 'one' the unitary principle behind the phenomena, then the language of poetry may be more important than the language of science.[10]

This statement points to the kind of language and level of understanding where it is possible to ask questions about the unified vision of reality. Coming from the pen of a scientist the statement is rather surprising and novel; and yet in some parts of culture, for instance in philosophy, the search for the unified vision of reality is old; it was never forgotten, perhaps with the exception of the nineteenth century, when the one-sided confidence of modern science created an artificial conflict, not only with religion but also with contemporary philosophy (in particular the philosophy of nature). The conflict was ultimately resolved in a rather sober way by a declaration of neutrality, well-illustrated by the following statement:

> The heavens referred to in the Bible have little to do with the heavens to which we send up aircrafts and rockets. In the astronomical universe, the earth is only a minute grain of dust in one of the countless galactic systems, but for us it is the center of the universe – it really is the center [...] The care to be taken in keeping the two languages, religious and scientific, apart from one another, should also include an avoidance of any weakening of their content by blending them. The correctness of tested scientific results cannot rationally be cast in doubt by religious thinking, and conversely, the ethical demands stemming from the heart of religious thinking ought not to be weakened by all too rational arguments from the field of science.[11]

This conclusion may be acceptable for science and religion as long as they agree to remain independent, but is not an answer to ecology, which depends on the understanding of environment in its wholeness.

Towards a new ecological knowledge

The real task facing ecology as a genuine discipline is a more appropriate knowledge of the natural world, which at the moment neither individual sciences nor religion can provide on their own. The more appropriate knowledge should be able to restate in a convincing manner the results of the individual sciences on a level where the individual results can be expressed in a common language, compatible with the language of religion. This is not an easy task. It is certainly not as easy as it may appear in the superficial talk about interdisciplinary research, which does not answer the most important question: what kind of vehicle or paradigm can integrate the mosaic of scientific knowledge on a level that can be shared with religion. In current debates the name of the paradigm that is expected to integrate our fragmented knowledge, including the ethical and religious issues, is 'environment'. And yet there is no clear consensus about the nature of environment or ecology. The dominant understanding is most often expressed in the following definition: 'Ecology is a branch of biology that studies relationships between living organisms and the non-living components of the environment in which they live.'[12] The inconclusive understanding of the nature of environment (ecology) is apparent in the shift from the earlier forms of environmental concerns and studies, dominated mostly by biological sciences to a new, extended vision of environment, which takes into consideration also the nature of the human world.[13] This shift, described as a move from a shallow to a deep ecology, brought into the understanding of environment the issues of human presence and personal ethics. However, even the most laudable intentions of deep ecology leave the results suspended between an ambiguous notion of ecological science (which nobody seems to define) and personal religious language. This brings us back to our question of the more appropriate ecological knowledge. It is curious and rather strange that the same issues addressed in current environmental or ecological studies have been investigated and articulated systematically and in great detail by the phenomenology and hermeneutics of the natural world for almost one hundred years, and yet the results are either unknown or ignored by most environmentalists. This may be explained by the fact that phenomenology is a philosophy that is usually outside the domain of the interest and competence of scientists, and by the fact that phenomenological studies don't present their results in the language of ecology.

Phenomenology of environment

It was mainly the critical response to the dogmatic belief that science is the only and ultimate criterion of truth that the attempts to restore the contextual foundations of science and the unified vision of reality emerged. The most rigorous and coherent of these was the movement known later as phenomenology. As is well known, phenomenology represents the most radical form of empiricism, the 'return to things themselves',[14] and the rehabilitation of philosophy in its role of laying the foundations of knowledge and situating it in the unifying context of the 'world'. The new understanding of world as the life-world or natural world of our existence is probably the most important contribution to the new way of thinking that became necessary in a situation increasingly dominated by a scientistic vision of reality, and by the growing awareness of the limits of such a vision. There is no need to describe the history of phenomenology, which is already well known today.[15] It is more important to comprehend and appreciate the profound meaning the return to the primary reality of the natural world has for the understanding of our current ecological crisis.

The natural world is not a thing or sum total of things that can be seen or studied in their explicit presence. It is an articulated continuum to which we all belong. The main characteristic of the natural world is its continuity in time and space and its permanent presence. A most explicit manifestation of this can be seen in language, revealing most clearly the structure of the natural world. In this world, we can move, in the same way as in language, into the past or future, survey different regions of reality, refer to almost anything in our experience and translate the experience into any language. This possibility also includes the language of science and religion. What is revealed in language points to a level of articulation that shows our involvement in the structuring of the natural world, as well as the level of reality where language meets the natural conditions, i.e., the given reality of embodiment in its most elementary form.[16]

The structure of the natural world is frequently described as a totality of references.[17] We may go one step further by emphasising the continuity of references between that which can be expressed in language, even the most abstract one, and its embodiment in the physical (natural) conditions of a specific place. The natural world then appears less as a descriptive monologue and more as a dialogue (reciprocity) of language and the silent language of the given natural conditions. The continuity and communicative nature of references are always present and play their role even in situations where we are not aware of them. This points to the fact, not always fully appreciated in modern times, that the natural world is not chaotic, but has its own intrinsic structure. The best demonstration can be found in the long history of cosmology and cosmogony or in the philosophical and theological interpretation of creation, where we can find the highly elaborate, hierarchically structured reality of the natural world (the Great Chain of Being[18]). This tradition was seriously disrupted in the eighteenth century, when traditional cosmology was replaced by the 'new cosmology', which was in fact astronomy, based on celestial mechanics. We are still living today with the consequences of that change. Our current preoccupation with environment and ecology is a late attempt to come to terms with the problematic consequences of the mosaic-like pattern of our knowledge and its application. The impressive results of modern science depend upon their development in relative isolation from the broader context of reality and from the consequences of their application. Ecology is a price we must pay for this kind of progress.

Phenomenology and the nature of the natural world

In a phenomenological understanding, the environment is treated as part of the natural world. In the natural world, the given natural conditions and our experience belong together in a relation of reciprocity, which reveals the depths of our involvement in the apparent neutrality and objectivity of the surrounding world—a belief characteristic of most contemporary environmental studies, determined almost without exception, as we have already seen, by the methods of natural science. In most environmental studies, even the issues of human ecology are studied as an extension of biologically oriented disciplines.[19]

In the light of phenomenology, the environment appears as the embodiment of our life, very much like a body, which sustains our common existence. In such an understanding—once we have left behind the distinction between the external and internal reality—it becomes very difficult to decide what is and what is not environment. Are we, as corporeal beings, in the environment or rather an indivisible part of it? Is it not true that our own bodies and our corporeal situation are in fact the environment of our feelings, imaginations, thoughts and, ultimately, of the human world as a whole? An affirmative answer to these questions changes radically the conventional understanding of the environment as something external, as a surrounding world situated outside our personal existence.

Treating the environment as a natural world opens the possibility to see better not only the relation between individual natural phenomena but also their relation to human intentions, experience and interventions. A good example was the recent symposium concerned with the changing reality of the rainforest.[20] In several of the most impressive contributions addressing the history, climate, plant and animal life and the life of the indigenous communities, it became clear how beneficial and yet difficult it is to integrate the individual pieces of knowledge and judge the possible result in view of the social, political and eventually religious values. It was interesting to notice that most of the contributions at this conference were presented on two different levels, one analytical and rigorous, the other poetic and intuitive, trying to grasp in a rather improvised manner the given natural world in its integrity and wholeness. This is the point where the philosophy of the natural world is in a better position to bring the two levels closer to one common language. On the most concrete level, we don't encounter the natural world as a multitude of ecosystems, but as a hierarchy of tangible situations, as a particular place or territory, river, forest, etc., in the wholeness of their concrete presence and not as an intellectual construct.

Situations represent the most complete way of understanding the conditions of our experience of the surrounding world and the human qualities of that world. They endow experience with durability, in relation to which other experiences and knowledge can acquire meaning and can form a memory and history. The temporal dimension makes the process of differentiation and stabilisation of situations more comprehensible. The deeper we move into the reality of situations, the more we discover that situations share their common precedents until we reach the level of primary, deep structures of the natural world, which are their ultimate comprehensible foundation. Here we find the primary meaning of natural phenomena, such as waters, vegetation, sun, stones, etc. The deep structures are the dimensions of culture that open the way to the unity of our experience and to the unity of our world. In its essence, deep structures are the product of an interpretation of primary symbols that are spontaneously formed and that preserve the memory of our first encounters with the cosmic conditions of our existence. The persistence of primary structures and symbols in the structure of the natural world contributes decisively to the formation of typical situations. The nature of typical situations is similar to the nature of archetypes or institutions. Apart from their ability to serve as a unifying vehicle of knowledge typical situations can also serve as a measure of sustainability. The complex and highly relative notion of sustainability can best be judged by the criteria of well-established cultural situations, of their internal coherence and integrity.

In the case of the rainforest, a good example of a typical situation is the life of indigenous people in changing circumstances. It is interesting to compare the life of those who live in the depth of the forest, sometimes without contact with the outside world, and those who moved to cities, accepting the conditions of modern life. The third option, followed by several communities (tribes), is the limited acceptance of certain possibilities of modern life, but otherwise preserving the traditional way of life. Each of the options is related to a particular place, which gives it not only stability but also identity. This is particularly apparent in cases where the traditional way of life and the intimate knowledge of the forest represent a very rich and highly articulated world manifested in physically tangible situations. Practically all aspects of this elementary life are closely linked with customs and rituals reflecting not only the sacred aspects of life but also the sacred meaning of key natural phenomena, trees, rivers, sun and probably also stars. The integrity of such typical situations as hunting, fishing, ceremonies, etc. are all focused on the place of dwelling; and they hold together, in the form of a reciprocity between the natural and the spiritual phenomena. It is the integrity of the typical situations of the traditional ways of life that may explain their persistence in the partly modernised way of life. The phenomenon of persistence challenged by change opens a more fundamental question of sustainability and of the merit of change against the conservation of inherited traditions. The current debate about the need to protect the life of indigenous tribes, yet to also support the potential change of their life through a sustainable level of modernisation, illustrates the inconclusive nature of our judgments. As a result, the main question—what is a truly sustainable change—remains unanswered.

The judgments of sustainability always depend on values based on cultural norms, which cannot be substituted by personal experience or by abstract constructs such as the coherence of ecosystems, for instance. Cultural norms are created in the long life of cultures and their situational character can be grasped only in concrete situations. In order to understand better the nature of cultural norms and their role in the judgments of sustainability we must also take into account our personal point of view, based not only on genuine understanding but also on prejudices and personal interests. It is only too obvious that the interests of a developer differ fundamentally from the interests of a conservationist. The attempt to overcome such differences takes us inevitably into a broader context of reality and into the domain of ethics, where the judgments of sustainability culminate in the question of what is or is not proper or good.

These are all issues already studied for some time in philosophical hermeneutics, which has also contributed to a better understanding of the natural world and our role in it. The language of philosophical hermeneutics coincides, to a great extent, with the language of contemporary theology. While in philosophy hermeneutics is measured by its power to understand better the communicative truth hidden in the phenomenal world, in theology the role of hermeneutics is measured by its power to restate in undistorted form the actual truth of faith. How can science respond to the language of religion? By a philosophical dialogue in which the results of individual sciences are translated (restated) into the language and experience that can be shared with religion. The mediating role of philosophy creates a challenge to individual sciences in their attempt to speak about the same world, but also to religion in its possibility to get more involved in the problem of the nature of the natural world. The challenge to religion refers to already well-established hermeneutical theology where the sacred is not treated solely as a result of proclamation but also of manifestation, that is, of anything by which the sacred shows itself in the visible world. The manifestation of the sacred in natural phenomena is a reminiscence of the book of nature in the Medieval duality of two books of divine revelation, the book of scripture and the book of nature. To meet with science on the level of the natural world, theology must articulate its own understanding of the sacred dimensions of the natural world. Only then can a meaningful relation between religion and science be fully established.

Conclusion

The distance that separates today science and religion is a result of an historical development in which science created its own language, motivated by the interest to dominate and control reality. In this purely instrumental orientation, there is no room for issues that we encounter in our everyday life, in the natural world and in such important domains as ethics. This is a price that it is necessary to pay for the otherwise impressive and undisputed achievements of the natural sciences and their application. Their separation from the broader context of reality is compensated by the changing nature and role of the humanities, including theology, asserting gradually and more firmly their own specific nature and identity. The specific nature of the humanities is their ability to address the phenomenal reality of the natural world, the foundation and framework of the rest of our knowledge. This is reaffirmed by the words of a contemporary philosopher: 'We cannot escape the natural world as a fundamental condition. Our task remains to integrate and situate the theoretical knowledge and the technical possibilities of human beings in their praxis';[21] in other words, in their practical existence in the natural world and in the most appropriate knowledge of this world. To integrate and situate the theoretical knowledge on the broadest and most concrete level of reality is, as we have already seen, the main task of philosophical hermeneutics, which, in its universality, includes theology. In this mode of understanding, ecological knowledge is no longer isolated from but culminates in theology. This cannot be achieved by individual sciences or by theology themselves, but only in a philosophical (hermeneutical) interpretation of both.

Notes

1   Roger Bacon, *Opus majus*, trans. Robert Belle Burke, Philadelphia, PA: University of Pennsylvania Press, 1928, p. 36.
2   Isaac Newton, *Philosophiae naturalis principia mathematica*, London, 1687, 1713 and 1726.
3   Bacon, op. cit., pp. 233–34 and p. 240.
4   [Ed.] Famously depicted in the frontispiece of the Codex Vindobonensis 2554 *Bible Moralisée*, 1220–30. See also Thomas Aquinas, *Summa theologia*, I, Quaestio 27, reply to objection 3 (concerning the procession of God): 'Deus autem, qui est primum principium rerum, comparatur ad res creatas ut artifex ad artificia [God, Who is the first principle of all things, may be compared to things created as the architect is to things designed].'
5   Cf. William A. Wallace, *Galileo and his Sources, The Heritage of the Collegio Romano in Galileo's Science*, Princeton, NJ: Princeton University Press, 1984.
6   Galileo Galilei, *Dialogue Concerning the Two Chief World Systems – Ptolemaic & Copernican*, trans. Stillman Drake, Berkeley: University of California Press, 1967, p. 103.

7   Johann Gottfried Herder, *Älteste Urkunde des Menschengeschlechts, Säm-mtliche Werke*, ed. Bernhard Suphan, Berlin: Wiedmann, 1877–1913, Vol. VI, p. 202.

8   Alexandre Koyré, *Newtonian Studies*, Cambridge, MA: Harvard University Press, 1965, p. 23–24.

9   Werner Heisenberg, *Across the Frontiers*, trans. Peter Heath, New York: Harper & Row, 1974, p. 120.

10   Ibid., pp. 120–21.

11   Ibid., pp. 226–27.

12   [Ed.] The exact source of this definition could not be located; it is, however, completely conventional.

13   Cf. Arne Naess, *Ecology, Community* and *Lifestyle*, Cambridge: Cambridge University Press, 1994.

14   [Ed.] See, e.g., Edmund Husserl, *Logical Investigations*, ed. Dermot Moran, 2 vols., Abingdon: Routledge, 2001, p. 168.

15   Cf. Gerd Brand, *Die Lebenswelt*, Berlin: W. de Gruyter and Co., 1971; and Hubert Hohl, *Lebenswelt und Geschichte*, Freiberg and Munich: Karl Alher GmbH, 1962.

16   Here it is possible to see an analogy between the Greek notion of *physis* and its articulation through *logos* and our own notion of Being (world) and its articulation through language. This possibility is discussed by Otto Pöggeler as 'topology of Being' in *Martin Heidegger's Path of Thinking*, trans. Daniel Magurshak and Sigmund Barber, Atlantic Highlands, NJ: Humanities Press International, 1989, pp. 227–43.

17   See, for example, Martin Heidegger, *Being and Time*, trans. John Macquarrie and Edward Robinson, Oxford: Basil Blackwell, 1967, pp. 102–22; and Hans-Georg Gadamer, *Truth and Method*, trans. William Glen-Doepel, ed. John Cumming and Garret Barden, London: Sheed & Ward, 1975, pp. 397–414.

18   Arthur O. Lovejoy, *The Great Chain of Being*, Cambridge, MA: Harvard University Press, 1974.

19   See Anna Bramwell, *Ecology in the Twentieth Century: A History*, New Haven, CT: Yale University Press, 1989.

20   [Ed.] Religion, Science and the Environment Symposium on the Amazon, 13–20 July 2006; see http://www.rsesymposia.org/more.php?pcatid=45&catid=52.

21   [Ed.] Again, the precise quotation could not be located. However, the 'contemporary philosopher' mentioned by Vesely must be Jan Patočka, who worked on these themes most consistently and was, of course, Vesely's teacher in Prague. It is possible Vesely was translating from a Czech manuscript or even his own seminar notes. See, for example, the essays by Patočka, 'Edmund Husserl's Philosophy of the Crisis of the Sciences and His Conception of a Phenomenology of the "Life-World"', and 'The "Natural" World and Phenomenology', collected in Erazim Kohák, *Jan Patočka Philosophy and Selected Writings*, Chicago, IL: University of Chicago Press, 1989, pp. 223–73.

5 Architecture and Ethics in the Age of Fragmentation

In current practice, architecture is not easily associated with the notion of ethics. To most practitioners involved in pragmatic daily tasks, the question of ethics may appear as an academic occupation that has very little to do with the daily running of things. And yet the same practitioners are answering ethical questions almost every day of their professional lives, most often using different terms and quite often without being aware of it.

The reasons for the curious presence-absence of ethical questions in our field can be found in the development that absorbed modern architecture into a broader framework of technical thinking and production. The main characteristic of technical thinking is the systematic emancipation from the impediments of everyday life and the practical world. In a framework defined by the relative autonomy and universality of technical thinking, there is no room for ethical questions, which can only be answered in view of a particular concrete situation. There is a close analogy between architecture and legal or medical application of knowledge. And yet, even the most emancipated techniques are not part of some ideal reality situated beyond good and evil. There is always somebody who makes the decision about the use and application of technical knowledge. However, it is far from clear what is the ground on which these decisions are made. In view of the way architecture is taught and practised today, it is unlikely that the ground can be found in the domain of architecture itself. Under the pressures of economic and technological changes, our vision of architecture is mostly dominated by the economy and efficiency of solutions, by the marketable appearance of buildings and by the irrepressible subjectivity of experimental projects. It is true of course that there are schools and practices around the world where other than technical and purely economic criteria are given

DOI: 10.4324/9781003272090-6

preference. The most obvious are political, cultural or ecological criteria. However, the success of the more broadly established vision of architecture is frequently hampered by the inability or impossibility to reconcile the intentions with the built results due to controversial programmes, fake ecological criteria, artificial bureaucracy involved in the execution of projects, pluralism and irreconcilability of individual positions that reduce the ethical relevance of the results.

If we assume that ethical considerations are directly linked with the consensus about the possibilities of co-existence and about the nature of common well-being, then it is quite obvious how difficult it is to reconcile genuine ethical intentions with the conflict of different values, so characteristic of our time. What makes this ethically problematic is the one-sided emphasis on difference on behalf of identity, on what separates us rather than what unites us.

When one looks around it appears that 'everyone emotionally or intellectually, politically or economically grabs his fragment, which is partially real and creates a total reality with it. The splintered identities, the competing ideologies, the fractured parties and the glaring, cluttered advertising of competing businesses, assault the person and the society from a thousand sides.'[1] It is characteristic that architects themselves are more aware of the differences that separate them and give their work a dimension of novelty and originality. This leaves behind the common references and goals that contribute to the long-term cultural relevance of their work. The exclusive emphasis on difference and originality leads not only to the questionable merit of the results, but also to their separation from the common world that we all, in one way or another, share.

The presence of the shared world behind the apparently inevitable fragmentation of contemporary culture is well illustrated by a recent survey to formulate new ethical principles for the late twentieth century. The inquiry conducted among young university students resulted in the formulation of new principles, which were almost identical with the traditional Christian commandments.[1a] The survey shows that ethics is rooted in the living ethos that is present in the depths of our culture and thus influences all its aspects. This is important to emphasise against the conventional treatment of ethics studied by the philosophers. From the point of view of our own discipline, ethics is part of a practical world, the world in which we live our everyday life and where architecture itself has its origin. For this reason, it would be better to speak about the ethical understanding of architecture rather than architecture and ethics as two different domains. The ethical understanding of architecture is a natural part of an approach that does not see architecture as an extension of technical thinking and knowledge but as a reflection and embodiment of practical life. What is practical life? In its original sense, practical life coincides with the Greek notion of *praxis*.

The roots of ethics in *praxis*

The Classical notion of *praxis* belongs to the fundamental constitution of human beings and their situation in the world, and it is mostly for that reason that it should not be confused with its modern equivalent, which is seen merely as an application of theoretical knowledge. *Praxis* does not depend exclusively on the abstract knowledge of norms but is always concretely, i.e., practically motivated. 'In every culture a series of things is taken for granted and lies fully beyond the explicit consciousness of anyone, and even in the greatest dissolution of traditional norms, mores and customs, the degree to which things held in common still determine everyone is only more concealed.'[2]

This is apparent to anyone who takes seriously the creative possibilities of a project, its programme or brief, which defines not only the content, but also, as we know, to a great extent the success of the project. The close affinity between *praxis* and typical situations shows that *praxis* always belongs to a world that it articulates and thus brings about, and on the situation. Even when it is more specifically or abstractly defined, the situation is always practical. The practical nature of situations is revealed not only in the way people act or in what they do in a particular setting but also in the structure of the setting itself. Practical situation is a place 'where people are not only doing or experiencing something but includes also things which contribute to the fulfilment of human life.'[3] This includes everything associated with human activity, for instance the table on which we take our everyday meal or the walls of a room which protect the intimacy of our conversations.

The reason for the restoration of the practical nature of situations as a primary vehicle of design is to move away from the inconclusive play with abstract forms and functions. Once separated from the unity of practical life and cultivated in that separation, the forms and their functions can never satisfactorily be integrated with the concrete reality of architecture. The tendency to express the richness of life through transparent, clearly defined functions is a result of a change in which the traditional understanding of creativity, based on the creative imitation of *praxis* (*mimesis* of *praxis*) and poetic knowledge (*techne poietike*) was replaced by the imitation of rationally formulated standards and theoretical knowledge (*techne theoretike*). This led to a degeneration of practice into technique and to a general impoverishment of culture.

However, despite this change, even today 'the normative character of practice and hence the efficacy of practical reason is "in practice" still a lot greater than theory thinks it is', as Hans-Georg Gadamer writes. And he continues:

> It certainly looks at first as if we are being overwhelmed in our economic and social system by a rationalization of all the relations of life that follows an immanent structural compulsion so that we are always making new inventions, and we are always increasing the range of our technical activity without being able to see our way out of this vicious circle. Far-seeing people already consider this a fatal path down which humanity is heading.[4]

The fatality of this path is clearly visible in some developments and tendencies in contemporary architecture, where the broader purpose of space is reduced to clearly defined functions closely co-ordinated with the abstract organisation of space. The ideal fulfilment of this tendency is a comprehensive co-ordination in which the purpose of a particular space becomes identical with the quantifiable characteristics of space. Once this has been achieved, it is possible to extend the identity of the function and the structure of space into the domain of purely conceptual configuration, and eventually to the point where the sequence can be inverted so that the structure of space can generate its own purpose. The acquisition of power over the complexities of life may be technically exciting but it doesn't follow that it is also practical. In fact, technical success very often increases the tension between newly created environments and our practical life.

The source of the tension is not only the speed of technical development but also the stability and relatively slow change in the deeper levels of our life and in the natural world. Practical situations are formed mostly spontaneously. On the deeper level, situations in which we act and form our ethical attitudes come to existence not only through the exploration of new situational possibilities, individual preferences, intentions and desires but also by the given conditions of our everyday life. In the depths of reality, these conditions tend to challenge our creative freedom and it is for that reason that instead of freedom we should rather speak about the spontaneity of the creative movement, in which there is not a clear distinction between our own creativity and the creative power of nature. The spontaneity of the creative process illustrates very well the formation of ethically oriented architectural solutions, in other words it illustrates how ethics is present in the very heart of the making of architecture. Here modern thinking comes very close to the understanding of creativity in Aristotle's *Poetics*. For Aristotle, the work of art is a creative interpretation of practical human life. In Greek terms, the work of art is a *mimesis* of *praxis*. In Aristotle's own words when discussing tragedy, 'it is mainly because a play [work of art] is a representation [*mimesis*] of action [*praxis*] that it also, for that reason, represents people as doing something or experiencing something [*prattontes*].' In Aristotle's understanding, *praxis* is living and acting in accordance with ethical principles.[5]

This is a good place to establish more clearly the difference between ethics and ethos. In the current understanding, ethics is most often associated with ethical rules or values, and even more often with the philosophical or scientific disciplines dealing with ethical issues. On the other hand, ethos, on which ethics always depends, is our spontaneous everyday ethical behaviour, based on accumulated experience, on habits, customs, faith and attitudes. Ethos cannot be taught, it can be acquired only in practical life, which is always structured in particular situations such as the home, school, church, public spaces, streets, etc. It is probably not a coincidence that this brings us very close to the way we design, in following the requirements of individual situations such as the private house, public buildings, concert halls and so on. The formation and cultivation of ethos leads to the formation of cultural norms of conduct, which may vary from culture to culture and even more in respect of individual situations. And yet the main characteristics of ethos are usually preserved in all of them and are, to a great extent, predictable in view of individual situations. We behave always according to the nature of a particular place or situation. The conforming power of situations is a fascinating phenomenon. Is it possible to explain it?

Situations represent the most complete way of understanding the condition of our experience of the surrounding world and the human qualities of the world. Situations also endow experience with durability, in relation to which other experiences can acquire meaning and can form memory and history. The temporal dimension makes the process of differentiation and stabilisation of situations more comprehensible. The deeper we move into history, the more the situations share their common precedents until we reach the level of myth, which is their ultimate comprehensible foundation. Myth is the dimension of culture that opens the way to a unity of our experience and to the unity of our world. In its essence, myth is an interpretation of primary symbols, which are spontaneously formed, and which preserve the memory of our first encounters with the cosmic condition of our existence. The persistence of primary symbols, particularly in the field of architecture, contributes decisively to the formation of secondary symbols, and finally to the formation of paradigmatic situations. The nature of paradigmatic situations is similar to the nature of institutions, deep structures or archetypes.

The role of the paradigmatic structure of a spatial situation is comparable with the role of poetic *mythos* in a poem. Both have the power to organise individual events and elements of *praxis* into a synthesis and give them higher and more universal meaning. The formation of poetic *mythos* or paradigm represents the first half of the creative cycle, of which the innovative interpretation of poetic *mythos* or paradigm is the second half. This is quite clearly the meaning of the following statement from the *Poetics*: 'the poet must be a maker not of verses but of mythos since he is a poet in virtue of his mimesis, and what he imitates is praxis.'[6] The prominent position given to poetic *mythos* (theme, plot) illustrates how important is the concept of representation in the creative process and to what extent, therefore, the poetic *mythos* 'is the first principle and as it were the soul of tragedy. Character comes second. It is much the same also in painting.'[7] Is it not also the same in architecture?

We have already mentioned the analogy between the structure of the work of art, based on poetic *mythos* and the structuring role of situation in architecture. How close is the analogy we are reminded by Plato, who compares the maker of the city with the artist. 'Respected visitors', he writes, 'we are ourselves authors of a tragedy, and that the finest and best we know how to make. In fact, our whole city [*polis*] has been constructed as a dramatization of a noble and perfect life; that is what we hold to be in truth the most real of tragedies. Thus, you are poets, and we also are poets in the same style, rival artists and rival actors, and that in the finest of all dramas, one which indeed can be produced only by a code of true law – or at least that is our faith.'[8]

The presence of ethos in the making of architecture is not a modern discovery, it has a history, which culminates in the term 'character' in the eighteenth century, a term still used today. It is important, at this point, to remember that the original Greek meaning of *ethos* is the habit of dwelling, the way of life or character. In architecture the term 'character' appears only in the seventeenth century as a substitute for earlier terms, such as the French *convenance* and *bienséance* (suitability), and earlier still *decorum* (propriety), which is the Latin equivalent of the Greek *prepon*. In the early eighteenth-century, Germain Boffrand describes character in the following manner: 'a man who does not know the different characters and who is unable to sense their presence in his buildings is not an architect.'[9]

Decorum (propriety) is inseparable from moral goodness for 'what is proper is morally right and what is morally right is proper. The nature of the difference between morality and propriety can be more easily felt than expressed. For whatever propriety may be, it is manifested only when there is pre-existing moral rectitude.'[10] What is 'morally good' is nothing else than a harmonious fulfilment of the inner possibilities of human nature, a process which becomes part of the realisation of that which appears as beautiful manifested as *prepon*. In its fully articulated sense, *prepon* means a harmonious participation in the order of reality and the outward expression of that order. The primary meaning of *prepon*/decorum was preserved in European architecture well into the eighteenth century and in a limited way in the modern notion of character.

Character is a notion that has emerged from a cultural field encompassing not only architecture and painting, but also rhetoric, poetry and philosophy. It was loaded with a range of meanings that architecture on its own could not readily absorb. The simplification of the earlier modes of representation was a first consequence. The aestheticisation of character was a second. This is clear in Germain Boffrand's statement, which may even be taken for a definition of character: 'Architecture, although its object seems only to be the use of that which is material, is capable of different genres, which serve to animate its basic solutions by means of the different characters that it can express. A building expresses through its composition, as if on a stage, whether the scene is pastoral or comic, whether it is a temple or palace [...] It is the same in poetry: here also are different genres, and the style of one does not contradict the style of the other. Horace gave us excellent principles for this in his *Art of Poetry*.'[11] The ambition to subsume the traditional metaphysics and poetics of architecture into the aesthetics of character created a temporary illusion of order, but in the long run proved to be a basis of relativism, arbitrariness and confusion. The general aestheticisation of character made it vulnerable to the operations of taxonomy, in which it became possible to isolate individual manifestations of character from the context of tradition and from the culturally established norms. This was already evident to J.F. Blondel, who wrote: 'after all it matters little whether our monuments resemble former architecture, ancient, Gothic, or modern, provided that they have a satisfactory effect and a character suited to each genre of edifice.'[12]

The deeper relation of character to the inherited culture was eventually replaced by a detached image that could be manipulated with a much greater degree of freedom and persuasive power. As Blondel admits, 'a building can by its appearance take away, move and so to speak raise the soul of the spectator, carrying it to a contemplative admiration which he himself would not be able to explain from the first sight (*coup d'oeil*) even though he were sufficiently instructed in a profound knowledge of art.'[13]

The emancipation and formalisation of character asks for a more focused and precise definition of appearances, a demand fulfilled by the notion of style. The aesthetic interpretation of character and its eventual transformation into 'style', with all the implied arbitrariness of historicism and arbitrariness of choice, is part of the general fragmentation of modern culture.

The ethical role of the fragment

There is a tendency to see fragmentation as a result of isolation, disintegration and thus as potential chaos. It is not difficult to recognise that fragmentation is one of the main characteristics of our modern predicament. But, at the same time, it is clear that the process of fragmentation is more complex, subtle and contradictory.

'Fragmentation' has in principle a similar meaning to 'disintegration'. But in accepting this, we would have to account for the fact that, in so many areas of culture, apparent fragmentation has played an opposite role, contributing to the formation of meaning and to the sense of wholeness. We need only think of the works of Synthetic Cubism, Surrealism, the art of collage or of similar tendencies and achievements in contemporary literature, poetry, music and, to some extent, in architecture. All these illustrate that the phenomenon of fragmentation has more than one meaning and that mere appearance is not a sufficient criterion by which to judge what kind of meaning is before us.

The fragmentation taking place in Analytical Cubism or through the use of an isolated fragment in Synthetic Cubism is an articulation of the world. What is apparent even in the first stage of Cubism (1908–10) (Fig. 5.1) is the elementary non-perspectival structure of a world represented through the particular settings of the still lifes, portraits or landscapes. What makes these settings radically non-perspectival is

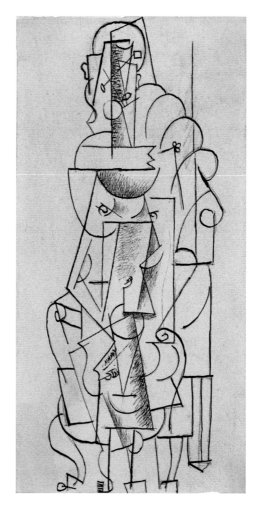

5.1 Pablo Picasso, *Seated Woman*, 1912.

their situational character, which is neither arbitrary nor a result of a pure construction. The setting follows instead the deep logic of a particular situational structure, into which each object or fragment is placed in accordance with its situational meaning. This can be compared with the way we organise our familiar living or working space. It is in the situational structure of Cubist space that the topography of familiar settings meets the fragment in its metaphorical role. This is apparent in the following description by Georges Braque: 'I started by painting a space and then by furnishing it. The object is a dead thing. It only comes alive when it is activated. Find the common ground between things. That is what poetry is, don't you see?'[14] If the common ground of things is space, it is not a space that can be understood through geometry or as a formal structure, but as a living structure in which the metaphorical power of the fragment plays a decisive role. This becomes clear in Synthetic Cubism (Fig. 5.2), in the art of collage and later in Surrealism.

The formation of space in Synthetic Cubism and in the early development of collage is almost entirely determined by the situational meaning of individual fragments. The creative process can be compared to a visual discourse that depends on a few critical points of reference (*points de repère*), usually fragments of a familiar reality,

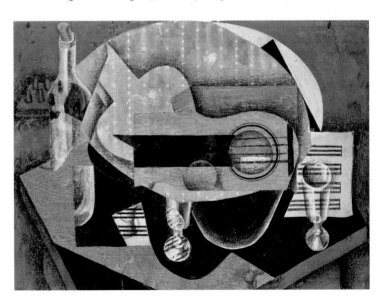

5.2 Juan Gris, *A Guitar, Glasses and a Bottle*, 1913.

developed through a sequence of metaphorical steps into a more complex configuration. The complexity consists in the references generated by the metaphorical possibilities that enable the recognition of sameness and difference in the context of a world opened up by the main theme—appearing most often in the title of the work— and represented initially by the chosen fragments. There is no obvious intention to restore the unity of some object in the process. On the contrary, the fragmentary presence of a particular object should be seen as a thing in its thingness—as it would be, for example, in contemporary hermeneutics. In the hermeneutical understanding, the thingness of a thing is its purpose and serviceability, which includes human attitudes, dreams, aspirations and so on. These, taken together, represent a world to which a thing belongs and which in turn belongs to it. The world to which a particular thing belongs is inexhaustible, and it is for this reason that the creation—as well as the reading—of a Cubist painting is always open to further revelations. This seems to be the message of the following statement by Braque: 'You can always invert the facts. There are relationships between objects that sometimes give us the feeling of infinity in painting. The objects themselves fade next to these relationships. Life is revealed in all its nakedness as if outside of our thoughts. I'm not searching for definition, I tend towards infinition.'[15]

Is it reasonable or relevant to ask what the possible goal of 'infinition' is, and where may it lead? Anybody who works with the metaphoricity and restorative possibilities of fragments is like the author of an aphorism, who, as one modern scholar writes, 'holds in his hands the potsherds of a vessel so large and so shattered that from its thousand fragments he finds it almost impossible to tell what shape the vessel once had. He makes it his task to contemplate each and try to fit them together as best as he can. Sometimes he is helped by their shape, sometimes he works by bright ideas, sometimes a dim memory stirs in him.'[16] This, I think, is a good description of the position of any genuine artist of our times. Situated in the heart of a culture that has become introverted and fragmented, the artist is faced with a deep dilemma, knowing that the relevance of his or her art is closely linked not only with its cultural authenticity but also with public recognition and thus its universal validity. The artist can overcome this dilemma by accepting the current civilisational notion of universality, which is based on instrumental reason and is mostly formal, empty of any particular content. This is the line followed by Constructivism, or neo-Plasticism, for instance. But art can also overcome the limits of its isolation through a restorative work, by recognising the presence of the latent world waiting for articulation.[17] While the first approach has produced art with a certain level of universality but without a particular content (only formal content), the second has created art that has a rich content, but its universality is not yet fully visible and recognised. We still tend to see the achievements of Cubism, the art of collage and Surrealism as private constructions or as a regress to the realm of private dreams. What we do not grasp clearly enough is how close these movements—which represent a long and consistent tradition—came to the genuine creative nucleus of modern culture.

The metaphoricity of the fragment not only pertains to the domain of the arts but is also a germ of a new universal restorative power relevant to our culture as a whole. This potential was recognised by the Surrealists and, on a broader scale, by modern hermeneutics.[18] In the thinking of the Surrealists, the restorative power of the fragment was closely linked with the notion of poetic analogy. In André Breton's words, 'poetic analogy [...] transgresses the deductive laws in order to make the mind apprehend the interdependence of two objects of thought situated on different planes, between which the logical functioning of the mind is unlikely to throw a bridge, in fact opposes *a priori* any bridge that might be thrown.'[19] 'Poetic analogy' here refers primarily to the art of collage. Though collage itself originated in the early stages of Synthetic Cubism (1911–12), it was the Dadaists and later the Surrealists who made it a medium in its own right (Fig. 5.3). In the peak period of its development, collage became a visual text not unlike a poetic text, with which it was always closely linked. The metaphorical and often aphoristic nature of collage can be recognised in Max Ernst's commentary on the 'mechanism' of collage: 'I'm tempted to see in collage the chance meeting of two distant realities on an unfamiliar plane, or to use a shorter term, the culture of systematic displacement and its effect.'[20] The 'culture of systematic displacement' is only a more explicit version of the sequence of metaphorical steps that structured the situational space of early Cubism.

The continuity between Cubism and Surrealism is nowhere more apparent than in the metaphorical nature and role of the fragment and the role of the analogical or metaphorical image. The analogical image that illuminates partial similarities cannot be seen as a simple equation; it moves and mediates between the two realities (fragments) present in a way that is never reversible. 'The greater and

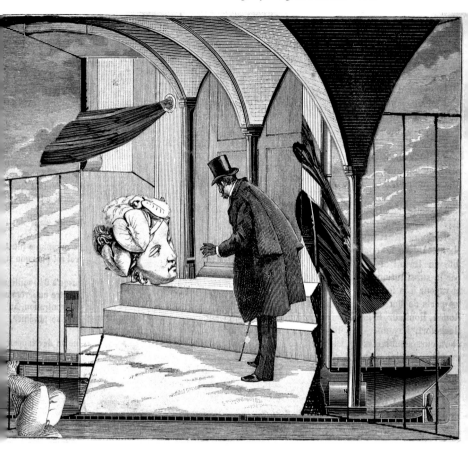

5.3 Max Ernst, *On voit filer plus d'un notaire laissant tomber sa voix en cadence*, 1929.

truer the distance between two juxtaposed realities, the stronger will be the image and the greater will be its emotive power and reality.'[21] It is interesting to compare this statement by Pierre Reverdy, which refers to poetry and possibly to late Cubist paintings, with a comment by Breton on Ernst's collages on the occasion of their first exhibition in Paris in 1920: 'The marvellous faculty of reaching two distant realities without leaving the field of our experience and their coming together, of drawing out a spark, of putting within reach of our senses figures carrying the same intensity, the same relief as the other figures, and in depriving ourselves of a system of reference, of displacing ourselves in our own memory – that is what provisionally holds us.'[22]

The movement away from the established system of references creates in collage conditions for the formation of a situational space whose controversial identity is more explicit than was the case in Cubism. The strange, enigmatic reality of Surrealist space often includes not only elements of illusionism but also explicit architectural references. This is a logical outcome of a development that became in Surrealism a more complete encounter with the reality of everyday life. In this encounter, the work of art was extended into the work of life, where different circumstances played a role and where the 'latent world waiting for articulation' could be activated in a more global manner. I am thinking here of the Surrealist activities which took place outside the walls of studios or on the streets of Paris, in the theatres, films, exhibitions and so on. The unpredictability of the encounters that became possible in these environments had its source in the anonymity of circumstances much richer and more rewarding than the limited realm of personal experience and memory. It was the concreteness of these circumstances, their spatial and corporeal nature, that brought the poetic interpretation of reality into the domain of architecture.

In the realm of spatial and corporeal phenomena, the Surrealists discovered the source of primary creativity, embodied in the image of the crystal. As Breton stated, 'The great secret of the environment of things can be discovered in this way: the crystal possesses the key to every liberty.'[23] This enigmatic statement is partly clarified through a comment made by Breton in another context: 'I have never stopped advocating creation, spontaneous action, insofar as the crystal, non-perfectible by definition, is the perfect example of it [...] Here the inanimate is so close to the animate that the imagination is free to play infinitely with these apparently mineral forms.'[24] The crystal became for the Surrealists a supreme metaphor of spontaneity, imagination and creativity. It also became a principle of order more primordial than the order of reason. The facets of a crystal, in their way as anonymous as the fragments of a city, appear as a forest of symbols, a world like a 'cryptogram which remains indecipherable only so long as one is not thoroughly familiar with the tool that permits one to pass at will from one piece of reality to another.'[25] The tool that permits us to move through the forest of symbols and indices is analogy. Analogy can reveal the deep relation between distant realities which the logical functioning of our mind cannot link together. In the exploration of analogies, the Surrealists discovered the anonymity of natural creativity, and also, without being fully aware of it, the latent world, where our imagination and its organising power have their source.[26] In the narrative journey through Paris, the poetic experience of particular places opened a sequence of analogical readings that led eventually to the formation of a coherent poetics of analogies.

The history of Surrealism has interesting similarities with the history of the positive fragment, which began with the discovery of the restorative power of the word, followed by the discovery of the same power in the image, and finally, in the space of the city. It is a strange irony that the achievements of the Surrealists are seen, even today, as subjective and arbitrary, merely as interesting interpretations of reality. Such a view fails to recognise that Surrealism represents the most admirable effort of the twentieth century to bring the latent world of our common existence into our awareness, not only in the domain of art, but also in the domain of everyday practical life. That we have not understood this message may partly explain why the restorative role of the fragment was recognised in architecture much later than it was in literature or painting. The articulation of the latent world, which became deeply introverted and very personal, was difficult to follow in areas of culture much more open to external constraints, public scrutiny and shared understanding.

The movement towards a situational understanding of space was also hampered by the perspectival and object-oriented thinking that has dominated most of modern and contemporary architecture. It is true that many modern architects moved away from traditional perspectivism and that many also used fragments in their work. However, in most cases the effort was anecdotal, limited and without a clear restorative intention.

The communicative space of the practical world

The movement away from the rigid conditions of perspectivity and functionality of space and the attempts to recover meaning through the use of fragments represent a tendency that has reached almost inflationary proportions in recent years, mostly because they are rarely based on a proper understanding of what is involved. In too many cases, fragments are used purely as formal devices or only as a source of experimental possibilities, which may produce interesting solutions but not necessarily a meaningful work. But how can we judge what is 'meaningful'?

Meaning depends on the continuity of communicative movement between individual elements and on their relation to the pre-existing latent world. The continuity of communicative movement manifests itself in the legibility of concrete architectural space in the same way as it does in a poem or a collage. In that sense, the meaning of a work can be judged by the extent of its legibility. The communicative movement between individual elements of architectural space—its legibility—creates a communicative space, ruled by the situational structure of typical elements and their metaphorical meaning. However, the creation of a communicative space, the soul of the practical world, is not only a question of good intentions. It depends to a great extent on a deeper understanding of the given cultural conditions and their interpretation. Architecture, perhaps more than any other discipline, is deeply rooted in the reality of the practical world and, consequently, in the continuity of latent culture and tradition. Under such conditions, the radicality of creative achievement cannot be measured by the extent of its innovation or the sharpness of its solutions. It is important to remember that even Surrealism in its effort to overthrow conventional modes of representation did not completely abolish traditional illusionism and perspectivity, and that this sense of continuity was part of its strength rather than a weakness.

We have already seen that one of the main conditions of a well-articulated practical world and culture is the continuity of communicative space, where the meaning of positive fragments is ultimately established. It was mainly for these reasons that communicative space became the main theme of a project for Spitalfields in London, one of our diploma projects at the Department of Architecture in Cambridge in 1988–89.[27] The point of departure was a vision of space not as we would like to see it, but as it is given to us today in its most typical representation as highly abstract programmes, environmental analysis, calculations and diagrams, formal plans, sections, axonometrics and other geometrical approximations. It is deeply ironic that these abstract and partial representations are so often presented as complete and self-sufficient. This is no doubt the main source of the confusion and negative fragmentation evident in the current architectural scene. What makes this scene most confusing is the difficulty of identifying the true fragmentary nature of particular representations.

The best way to reveal the fragmentary nature of a representation is through a dialogue with the concrete reality of a particular space. In such a dialogue even the most abstract or fragmentary vision of space may be identified as a potentially positive fragment and engaged in a genuine communicative process. How this can be done is illustrated in the Spitalfields project (Fig. 5.4). The market is situated on the

5.4 Cambridge diploma studio, Spitalfields project, 1988. Model.

edge of the City of London, where its (then) most recent commercial expansion had taken place; while, on the other side it borders a community whose population has tried repeatedly over several hundred years to establish its own urban identity. The clash between commercial urban interests and civic interests is typical of most contemporary cities, and there is no obvious way to reconcile them. Their incompatibility is a manifestation of a more fundamental problem: the incompatibility of the fragmentary nature of many urban structures and systems with the situated nature of urban life. The Spitalfields project illustrates how such incompatibilities may be reduced and even eliminated if the current city of isolated fragments is seen in the light of the restorative potential of the fragments, and with the awareness that such a new vision cannot be realised instantly. Time is a key to addressing the difficulty and complexity of the problem.

On a small scale, this process can be illustrated by a project for a shadow theatre (Fig. 5.5). Here the spatial organisation of the performance space is represented in the first stage by conventional axonometrics. However, what could be seen as a complete representation is taken as a point of departure for an imaginative dialogue with the deeper structure and content of the space. It is at the limits of geometrical representation that we discover a world in which geometry itself is situated. In the case of the shadow theatre, it is a world where the performance and its visibility are not yet reduced to a predictable representation, stereotype or cliché. The movement of figures and their shadows create their own space, which does not follow the rules of geometry, but only the rules of communicative space. The final structure of the space is the result of a process whereby the relations between the figures, lights, audience and projection screens create a series of possible settings that may eventually be translated into a plausible configuration. Unlike conventional perspectival space, communicative space generated by positive fragments has the capacity to hold together a plausible solution and a series of possible ones. This power depends almost entirely on the metaphorical articulation of the space. It is for this reason that the metaphorical exploration of each particular space has been used as an important heuristic stage for the final design.

In a proposal for a museum of Surrealist art, which could be treated as a collection of neutral fragments, each part of the museum is handled instead as a segment of a situation linked metaphorically with other segments. The process of metaphorical interpretation begins in the workshop for metal plating situated in the lower part of the museum, exploiting a deep analogy between the transformation of materials and

5.5 Adam Robarts, Spitalfields project, 1988. Shadow theatre.

the poetic metamorphosis in the artworks.[28] How preliminary meta-phorical studies contribute to the richness, quality and meaning of the ultimate solution can be seen in a project for a centre for experimental music (Fig. 5.6). In one of the final drawings, we can see the attempt to establish a communication between the physiognomy of the room, the

5.6 Elspeth Latimer, Spitalfields project, 1988. Centre for experimental music.

light, the sound and finally between the room and the outside world (garden). The most interesting discovery was the mediating role of light. In the final arrangement, light penetrates into the room through an aviary situated behind a large window. Animated and articulated by the movement of the vegetation and the movement and sound of the birds, this provides a medium by which it is possible to see the link between the visual and acoustic articulation of the room.

The metaphorical links established between the individual elements of the space reveal their deeper common ground in the synaesthesis that is the key to understanding and restoring communicative space. It is encouraging to see that behind the silence of mutually isolated negative fragments there is a potential world of communication that can be, under certain conditions, articulated and restored. The role of architecture and visual arts in the restoration of communicative space illustrates how it is possible to overcome the current state of fragmentation, not only in the sphere of arts but in culture as a whole.

Returning to our original question, what constitutes an ethical understanding of architecture, we may repeat that it is the interpretation and embodiment of practical life; and add that practical life itself is a realm where such a question can be asked, because ethics, the teaching about the right way to live, presupposes its concretisation within a living ethos.[29]

Notes

1 Max L. Stackhouse, *Ethics and the Urban Ethos: An Essay in Social Theory and Theological Reconstruction*, Boston, MA: Beacon, 1972, p. 3.

1a [Ed.] Vesely does not offer a reference. We have been unable to confirm what he had in mind, but a 2006 study from the University of South Florida indicates similar results: https://core.ac.uk/download/pdf/154468202.pdf

2 Hans-Georg Gadamer, 'What is Practice? The Conditions of Social Reason', in *Reason in the Age of Science*, trans. Frederick G. Lawrence, Cambridge, MA: MIT Press, 1981, p. 82.

3 The reciprocity of man 'as acting' and all things 'as in act' is discussed in Ernesto Grassi, *Die Theorie des Schönen in der Antike*, Köln: Du Mont, 1962, p. 127; Paul Ricoeur, *The Rule of Metaphor*, trans. Robert Czerny et al., London: Routledge & Paul Kegan, 1978, pp. 42–43; Aristotle, *Art of Rhetoric*, trans. John H. Freese, Loeb Classical Library, Cambridge, MA: Harvard University Press, 1975, 1411b24.

4 Gadamer, op. cit., p. 83.

5 Aristotle, *Poetics*, trans. Stephen Halliwell et al., Loeb Classical Library, Cambridge, MA: Harvard University Press, 1965, 1450b22.

6 Ibid., 1451b10.

7 Ibid., 1450a19.

8 Plato, *Laws*, trans. Alfred E. Taylor, Everyman's Library, London: J. M. Dent and Sons, 1934, 817b.

9 Germain Boffrand, *Livre d'architecture*, Paris, 1745, p. 26. [trans. Vesely]

10 M. Tullius Cicero, *De Officiis*, with an English translation, ed. Walter Miller, Cambridge, MA: Harvard University Press, 1913, Book I, Section 94.

11 Boffrand, op. cit., p. 16.

12 Jacques-François Blondel, *Cours d'architecture, Tome second*, Paris: Chez Desaint, 1771, p. 318. [Ed. The remark appears in a discussion of Latin-cross churches, in which Blondel discovers the virtues of Gothic architecture].

13 Ibid., *Tome premier*, p. 378.

14 Braque, quoted in Bernard Zürcher, *Georges Braque: Life and Work*, trans. Simon Nye, New York: Rizzoli, 1988, p. 154.

15 Ibid., p. 155.

16 Joseph P. Stern, *Lichtenberg: A Doctrine of Scattered Occasions*, London: Thames & Hudson, 1963, p. 275.

17 The question of civilisational universality and its relation to the life of particular cultures has been discussed by Paul Ricoeur in 'Universal Civilization and National Cultures', in *History and Truth*, trans. Charles A. Kelbley, Evanston, IL: Northwestern University Press, 1965, pp. 271–87.

18 For a relatively recent discussion of the role of metaphor in modern culture see Joel Weinsheimer, 'Gadamer's Metaphorical Hermeneutics', in *Gadamer and Hermeneutics*, ed. Hugh J. Silverman, London: Routledge, 1991, pp. 181–202. The classic work on metaphor is still Paul Ricoeur, *The Rule of Metaphor: Multidisciplinary Studies in the Creation of Meaning in Language*, trans. Robert Czerny et al., London: Routledge & Kegan Paul, 1978.

19 André Breton, *La clé des champs*, 1953; reprint, Paris: Pauvert, 1979, p. 13 [trans. Vesely].

20 Max Ernst, *Beyond Painting*, The Documents of Modern Art vol. 7, New York: Wittenborn Schultz, 1948, p. 13.

21 Paul Reverdy, 'L'image', *Nord-Sud*, 13 March 1918; reprinted in his *Oeuvres complètes*, Paris: Flammarion, 1975, p. 73 [trans. Vesely].

22 Breton quoted in Ernst, op. cit., p. 13.

23 André Breton, *Surrealism and Painting*, trans. Simon Watson Taylor, New York: Harper & Row, 1972, p. 205.

24 André Breton, *Mad Love*, trans. Mary Anne Caws, Lincoln, NE: University of Nebraska Press, 1986, p. 11.

25 André Breton, *The Manifestoes of Surrealism*, trans. Richard Seaver and Helen R. Lane, Ann Arbor, MI: University of Michigan Press, 1974, p. 303.

26 'All the will of the artist is powerless to reduce the opposition that nature's unknown ends set against his own aims. The feeling of being set in motion, not to say being played with, by forces which exceed ours will not, in poetry and in art, cease to become more acute or overwhelming: "It is false to say: I think. One ought to say: I am thought." Since then, ample room has been given to the question: "what can we create - is it ours?"' André Breton and Gérard Legrand, *L'art magique*, Paris: Club Français du Livre, 1957, p. 93 [trans. Vesely].

27 The area of Spitalfields was made available for development because the vegetable and fruit market originally on site was transferred to the outskirts of London in 1991. Civic and commercial interests were battling for decades over the nature of the new development. The alternative proposal presented here is a synthesis of individual contributions made by Cambridge architecture diploma students taught by Vesely across two years, 1988–89.

28 The role of imagination in this kind of transformation was studied and discussed in great detail by Gaston Bachelard under the heading of 'material imagination' in his 'L'imagination matérielle et l'imagination parlée', in *La terre et les rêveries de la volonté*, Paris: J. Corti, 1948, pp. 1–17.

29 See Gadamer, 'Hermeneutics as Practical Philosophy', in *Reason in the Age of Science*, op. cit., pp. 88–112.

6   The Hermeneutics
of the Latent World
of Architecture

The hidden harmony is stronger than the visible one.

(Heraclitus)[1]

How can we understand the relation of architecture and phenomenology? A key and a possible answer can be found in the concept of
world (described in the phenomenological tradition as *lebenswelt*, in
English translation as 'life' or 'lived world', sometimes also as 'natural world'). Life-world is the first philosophical term bringing modern thinking close to the nature of architecture. As a reference to the
totality of the everyday life and as an articulated spatial continuum,
the concept of world represents a decisive step beyond the conventional concept of space. The result of this step is a discovery and
disclosure of the phenomenal foundations of space in the spatiality of
the world. It is well known that the term *lebenswelt* was for the first
time systematically discussed by Husserl (the term itself was taken
from Richard Avenarius, *Der menschliche Weltbegriff*, *The Human
Concept of World*[2]). Husserl acknowledged that his interpretation
may not be the last. This is clearly expressed in the description of
his attitude and interpretation of world (*lebenswelt*): 'We always live
in the life-world, normally there is no reason for making it explicitly
thematic for ourselves universally as world. Conscious of the world as
a horizon, we live for our particular ends, whether as momentary and
changing ones or as an enduring goal that guides us.'[3] In Part II of
The Crisis, Husserl remarks: 'This manner of clarifying [the] history
[of the world] by inquiring back into the primal establishment of the
goals which bind together the chain of future generations, insofar as
the goals live on in sedimented forms yet can be reawakened again
and again and, in their new vitality, be criticised […]'[4]

DOI: 10.4324/9781003272090-7

The response, in part a criticism of Husserl, but at the same time a radically new understanding of world that represents a new epoch in modern thinking, was formulated by Martin Heidegger. We are familiar with his break from Husserl's transcendental subjectivism, the interpretation of the world in terms of four regions (*das Geviert*—[lit. 'quartered']—gods, mortals, heaven and earth), and the use of this scheme in the understanding of the works of art and the nature of things.[5] It is interesting that in his later writings Heidegger articulates the problem of Being, the main theme of his philosophy, as the four regions of the fourfold, which, as he understands, constitute the world and are gathered at the point of intersection of the cross over Being.[6] The intersection of the cross is a place of *Er-eignis*, the togetherness of humans, understood as *Dasein* and world within the fourfold of the world, for which Being, as he in the end admits, has always remained a provisional name.[7] It is rather critical that, for Heidegger, the mode of being of humans, and by implication of world does not have a body or corporeality, in other words, they are not embodied phenomena. In *Being and Time*, he says explicitly: 'The bodily nature hides a whole problematic of its own, though we shall not treat it here.'[8] As we know he never returned to it in any consistent way. As Hans-Georg Gadamer confirms:

> [...] the philosophical tradition to which I too belong both as a phenomenologist and student of Husserl and Heidegger, has done little to illuminate the theme of the body and embodiment and its peculiar obscurity. It is no accident that Heidegger himself was forced to admit that he had not reflected on the theme of the body or concentrated his intellectual power on it to the same extent as he had on so many other essential themes of human existence.[9]

In his later years, Gadamer returned to the theme of embodiment, but the results of his thinking, though interesting, remain rather fragmentary as far as the overall nature of world is concerned. As late as 1986, he writes:

> The phrase 'the body and embodiment', like the 'living body and life', sounds almost like a play on words and thus acquires for us an almost mysterious presence. It vividly presents the absolute inseparability of the living body and life itself. We should perhaps even ask ourselves whether questions concerning

the existence off the soul, indeed any talk of the soul at all, could ever arise if we did not experience the body both as something living and as something subject to decay.[10]

That the world was traditionally structured in reference to corporeality is well illustrated by the long tradition of the link (reciprocity of micro and macrocosm. In this tradition, the human body, the microcosm, is a manifestation or exemplum of reality as a whole. This was encapsulated during the Middle Ages in the phrase, *mundus minor exemplum est – maiores mundi ordine*.[11] In his commentary on Plato's Timaeus, Chalcidius speaks summarily about man as *mundus brevem*—man as the abbreviation of the world.[12]

The corporeality of the lived world

It is true that the theme of corporeality, or embodiment, was included in the studies of anthropology—Arnold Gehlen, Helmuth Plessner—psychiatry—Kurt Goldstein, Ludwig Binswanger—and philosophy—Gabriel Marcel, Maurice Merleau-Ponty, Emmanuel Levinas—to mention the most obvious examples; but none of them, including Merleau-Ponty, whose contribution to the understanding of corporeality is particularly unique and profound, created a coherent new understanding of world. The exception is the recently discovered and, so far, less known Czech philosopher Jan Patočka, who devoted most of his later life to the problem of embodiment.[13] His interpretation (understanding) of the world is based on what he describes as 'the ontological movement of human existence'. In the words of James Dodd: 'The goal here is rather to grasp a more originary sense in which we are creatures "of" the world, to capture in our descriptions that sense in which our life still bears the trace within it of that out of which we have been individuated–and thus, as Patočka says, to win for ourselves a "more radical" concept of the world, of the "wherein" (*Worin*) of Dasein, than that of Heidegger.'[14] As a first important step, Patočka replaced the Heideggerian notion of thrownness, defined as being-in-the-world with being-*of*-the world. Humans, in Patočka's understanding, are integrated into the world already by virtue of their corporeity: 'Precisely, corporeity is what places humans into the world as intrinsically living beings, living a life.'[15] To live a life depends not only on our corporeality, but also on our spatiality, which allows us to move around. In a deeper sense all three, corporeality, spatiality and movement belong together as the main characteristics of the human situation. What is meant by human situation?[16] Situation is a place where our world manifests itself, comes to visibility and presence. In the same way as language, world comes to presence (actuality), only where we ourselves are (situated). We can ask the same question about the world as we can about language: where is language when we are not using it? Answer: it is always available, but only potentially in the sphere (domain) of our latent world.

Human situations represent the most complete way of understanding the condition and nature of our experience of the surrounding world and the human qualities of the world. Situations endow experience with durability in relation to which other experiences can acquire meaning and can form a memory and history. The temporal dimension makes the process of differentiation and stabilisation of situations more comprehensible. The deeper we move into history, the more situations share their common precedents until we reach the level of poetry and myth, which are their ultimate comprehensible foundation. Myth as well as poetry, narratives, creation stories and legends are the dimension of culture which opens the way to a unity of our experience and to the unity of our world. In their essence, myth and poetry are an interpretation of primary symbols which are spontaneously formed, and which preserve the memory of our first encounters with the cosmic conditions of our existence. The persistence of primary symbols, particularly in the field of architecture, contributes decisively to the formation of secondary symbols and finally to the formation of typical (paradigmatic) situations. The nature of paradigmatic situations is similar to the nature of institutions, deep structures or archetypes.

We may look closely at a concrete example—a French café, which I have chosen as a place where in modern times our world was, and probably still is, articulated and shared most explicitly, in a way that it was in the past in religious centres, theatres, fraternities, etc. (Fig. 6.1). It is obvious that the essential nature of the café is only partly revealed in its visible appearance; for the most part it is hidden in the field of references to the social and cultural life related to the place. They are the settings for informal meetings ranging from the creative to the subversive in politics, the arts, philosophy, etc. One needs only recall some famous Parisian examples such as the Café Procope, favoured by the arrival across the street of the Comédie-Française in 1689, where the *Encyclopédistes* met, or the contribution to the French Revolution of the theatres, shops and cafés assembled by Phillipe Égalité

6.1 Ilya Repin, *A Parisian Café*, 1875.

in the Palais Royal, or the importance to the Impressionists of their gatherings at the Café Guerbois and La Nouvelle Athènes.

Any attempt to understand the character, identity or meaning of the situation, and its spatial setting, using conventional architectural typologies is futile. The essential reality of the situation is not entirely revealed in its visible appearance, it cannot be observed or studied just on that level. Its representational, ontological structure can be grasped through a pre-understanding based on our familiarity with the situation and with the segment of world to which it belongs. Pre-understanding in this case is a sedimented experience of the world acquired through our involvement in the events of the everyday life.[17] The identity of the French café is to a great extent defined by its institutional nature, rooted in the habits, customs and ritual aspects of French life. The formation of identity is a result of a long process in which the invisible aspects of culture and the way of life are embodied in the visible fabric of the place (café) in a similar way as is language embodied in the written text. The visible 'text' of the café reveals certain common, deep characteristics, such as its location, relation to the life of the street, transparency of enclosure, certain degree of theatricality expressed in the need to see the life of the outside world, but also a need to be seen in it like an actor, the ambiguity of inside and outside expressed not only in the transparency of enclosure, but also in the choice of furniture, etc. These are only some of the characteristics which contribute to the identity and meaning of the French café as a culturally distinct typical situation.

The most important characteristics of typical situations are their ability to reveal the deepest strata of our experience and their relative stability, which Merleau-Ponty termed 'constancy', or in our terms, 'typicality' or 'paradigmatic nature'. In a global understanding, situations can be seen as places where the world comes to visibility as an articulated continuum, as a structured totality of references, and as a communicative space of culture. There is an understandable temptation to see the global experience of situations in terms of global style, character, affection, or in Heideggerian terms, of mood. In moods the situation in which we are presents itself not as something that has to do solely with our corporeity but rather as something that has to do with our environment and with the world at large.[18] It may be useful to remember that the term 'mood' is derived from German *Stimmung*. In his *Classical and Christian Ideas of World Harmony, Prolegomena to an Interpretation of the Word Stimmung*, Leo Spitzer has this to say: 'If we are to delve now into the historic foundations of *Stimmung* we find the surprising fact that the German word, however individual may be its use today, and however wide its semantic range, is simply indebted to the all-embracing ancient and Christian tradition of harmony, which is at the bottom of all the main European languages.'[19] It is certainly possible to open the global experience of situations on the level of *Stimmung* or mood, but this would help us only to understand the background of the articulation of the world, and not the articulation itself, which we want to understand better (as our main interest). The role of *Stimmung* in this understanding can be compared with the darkness of the cinema, needed to make the image on the screen visible.[20]

The image on the screen is, in our case, the ongoing articulation of our world. This takes place already on the non-verbal level through gestures and significant movements (embodied in rituals, drama, dance, but also in the corresponding configuration of space). All of that leads to the discovery of similarities, metaphorical and analogical relations and finally to the formation of the communicative space of the world and culture as a whole. The communicative space is formed by movement which can be, for that reason, described as communicative. The privileged place of movement in understanding the nature of the created reality was recognised already by Aristotle and in modern times by Leibniz, the most representative thinker of the early Enlightenment who held firmly against Descartes, that motion and not extension (*res extensa*) defines physical bodies and the reality of the created world.

The ability of communicative movement to establish (discover) relations between the different levels and distant parts of reality can be best illustrated by a situation in which a text is dictated to another person who writes it down and reads it back to us. In such a situation we don't translate the audible meaning into the movement of our hands and then into a visual representation which we can read. We recognise the physiognomy of the audible and visual patterns in such a way that the sequence of hearing, writing and reading becomes a modulation of the audible, motoric and visual space, all of them sharing a common articulated movement, 'without there being any need to spell the word or specify the movement in detail in order to translate one into the other'.[21] The translation is more like a melody played in different keys.

As with all movements, communicative movement has its inevitable final referent, that to which it relates. As moving beings, we are drawn to something that is motionless, that is eternally the unshakable ground—the earth (see Husserl's manuscript 'Foundational Investigations of the Phenomenological Origin of the Spatiality of Nature: The Originary Ark, the Earth, Does Not Move'[22]). Jan Patočka writes:

> The earth is the referent of bodily movement as such, as that which is not in motion, which is firm. At the same time, we experience the earth as a power ... [as] something that has no counterpart in our lived experience. It is a power as the earth that feeds us, something that penetrates us globally. By our nature, by the structuring of our life, we are earth-bound. The corporeity of what we strive for in our life testifies to the power of the earth in us.[23]

The earth as the ultimate source of movement is a reference and not a ground. It is as reference that earth motivates and defines the

articulation of the world in a history of representations known better
as cosmologies. In European history cosmologies were only a framework and foundation for history and for theoretical thinking. It was
in the communication between these three levels (cosmology, history and theoretical thinking) that the world of different epochs was
articulated.

It is difficult to resist the admiration of the complexity, richness
and coherence of the world of some epochs such as the Classical world
of Greece, the world of Medieval cathedrals, Renaissance Humanism
in Italy and many others. Is it not possible that some of them could
serve as a good illustration of the 'discovered' life-world of modern
phenomenology? And is it not also possible that some of them could
tell us more about our own lived-world than the best of contemporary philosophical interpretations? Unfortunately, such questions
were not asked by most philosophers for a number of reasons. The
most obvious reason for not asking such questions was the assumption that our knowledge and understanding of history were superior
to everything in the past and that the continuity with the past was
disrupted (deformed) by the metaphysical nature of modern thinking. Gadamer speaks about the relevance of Aristotle for contemporary hermeneutics, what about the rest of the Greek culture? It was
mostly the strong influence and authority of Heidegger that blocked
more critical inquiry in our own field and yet there could be heard
already in his lifetime some critical voices. From a number of such
critical voices, criticising mostly Heidegger's generalisation of the
history of Being and its forgetfulness, I have chosen two closest to
Heidegger's own position.

Gadamer raised his doubts about Heidegger's generalisation in
many places, perhaps most clearly in the following:

[Behind the language of metaphysics of modern times] is a
language of the Indo-European peoples, which makes the
metaphysical thinking capable of being formulated. But can a
language or a family of languages ever properly be called the
language of metaphysical thinking, just because metaphysics was
thought, or what would be more, anticipated in it? Is not language always the language of the homeland and the process of
becoming-at-home in the world? And does this fact not mean
that language knows no restrictions and never breaks down,
because it holds infinite possibilities of utterance in readiness? It
seems to me that the hermeneutical dimension enters here and

demonstrates its inner infinity in the speaking that takes place in the dialog.[24]

In his polemic with Heidegger's understanding (interpretation) of humanism Ernesto Grassi complements Gadamer's defence of the non-metaphysical nature of language (particularly on the poetic level), against Heidegger's. As Grassi sees it, there are misunderstandings, expressed very clearly in the 'Letter on Humanism', where Heidegger states: 'Humanism does *not* ask about *Being's relationship to man* and his essential nature. Humanism even hinders asking this question because *on the basis of its own origins in metaphysics*, it neither recognises nor understands the question.'[25] Heidegger understood 'Humanism' to be only a superficial rediscovery, a Humanism in which, for example, the essence and function of poetry play no fundamental role. In Grassi's view, Heidegger refers to a tradition 'which he did not himself know and which he misunderstood whenever he referred to it'.[26] In a better informed and critical understanding, Grassi argues, 'One of the central problems of Humanism is not man, but the question of the original context, the horizon of openness in which man and his world appear.'[27] And further: 'In the Humanist tradition, there was always a central concern for the problem of the primacy of unhiddenness, openness, that in which historical *Dasein* can first appear. For this reason, we need to reassess and revise the historical categories which still govern our thinking.'[28]

One revised category that we may already put forward is 'continuity', continuity between the contemporary philosophical understanding of the world and its historical antecedents in the past. The articulation of worlds, in which architecture always played a decisive role, were, until the end of the seventeenth century, dominated by cosmological thinking. This meant, in reality, that history and theoretical thinking were articulated always in the framework of a particular cosmology and that all the main principles, such as order, proportions, harmony, etc. were derived from the cosmic (natural) conditions, as the ultimate level of their embodiment.

The transformation of traditional cosmology into astronomy in the seventeenth century emptied (deprived) the traditional architectural principles (proportions, harmony, order, etc.) of their original meaning and led to a shift towards a new frame of reference, which can be described as historical. In the new historical thinking the traditional architectural principles, reflecting cosmic conditions, were replaced by the search for origins, such as the Solomonic temple, the primitive hut, etc. The growing relativism of the historical thinking led at the turn of the nineteenth century to a search for new objectivity, replacing historical by theoretical thinking. It is from this position, which we still share today, that history and cosmic conditions appear as latent world. The reference to history and cosmic conditions from a theoretical point of view can be illustrated by many modern (and recent) examples. Perhaps the most interesting are examples that belong to what has been labelled (designated) as the Deconstructivist movement. Following the idealistic vision of creativity, Alois Riegl, Viennese art historian writes: 'All artistic creation is thus essentially nothing other than a competition with nature, and the fundamental law according to which nature forms dead matter is that of crystallization.'[29] Crystallisation is seen by Riegl as a cosmic principle which brings together nature and art. In the retrospective assessment of the early avant-garde, influenced very strongly by French Cubism, Ozenfant writes:

> On the whole, one can detect a tendency which might be described metaphorically as a tendency towards the crystal. The crystal in nature is one of the phenomena that touch us most, because it clearly exemplifies its movement towards geometrical organisation. Nature sometimes reveals to us how its forms are built up by the interplay of internal and external forces. The crystal grows and stops growing, in accordance with the theoretical forms of geometry; man takes delight in these forms because he finds in them what seems to be a confirmation for his abstract geometrical concepts. Nature and the human mind find common ground in the crystal as they do in the cell and as they do wherever order is so perceptible to the human senses that it confirms those laws which human reason loves to propound in order to explain nature.[30]

What is very clear in this statement is a reference to the primary cosmic conditions of creativity but in a very selective manner. The natural conditions are seen from a detached, theoretical point of view and appear thus only as formal, without genuine corporeality and the mediating role of history. The result is a reference to natural-cosmic conditions, true, but only in terms of their theoretical reality. The *real* presence and role of the natural conditions, as well as the role of history remain latent—contributing, as a result, to the formation of the latent world of our current culture.

For a better understanding of the latent presence of the life-world in the contemporary culture and its possible equivalents in the past, we have to look more closely at the transformation of cosmologically based to historically based thinking and finally to a theoretical one. As we have already mentioned, architectural thinking was, until the end of the seventeenth century, formed in reference to the natural conditions, most often described simply as 'nature'. The reference to natural conditions took place in the framework of a cosmos articulated as cosmology. As far as architecture is concerned, the order, proportions and harmony were defined primarily by Plato's *Timaeus* modified later in the Neoplatonic and Aristotelian orientation of thinking and developed into a long tradition of Christian cosmology.[31] Christian cosmology was based on the conception of the world as a finite, closed and hierarchically ordered whole, in which the hierarchy of values determined the hierarchy and structure of Being, rising from the dark, heavy and imperfect earth to the higher and higher perfection of the stars and heavenly spheres. The result was an articulated continuum dominated by communication between different regions and levels of the world situated in the corporeality of the cosmic conditions.

From cosmology to history and theory

The development of cosmology during the seventeenth century concentrated on the universality of cosmic laws and formation of the new, heliocentric system in a process that replaced cosmology with astronomy based on the principles of celestial mechanics. The new astronomic systems (still referred to even today rather wrongly as new cosmology) became an 'indefinite and even infinite universe which is bound together by the identity of its fundamental components and laws, and in which all these components are placed on the same level of being. This, in turn, implies the discarding by scientific thought of all considerations based upon value-concepts, such as perfection, harmony, meaning and aim, and finally the utter devalorization of being, the divorce of the world of value and the world of facts.'[32]

As a consequence of the seventeenth-century transformation, humans lost the world in which they were living and about which they were thinking; and they had to transform and replace not only their fundamental concepts and attributes, but even the very framework of thought. The transformation can be described in more simple terms as the destruction of the cosmos. The same forces that contributed to the destruction of the cosmos created conditions for the rise and, later, the domination of history, as a new framework of culture. The rise of history coincided with the changing nature of cosmology (nature), which, apart from the shift to astronomy, changed in a process that can be described as temporalisation. Defined by the new sense of individuality, change and the possibility of progress, temporalisation affected culture as a whole. The most critical effect was the impact temporalisation had on cosmology. The traditional sense of cosmic order as relatively stable and permanent was undermined by the discovery of signs of change and temporal development (leading to the sense of progress and to the anticipation of evolution).

The main signs of change were found in the domain of palaeontology, in the enigmatic nature of fossils, etc. The biblical creation of the world (genesis) itself acquired a date, debated among others by such well known scientists as Hooke, Boyle and Newton. In the process of temporalisation all the main aspects of the cosmos were substituted by historical equivalents. The paradigmatic vertical hierarchical structure was substituted by a horizontal historical process in which the disintegration of the cosmos lead to the disembodiment of the world. This transformation represented a threshold of a new epoch, in which the harmony and beauty of the traditional world revealed gradually in a dialectical process became a field of historic and aesthetic experience and judgment, based on the cultivation of taste and on the role of genius. It was in this context that traditional interpretation of the cosmic conditions was replaced by the motifs referring to historical origins mentioned above.

To illustrate the nature of this change we could refer to Claude Perrault as one of the first to acknowledge the relativity of architectural order and the new phenomena, such as conventional beauty or taste. The work of Fischer von Erlach provides a more explicit example. In his *Entwurf einer historischen Architektur*, published in 1721, Fischer assembled the first true history of architecture (Fig. 6.2). His treatise was a personal interpretation, based upon historical and archaeological reconstructions and, to a great extent, upon invention. Fischer describes his treatise in the following words: 'This essay of diverse architecture will not only please the eye of the curious and those of good taste but will embellish their minds .... Artists will here see that nations dissent no less in their taste for architecture, than in food and raiment,

6.2 Fischer von Erlach, *Entwurf einer historischen Architektur*, 1721. The temple of Solomon.

and, comparing one with the other, they themselves may make a judicious choice.'[33]

The terms that now define the nature of architectural design are not only conventional beauty and taste (*bon gout*) but most of all 'character' (leading later to the modern concept of style). Germain Boffrand wrote in 1745 that, 'a man who does not know the different characters, and who is unable to sense their presence in his buildings, is not an architect;'[34] and further:

> Architecture, although its object seems only to be the use of that which is material, is capable of different genres, which serve to animate its basic solutions by means of the different characters that it can express. A building expresses through its composition, as if on a stage, whether the scene is pastoral or comic, whether it is a temple or palace .... It is the same in poetry: here also are different genres, and the style of one does not contradict the style of the other.[35]

The attempt to subsume the traditional poetics of architecture into the aesthetics of character created an illusion of order, but, in the long run, proved to be the basis for relativism, arbitrariness and confusion. This was already evident to J.F. Blondel, who wrote: 'after all it matters little whether our monuments resemble former architecture, ancient, Gothic, or modern, provided that they have a satisfactory effect and a character suited to each genre of edifice.'[36] The aesthetic treatment of character made it vulnerable to the operations of taxonomy, in which it became possible to isolate individual manifestations of character from the context of tradition and from the culturally established norms.

The relativism and, in the end, sheer arbitrariness of historical interpretation led already at the beginning of the nineteenth century to a new search for objectivity. This is apparent most clearly in the work of J.L.N. Durand, his *Recueil et parallèle*[37] and in the *Précis*, where he writes:

> We shall see how architectural elements should be combined with one another, how they are assembled each in relation to the whole, horizontally as well as vertically; and in the second place, how, through these combinations, a formation of such different parts of the building as porticoes, atriums, vestibules, interior and exterior stairs, rooms of every kind, courts, grottoes and fountains is achieved. Once we have noted this part well, we shall then see how they combine in turn in the composition of the entire building.[38] (Figs. 1.4 and 1.5)

The foundation of a new architectural order was based on the assumption that history had run its course and reached a standstill at the end of the eighteenth century. History, therefore, could be transformed into a new form of understanding—into a theory, which would be a recapitulation and consummation of its past as well as the foundation of a new architectural order. The transformation of history into a theory represents the latest stage of architectural thinking, a stage in which the phenomenological understanding of the world has its origin. At this stage, in our modern world, natural (cosmic) conditions and history are seen from a theoretical point of view, which means that their roots in the corporeality of the natural world and the continuity of reference to these roots are still visible, but only as latent. This is well illustrated in the following example.

Scharoun's Berlin Philharmonie was no doubt deeply influenced by the history and the natural conditions of music auditoria, and

6.3 Hans Scharoun, Berlin Philharmonie, 1963. Main auditorium.

yet Scharoun describes the process of its making as a direct dialogue with the nature of space seen as a landscape (Fig. 6.3). The
construction', he writes, 'follows the pattern of a landscape with the
auditorium seen as a valley and there at its bottom is the orchestra
surrounded by a sprawling vineyard climbing the sides of its neigh-
bouring hills. The ceiling, resembling a tent, encounters the landscape like a skyscape.'[39]

This example brings us back to the initial question—under what
conditions can we recover the continuity between the phenomenology of the life-world and its historical precedents? The first condition
is to turn the silence of the latent world into communication between
theoretical, historical and cosmological thinking. The second condition is to extend the horizon of our life-world into the horizon
of latent traditions and discover the relevant continuities of design
principles and their meaning. This is a hermeneutical task known
as the fusion of horizons.[40] In the opening and fusion of horizons
we are likely to discover many surprising continuities particularly
with the world of Baroque, still articulated metaphorically and structured hierarchically as a plenum, as well as with the long tradition
of architectural thinking, articulated in the framework of European
humanism.

Appendix: The city as an exemplary situation

All that has been said so far can be best illustrated by the example of the city, which can be seen as a critical situation, critical, because all other situations that we encounter in architecture such as dwelling, working places, theatres, music halls, etc. are directly or indirectly

6.4 Jean Fouquet, *The Right Hand of God Protecting the Faithful*, 1452–60.

subordinated to it. Seen historically, the city is a framework in which the formation of our civilisation and culture as we know it took place[41] (Fig. 6.4). Serving as a place making possible social integration, public interchange and cooperation, the city symbolised, in most cultures, the representation (centre) of the universe; and it remains, down to our day, a reflection of the universe in its geographic layout, orientation and configuration. We should perhaps mention and emphasise that the city as a reflection of the universe includes gardens, landscape and countryside which always did, and do even today, contribute to the full context of the city.

The reference to the city as a reflection of the universe may appear today as a lost distant memory as long as we do not acknowledge that the reality of the city is not homogenous but stratified, that the surface strata are more open to change than the deeper ones, which show a high degree of continuity and identity with the older past. This can be seen very well in the history of the main element of the city, the street, its changing character, but at the same time a surprising continuity of its presence and relative lack of change. It is perhaps not an overstatement to see the street as the main structuring element in the development of cities. We can appreciate its dominating role in the formation of cities, its accumulated complexity and richness particularly at a time, when the street was abolished either altogether or replaced by problematic equivalents. The ensuing vacuum and unsuccessful attempts to substitute the absence of the street with problematic equivalents, so characteristic for modern city planning, reveals the fact that the street has its roots in the natural conditions of its own existence and, what is equally important, cannot be treated as an isolated element, but only as part of the situational structure of the city as a whole. In the situational structure of the city, the street plays a mediating role. It mediates between individual buildings by creating a space they can share. The mediation continues usually in a hierarchical sequence from urban segment to district or quarter and finally the city as a whole. There is a close link between the hierarchical sequence of mediation and the phenomenon of sharing. We share that which is common, what we can participate in and what is equally accessible. This defines a natural tendency towards centrality where what is most common is usually situated. However, the process of mediation does not follow only the sequence of streets, but engages the fabric of the city in its depth, that is not only the urban exterior, but also the urban interior consisting of secondary streets and spaces, courtyards, gardens, etc. This very often complex layout creates a sequence of different, more appropriate conditions for shops, agencies, restaurants or cafés on the street, workshops or studios in the courtyards, intimate space in the gardens, etc.

The process of mediation can be seen as a process of communication. What is communicated takes place on the level of urban fabric, but this must be seen only as a mode of embodiment of the city life as a whole. The street and other urban spaces are only settings similar to stage sets for the events of everyday life, for markets, theatres in the open, processions, ceremonies, etc.[42] This brings us to the most important role of communication, the mediation between the more articulated forms of life and their embodiment in the fabric of the city. Gadamer describes the communicative role of architecture in a following way: 'Architecture gives shape to space. Space is what surrounds everything that exists in space. That is why architecture embraces all the other forms of representation: all works of plastic arts, all ornament. Moreover, to the representational arts of poetry music, acting and dancing it gives their place. By embracing all the arts, it everywhere asserts its presence.'[43]

Power of the earth and the question of identity

The power of architecture and city to assert their presence reflects the 'power of the earth' in our life, manifested on all levels of life. The most explicit manifestation of this power is the phenomenon of identity, appearing as regularity, constancy, stability or order. Identity plays a decisive role in the formation of typical human situations, and even more explicitly in logic, grammar, geometry and other mathematical disciplines.

We can see the presence of identity sometimes more clearly in the experience of architecture, works of art or literature from a distant past, which, despite the distance in time and the fact that we are living in a very different world, still have something to tell us. Contemporary hermeneutics describes this phenomenon as a fusion of horizons in which meaning is preserved on a deeper level due to the cultural continuity of reference. This is more clearly revealed, unsurprisingly, in literature or drama than in the visual arts. We can read ancient texts or perform Greek tragedy and understand them. Understanding is always a result of a dialogue or dialectics of identity and difference in which a plausible identity of meaning is, in the end, revealed. This dialogue is an ongoing process that coincides with what we know as interpretation. It is in the nature of

interpretation that its results are only probable. That much is true
for identities in general. The exception is formal identity, based on
the criteria of certainty (apodicticity), which constitutes the nature
of symbolic logic and mathematical disciplines. And yet even here
the formal identity is not as absolute as it may appear; it depends on
the deeper strata of reality to which it remains inevitably open. This
is very well illustrated by a modern mathematician, who writes: 'To
detach itself from these roots would in reality be to condemn itself
to asphyxia, to enclose itself in a kind of mortal solitude which
would result in the emptiness of a system void of all content'[44]; and
further:

> [...] the abstract is not the first. It is by a perpetual return
> to its intuitive origins and to the reality of its problems, by a
> close fidelity to the imperatives of this hidden life which trav-
> erses theories like fertilising sap, that mathematical thought
> reconquers, through the inevitable snares of a necessary
> abstraction, this original concrete which is always present
> at the core of its movements and which manifests in most
> characteristic fashion its permanent activity in the highest
> moments of creation.[45]

If we follow this argument and accept that even formal identity in
mathematics is not absolute and original, then we have to look for its
source elsewhere. We already know that identity is revealed in interpretation leading to results which are only probable. However, phenomenology tells us that such phenomena as identity are constituted
in a hierarchical sequence of steps each representing a foundation for
the next one in a movement that has its ultimate source in that which
does not move—earth. Earth not as an object but as a reference of
movement, which in the case of identity is revealed in the regularity
and periodicity of cosmic revolutions and cycles. We do not have to
look for historical evidence in philosophical texts, we can find it in a
well-known architectural treatise.

> All machinery is generated by nature and the revolution of the
> universe guides and controls it. Unless we could observe and
> contemplate the continuous motion of the sun, moon and the
> five planets; unless these revolved by the device of nature, we
> should not have known their light in due season nor the ripening
> of the harvest. Since then our fathers have observed this to be

so, they took precedence from nature, imitating them and led on
by what is divine, they developed the necessities of life by their
inventions.[46]

This understanding of the cosmic movement in relation to the
necessities of life can be complemented by the view of a modern
biologist:

> The evolutionary development of all living organisms, includ-
> ing man, took place under the influence of cosmic forces that
> have not changed appreciably for very long periods of time. As
> a result, most physiological processes are still geared to these
> forces, they exhibit cycles that have daily, seasonal and other
> periodicities clearly linked to the periodicities of the cosmos.
> As far as can be judged at the present time, the major biologi-
> cal periodicities derive from the daily rotation of the earth, its
> annual rotation around the sun and the monthly rotation of the
> moon around the earth.[47]

The attempts to understand, describe or visualise the mystery of
cosmic movement belong to the oldest modes of representation. We
can find them in ritual and in circular dance, in verbal descriptions
but most of all in visual diagrammatic representations of cosmos and
later in the construction of armillary spheres, etc. All of them are
symbolic representations of the ultimate source of regularity and
order (identity).

Conclusion

What is most interesting from our point of view is the tradition in
which the cosmos is represented as a city. The diagrammatic image of
the city is used very often as a representation of the cosmos. In older
literature, the making of the city and the creation of the world are
very often described in the same terms:

> When a city is being founded to satisfy the soaring ambition of
> some king ... there comes forward now and again some trained
> architect, who [...] first sketches in his own mind well-nigh all
> parts of the city that is to be wrought out [...] and like a good
> craftsman he begins to build the city of stones and timber, keep-
> ing his eye upon his pattern and making the visible and tangible

objects correspond in each case to the incorporeal ideas. Just
such must be our thoughts about God. We must suppose that
when He was minded to found the one great city He conceived
beforehand the model of its parts, and that out of these ...
He brought to completion a world discernible only by the
mind, and then, with that pattern, the world which our senses
perceive.[48]

Keith Lilley generalises this insight: 'What makes this interplay of 'city' and 'cosmos' especially significant is the way that
it took shape throughout the Middle Ages and beyond in the
reciprocity of the representation (imagery) of both city and cosmos.'[49] (Fig. 6.5).

As a symbolic representation of the cosmos, the city is not only a
representation but also a mediation of order (identity) in culture as a
whole. Is it possible to claim that what we have said so far is still true
today? In principle yes, but only as a latent possibility. The natural
conditions have not changed very much, our life is still conditioned

6.5 Hans Memling, *Scenes from the Passion of Christ*, 1470–71.

by the primary cosmic cycles. What has changed is the representation of reality and its applications in which the given natural conditions and their mediation through the hierarchy of reality and history have been suppressed and substituted by mathematical equivalents. However, even under those circumstances the natural conditions and history assert themselves in our everyday life, in language, in the formation of concepts, in institutions, political and economic life, as well as in scientific theories, in technological applications and in conceptual speculations. All these areas are, in modern times, challenged by mathematically based science and technology. As a result, architecture and the development of cities oscillate between the given natural conditions and their theoretical representation. The oscillation tends to become, occasionally, a mediating communication, but most often ends up in a subordination to the mainstream requirements dominated by technical and economic interests. This leaves us with an option with which we are familiar: communication within a limited sphere of reality, hoping to extend the communication into a broader sphere of current reality and design in the future.

Notes

1 [Ed.] Diels-Kranz B54, from Hippolytus, *Refutation of All Heresies* 9.9, trans. Vesely.
2 [Ed.] Reisland, Leipzig 1891.
3 Edmund Husserl, *The Crisis of European Sciences and Transcendental Philosophy*, trans. and intro. David Carr, Evanston, IL: Northwestern University Press, 1970, Appendix VII 'The Life-World and the World of Science', p. 379. Parts I and II originally 1936, Part III incomplete and posthumously in 1954 (see 'Translator's Introduction').
4 Husserl, op. cit., p. 71.
5 [Ed.] Cf. Martin Heidegger, 'Building, Dwelling, Thinking', originally a lecture in 1951, in *Martin Heidegger, Basic Writings*, ed. David Farrell Krell, Abingdon: Routledge, 1993, pp. 343–63. Note that the four-fold is not mentioned in the 1956 'Addendum' to 'The Origin of the Work of Art'.
6 [Ed.] Cf. Martin Heidegger, *The Question of Being*, trans. William Kleinbach and Jean T. Wilde, London: Vision Press Limited, 1959.
7 Martin Heidegger, *Vorträge und Aufsätze (1936–1953)*, ed. Friedrich-Wilhelm v. Herrmann, Frankfurt: Verlag Vittorio Klostermann, 2000, p. 229.
8 Martin Heidegger, *Being and Time*, trans. John Maquarrie & Edward Robinson, Oxford: Basil Blackwell, 1962, p. 143.
9 Hans-Georg Gadamer, 'Bodily Experience and the Limits of Objectivity', in *The Enigma of Health*, trans. Jason Gaiger and Nicholas Walker, Stanford, CA: Stanford University Press, 1996, p. 70.

10 Ibid., p. 71 [Ed. Vesely has a note to himself at this point, reading: 'Gadamer Merleau-Ponty relation'. David Leatherbarrow, who was among the scientific committee for the Kyoto Conference, kindly informs us that Vesely had asked Gadamer about the neglect of Merleau-Ponty and received an ambiguous answer that seemed to exhibit a preference for German language philosophy over French existentialism, in which Gadamer failed to distinguish Merleau-Ponty from Sartre].

11 Avicebron, *Fons vitae* III.2.10, in George Perrigo Conger, *Theories of Macrocosms and Microcosms in the History of Philosophy*, New York: Columbia University Press, 1922, p. 41.

12 Chalcidius, *Platonis Timaeum commentarius*, in Friedrich W. A. Mullach, *Fragmenta philosophorum graecorum*, Paris 1881, vol. II, CC cf. CCXXX, as cited in Conger, op. cit., p. 23.

13 Jan Patočka studied with Husserl and Heidegger, he collaborated with Eugen Fink and Ludwig Landgrebe, and was very close to Gadamer. He published already in 1936 his first *opus magnum* with the title, *The Natural World as a Philosophical Problem*, trans. Erika Adams, ed. Ivan Chvatík and Ľubica Učník, fwd. Ludwig Landgrebe, Evanston, IL: Northwestern University Press, 2016.

14 Introduction to Jan Patočka, *Body, Community, Language, World*, trans. and ed. Erazim Kohák, intro. James Dodd, Chicago and La Salle, IL: Open Court, 1998, p. XXVII.

15 Patočka, op. cit., p. 70.

16 Situations can be seen as settings, where people are not only doing or experience something, but which also includes things that contribute to the fulfilment of human life.

17 [Ed.] See, in general, Dalibor Vesely, *Architecture in the Age of Divided Representation*, Cambridge, MA: MIT Press, 2004, Chapter 2, particularly pp. 74 ff.

18 Patočka, op. cit., pp. 42–43.

19 Leo Spitzer, *Classical and Christian Ideas of World Harmony, Prolegomena to an Interpretation of the Word 'Stimmung'*, ed. Anna Granville Hatcher, Baltimore, MD: Johns Hopkins Press, p. 7.

20 Maurice Merleau-Ponty, *Phenomenology of Perception*, trans. Colin Smith, London: Routledge & Kegan Paul, 1962, p. 100: '... indeed its [the body's] is not, like that of external objects or like that of "spatial sensations", a *spatiality of position*, but a *spatiality of sensation* [emphasis original]'.

21 Ibid., p. 144.

22 Edmund Husserl, 'Foundational Investigations of the Phenomenological Origin of the Spatiality of Nature: The Originary Ark, the Earth, Does Not Move', in Maurice Merleau-Ponty, *Husserl at the Limits of Phenomenology, including Texts by Edmund Husserl*, ed. Leonard Lawlor and Bettina Bergo, Evanston, IL: Northwestern University Press, 2002, pp. 117–31.

23 Patočka, op. cit., p. 149.

24 Hans-Georg Gadamer, *Heidegger's Ways*, trans. John W. Stanley, introd. Dennis J. Schmidt, Albany, NY: State University of New York Press, 1994, p. 78 [Ed. Vesely corrects Gadamer's 'Indo-Germanic', a

term left over from the early philological debates, to 'Indo-European'. See Edwin Bryant, *The Quest for the Origins of Vedic Culture*, Oxford: Oxford University Press, 2001].

25 Emphasis added by Grassi in Ernesto Grassi, *Heidegger and the Question of Renaissance Humanism*, Center for Medieval & Renaissance Studies, New York: State University of New York at Binghamton, 1988, p. 32 [Ed. for the 'Letter on Humanism', cf. Heidegger, *Basic Writings*, op. cit., p. 226].

26 Grassi, op. cit., p. 30.

27 Ibid., p. 17.

28 Ibid., p. 29.

29 Alois Riegl, *Historische Grammatik der bildenden Künste*, ed. Karl M. Swoboda and Otto Pächt, Graz: Böhlau, 1966, p. 22 [trans. Vesely].

30 Amédée Ozenfant and Charles-Edouard Jeanneret, *La peinture moderne*, Paris: Les Éditions G. Crès et Cie, 1927, pp. 137–8 [trans. Vesely].

31 In his new, subtle and critical interpretation of Plato, Gadamer demonstrates clearly the non-metaphysical nature of Plato's philosophy, including his cosmology: 'In any case, it is clear: the schema of onto-theology or metaphysics is, as the word metaphysics already teaches, completely inadequate for Plato.' (Hans-Georg Gadamer, *Gesammelte Werke*, Band 7, Tubingen: Mohr Siebeck GmbH & Co. KG, 1991, p. 280 [trans. Vesely]).

32 Alexandre Koyré, *From the Closed World to the Infinite Universe*, Baltimore and London: The John Hopkins University Press, 1957, p. 2.

33 Johann Bernard Fischer von Erlach, *Entwurf einer historischen Architektur*, Vienna, 1721, Preface, p. 4 [trans. Vesely].

34 Germain Boffrand, *Book of Architecture*, trans. David Britt, ed. Carolyn van Eck, Aldershot: Ashgate, 2002 (orig. Paris, 1745), p. 10.

35 Germain Boffrand, op. cit., p. 8 [trans. modified by Vesely].

36 Jacques-François Blondel, *Cours d'architecture, Tome Second*, Paris: Chez Desaint, 1771, p. 318. [trans. Vesely]

37 Jean-Nicolas-Louis Durand, *Recueil et parallèle des édifices de tout genre, anciens et modernes: remarquables par leur beauté, par leur grandeur, ou par leur singularité, et dessinés sur une même échelle* by J.N.L. Durand, Paris, l'Imprimerie de Gillé fils, 1800.

38 Jean Nicolas Louis Durand, *Précis des leçons d'architecture données à l'École royale polytechnique*, Paris, 1809, Vol. 1, p. 29. [trans. Vesely]

39 Hans Scharoun, quoted in Peter Blundell-Jones, *Hans Scharoun*, London: Phaidon, 1995, p. 178.

40 [Ed.] See Hans-Georg Gadamer, *Truth and Method*, trans. William Glen-Doepel, ed. John Cumming and Garret Barden, London: Sheed and Ward, 1975, Second Part I.b.iv 'The principle of effective history', pp. 267 ff. This edition properly translates *Wirkungsgeschichte* as 'effective history' (as against 'history of effects' that can be found elsewhere), which was a significant inspiration for Vesely's 'latent world'.

41 Lewis Mumford, *The Culture of Cities*, Secker and Warburg, London, 1945; Giulio C. Argan, *Kunstgeschichte als Stadtgeschichte*, Paderborn:

Wilhelm Fink Verlag, 1989; Chiara Frugoni, *A Distant City*, trans. William McCuaig, Princeton, NJ: Princeton University Press, 1991.

42 Juliane Rietzsch, *All the world's a stage – Selbstdarstellung auf sozialen Netzwerkseiten: Eine Analyse der kommunikationswissenschaftlichen Literatur*, Munich: Grin Verlag, 2012; Peter Brook, *The Empty Space*, London: Penguin Modern Classics, 2008; Ian Macintosh, *Architecture, Actor and Audience*, Abingdon: Routledge, 1993; Edward Glaeser, *Triumph of the City*, New York: Macmillan Publishers, 2011.

43 Gadamer, *Truth and Method*, op. cit., p. 139.

44 Jean Ladrière, 'Mathématiques et formalisme', in *Revue des questions scientifiques*, Louvain, 20 October 1955, 538–73, trans. in *Phenomenology and the Natural Sciences*, Evanston, ed. Joseph J. Kockelmans and Theodore J. Kisiel, Evanston, IL: Northwestern University Press, 1970, p. 480.

45 Ibid., p. 483.

46 Vitruvius, *On Architecture II*, trans. Frank Granger, Loeb Edition, Cambridge, MA: Harvard University Press, 1934, Book X.C.1.4, pp. 276–77.

47 René Dubos, R., *Man Adapting*, New Haven, NJ: Yale University Press, 1965, p. 42.

48 Philo of Alexandria, 'On the Creation' (*De opificio mundi*), *Works Vol. I.*, trans. Francis H. Colson and George H. Whitaker, Cambridge, MA: Harvard University Press, 1981, pp. 15–17; cited in John B. Friedman, 'The Architect's Compass in Creation Miniatures of the Later Middle Ages', *Traditio XXX*, 1974, p. 425.

49 Keith D. Lilley, *City and Cosmos: The Medieval World in Urban Form*, London: Reaktion Books, 2009, p. 39.

7 Architecture as a Humanistic Discipline

Today architecture is treated most often as a technical discipline dominated by the knowledge of science seen as the ultimate criterion of truth and what is real. We are familiar with the reference to the 'real' world that we hear, almost as a cliché, so often today. What is meant by 'real' is usually the pragmatic reality of the everyday, defined by current politics, economics, market forces and technological developments. On a more sophisticated level, the real is defined more directly by the criteria of science. It is a standard and repeated experience that, in case of doubt, we ask science to be the ultimate arbiter of truth. And yet there is still another sense of what is real that we encounter in our everyday life, in personal relations, in friendship in our judgments of what is good or bad, in our faith and so on. It is mostly our intuition and common sense that point to a different reality, which we share to a great extent, but which we consider nevertheless mostly as personal or subjective and, therefore, find it difficult to give it an objective validity.

It is partly for this reason that some contemporary thinkers speak about modern citizens as citizens of two worlds. This is related only indirectly to the well-known discussion of C. P. Snow, outlined in his influential book, *The Two Cultures*.[1] Hans-Georg Gadamer has this to say about the citizens of two worlds:

> The forming of European civilisation by science implies not only a distinction, but brings with it a profound tension into the modern world. On the one hand, the tradition of our culture, which formed us, determines our self-understanding by means of its linguistic-conceptual structure which originated in Greek dialectics and metaphysics. On the other

DOI: 10.4324/9781003272090-8

hand, the modern empirical sciences have transformed our
world and our whole understanding of the world. The two
stand side by side.[2]

Ambiguity of the two worlds

The two worlds stand side by side in principle, but in everyday life
they very often overlap. The result is a state of ambiguity. This can
be best illustrated in our own field by concrete examples. In the
work of Daniel Libeskind, the critical, analytical vision frequently
overlaps with the romantic and personal inspiration. In his own
words: 'Contemporary formal systems present themselves as riddles -
unknown instruments for which usage is yet to be found. Today we
seldom start with particular conditions which we raise to a general
view; rather we descend from a general system to a particular
problem'.[3] This is complemented by the following statement: '[E]
ver since I encountered Johannes Kepler's study of the six cornered
snowflake, I have marvelled at the infinity of crystals that nature
created in every snowflake. Let me leave you with this thought:
All architecture is crystalline.'[4] Perhaps even more explicitly, illustrations of the state of ambiguity in our field can be found in the
work of Ivan Leonidov (Fig. 7.1). Leonidov's first period, defined
by the transparent constructivist rationality, differs fundamentally
from the second, defined by personal experience, cultural memory
and different levels of freedom to bring them to visibility. It is not
easy to clearly describe the nature of the difference, particularly in
view of the second period. There is, no doubt, an overlap of certain elements, but the transparent engineering approach melts into
a dream-like vision motivated by personalised human and cosmic
motives and values.

   The state of ambiguity changes once we move from the everyday to the more institutional levels, particularly to the domains of
academia and explicit knowledge. If we leave behind the tendency
to subordinate the humanities to the methods of the natural sciences,
we discover that the division between sciences and humanities is
taken for granted as a *fait accompli*. This division has its origin
in the seventeenth century, when the dilemma of science and the
humanities was created for the first time. At that time, the relatively unified culture was challenged by a radically new knowledge based on the mathematical criteria of truth. How did it come
about?

7.1 Ivan Leonidov, *Headquarters of Heavy Industry Moscow*, 1934 (top);
City of the Sun, 1943–57 (bottom).

Mathesis universalis

The new knowledge had its origins in the reaction to the sixteenth-century religious and cultural relativism, and in the search for the new universal foundations of faith and truth. Such foundations were found in the universality of mathematics (*mathesis universalis*), frequently referred to at that time as the 'queen of the sciences' (*regina scientiarum*), elevated sometimes in such names as *ars magna, are divina* or *scientia divina*.[5] These lofty names could not convince without supporting evidence from the physical world in which it became possible to speak of physics and metaphysics in the same terms, and theological problems could be, by implication, treated as metaphysical and eventually as physical (*theologia naturalis*).[6]

Universal mathematics (*mathesis universalis*) laid claim to cover the same area of knowledge as traditional logic—in other words, the area of all possible knowledge. The essence of the new knowledge was made—and seen as—compatible with the language of mathematics. The new knowledge was, in the end, turned into a universally applicable paradigm based on Newtonian mechanics. The consequences were summarised by one modern thinker in the following way:

> Yet there is something for which Newton - or better to say not Newton alone, but modern science in general - can still be made responsible: it is the splitting of our world in two [...] It did this by substituting for our world of quality and sense perception, the world in which we live, and love, and die, another world - the world of quantity, of reified geometry, a world in which, though there is a place for everything, there is no place for man. This, the world of science - the real world - became estranged and utterly divorced from the world of life, which science has been unable to explain - not even to explain away by calling it 'subjective'. True, these worlds are every day - and even more and more - connected by the *praxis*. Yet for *theory* they are divided by an abyss. Two worlds, this means two truths. Or no truth at all. This is a tragedy of modern mind which "solved the riddle of the universe" but only to replace it by another riddle, the riddle of itself.[7]

The dominating role and monologue of the Newtonian paradigm left the humanities in a deep shadow. This can be best illustrated by the new seventeenth-century attitude to poetry—the paradigm and essence of the humanities. Poetry was, at that time, considered to be rather dead, as the following statement illustrates: 'Prose is quite able to express anything you can say in verse; it is more precise, more to the point and it takes less time.'[8] And another contemporary opinion: 'When you begin reading a piece of poetry, remember you are reading the work of a purveyor of lies, whose aim it is to feed us on chimaeras or on truth so twisted and distorted that we are hard put to it to disentangle fact from fiction.'[9]

However, despite their secondary role in culture—based on the ideals of the Enlightenment—the humanities sustained their own life, though rather fragmented and mosaic-like. In the whole pleiades of names, humanistic tendencies and movements, we should mention the works of Giambattista Vico, Friedrich Schleiermacher, the Romantics, the German historical school and Wilhelm Dilthey. All contributed to the formation of modern humanities, and in particular to the establishment of modern hermeneutics embodied in the writings of Martin Heidegger and Hans-Georg Gadamer.[10]

Giambattista Vico and common sense

Gadamer sees the primary role of the humanistic tradition in *Bildung*, common sense, taste, and judgment (*Verstand* or good sense). In the field of architecture, the most relevant mediating link is common sense, which links modern hermeneutics with the work of thinkers like Vico. As Gadamer states: 'I have rightfully claimed for my own work the testimony of Vico'.[11] And further, in *Truth and Method*, Gadamer reminds us:

> There is something immediately evident about grounding philosophical and historical studies and the ways the human sciences work on the concept of the *sensus communis*. For their object, the moral and historical existence of humanity, as it takes shape in our words and deeds, is itself decisively determined by the *sensus communis*.[12]

Common sense is knowledge of the concrete, and it is concrete knowledge, because it is a sense acquired by living in a concrete community and determined by upholding the value of communal traditions. Common sense is historical in that it preserves tradition and not just as a datum of knowledge but as a principle of action. Common sense is closely linked with the meaning of common place and thus

7.2 Clementinum, Prague, the Baroque library (top); Jacques de Lajoue, *Le cabinet de physique de Bonnier de La Mosson*, 1734 (bottom).

with the topology of Being. Vico writes: 'Human choice, by its nature most uncertain, is made certain and determined by the common sense of men with respect to human needs or utilities, which are the two sources of the natural law of the gentiles.'[13] Moreover, 'common sense is judgment without reflection, shared by an entire class, an entire people, an entire nation, or the entire human race.'[14] Vico's common sense can be seen as an anticipation of Heidegger's pre-understanding, and in the framework of our own argument, it is an anticipation of the structure of the latent world, manifested in typical situations.

The separation of science and the humanities

In science, an attempt to understand the given phenomena observed in nature became a problem in the second half of the nineteenth century, when the gap between the world of science and the natural world was for the first time strongly felt. It is interesting, but perhaps not entirely surprising, that the first to raise the issue of the gap were the scientists. One of them was Hermann Helmholtz, who, in a lecture delivered in 1862 and entitled 'On the relation of the Natural Sciences to the whole of Science', drew a distinction between natural sciences and humanities based not on different methods but on the difference of their subject.[15] Another step, much closer to the formation of modern phenomenology, was the contribution of Richard Avenarius, who represents the culmination of nineteenth-century positivism in a form that he described as 'empirio-criticism'.[16] He was the first to use the term *Weltbegriff* (*der menschliche Weltbegriff*) to convey the human concept of world adopted by Husserl as *Lebenswelt* (lived world). What is interesting and rather profound is that Avenarius thought that all the different positions in our highly differentiated, syncretic world, are only variations of the common, given natural world.[17]

I have mentioned the role of science in the formation of the specificity of the humanities to correct the prevailing view that phenomenology as a philosophy was at the margins of that formation. This became true for phenomenology only in its later stages. We should remember that Husserl himself was a mathematician before he became a philosopher. The first intention of phenomenology was to lay foundations for a rigorous, universal science, capable to resolve the crisis in the sphere of knowledge, manifested first as a problem of foundations of modern mathematics and logic, leading only later to the problem of the new foundations of knowledge in general.

The crisis of the foundation of science manifests itself also as an unresolved relation of the natural sciences and the humanities, and later, as a question of truth in simulations, in virtual realities and artificial intelligence.

It is perhaps not surprising that the first serious attempt to challenge the methodical monologue of positive empirical sciences came from the humanities and in particular from history, in its effort to overcome the dogma of historicism. The best examples of such an attempt are the written works of Gottfried Semper and the late work of Wilhelm Dilthey, who happened to appreciate Semper's *Der Stil in den technischen und tektonischen Künsten oder praktische Ästhetik* (2 Vols. 1861 and 1863), which he describes as an 'enlightening model for how an important historical problem could be solved in aesthetics', and, for that reason, considers Semper to be a real successor to Goethe.[18] There are many similarities between Semper's and Dilthey's thinking, such as the search for the simplest constituent elements of history and the use of the comparative method, but most of all the search for the scientific theory of history and art. For Dilthey, the paradigm of method and its scientific legitimacy was Kant's *Critique of Pure Reason*, which he tried to emulate with his own *Critique of Historical Reason*.[19] However, the result was not a success. Dilthey's articulation of historical reason did not help to overcome the conflict between a recognition of the historicity of the human world and the attempt to develop a method which could grasp the phenomenon of historicity. As Gadamer demonstrated, the second ambition cancels the first. Dilthey's contribution, and in some sense Semper's as well, represent a turning point in the theoretical thinking about the arts and humanities. Their search for the scientific method in these fields led to the demonstration of the limits of such an enterprise, and opened the door for a very different way of thinking about the humanities and arts, including architecture.

The new way of thinking was opened and cultivated mostly in the sphere of phenomenology and, later, in hermeneutics. In this traditional method, epistemology and theory are not entirely dismissed but become rather redundant. Their place is taken over by a more critical and subtle thinking, sensitive to the hermeneutical conditions of typical situations, the reciprocity of their universal and particular meaning, the formation of historical concepts and their creative interpretation. In the last years of his life, Dilthey came very close to Husserl and phenomenology. Though it was rather too late, his influence on the phenomenological movement, particularly on

Heidegger and Gadamer, was substantial. The sequence of Dilthey's influences illustrates the changes in the nature of phenomenological thinking and its development from the immanent transcendentalism of Husserl to Heidegger's and Gadamer's ontology based on language, and to the most recent stage of thinking, situated in the sphere of embodiment (corporeality) articulated most consistently so far by Jan Patočka, Maurice Merleau-Ponty and his followers Jean-Luc Marion, Renaud Barbaras, and others.

Contemporary foundations of the humanities

The critical terms of the phenomenological foundations of the humanities are the typicality of experience, based on *praxis* and embodied in typical (paradigmatic) situations. The 'typicality of experience' is a sedimented experience which always precedes a particular design decision and its form. Reading, for instance, is essential to the vision of a library, but always transcends it. It can take place elsewhere or even without it. On the other hand, the concept of a library without a vision and understanding of the conditions of reading, borrowing of books and the inner life of the library is empty. Library seen as a type is not an original reference; it is always preceded by the typicality of the particular experience of using the library (Fig. 7.2).

The typical experience has its origins in *praxis*. The Classical notion of *praxis* belongs to the fundamental constitution of human beings and their situation in the world. *Praxis* does not depend on the abstract knowledge of norms but is always concretely—that is, practically— motivated: 'In every culture a series of things is taken for granted and lies fully beyond the explicit consciousness of anyone, and even in the greatest dissolution of traditional forms, mores and customs the degree to which things held in common still determine everyone is only more concealed.'[20] The deeper meaning of *praxis* is living and acting in accordance with ethical principles. For a more specific understanding, it is necessary to see *praxis* as related to a particular place, where people are not only doing or experiencing something, but which also includes things that contribute to the fulfilment of human life. This includes everything associated with human activity, for instance the table on which we take our daily meal or the walls of a room which protect the intimacy of our conversation.

The relation of *praxis* to a particular place leads to the formation of *typical (paradigmatic) situations*. Situations act as receptacles of experience and of those events which sediment a meaning in them, a meaning not just as survivals and residues, but as the invitation to a sequence of future experiences. Situations endow experience with durability, in relation to which other experiences can acquire meaning and can form a memory and history. Situations are dependent and closely related to habits, traditions and customs. Their nature is similar to the nature of institutions, deep structures or archetypes. Situations represent the most complete way of understanding the condition of our experience of the surrounding world and the human qualities of the world. The close link between *praxis* and typical situations indicates that *praxis* always belongs to a world it articulates and thus brings about.

This level of articulation can be reached in a hermeneutical interpretation of the lived world as it is manifested in typical situations. On that level, articulation can be read as a language structured by similarities, metaphors and analogies, which may be described altogether as poetic paradigm. The poetic paradigm is a key to the understanding of the lived (natural) world in its wholeness. The natural world in not a thing or a sum total of things that can be seen or studied in their explicit presence. It is an articulated continuum to which we all belong. The main characteristic of the natural world is its continuity in time and space and its permanent presence. A most explicit manifestation of this can be seen in language, revealing most clearly the structure of the natural world. In this world, we can move, in the same way as in language, into the past or future, survey different regions of reality, refer to almost anything in our experience and translate the experience into any language. This possibility also includes the language of science and religion. What is revealed in language points to a level of articulation, which shows our involvement in the structuring of the natural world as well as the level of reality, where language meets the natural conditions—that is, the given reality of embodiment—in its most elementary form.

The role of the poetic paradigm in understanding the natural world in its wholeness is recognised not only by humanists and artists, but also by scientists. Werner Heisenberg refers to it when he speaks of the 'one' (common good), which is only a different name for the unifying role of praxis. He writes:

> In the last resort, even science must rely upon ordinary language, since it is the only language in which we can be sure of really grasping the phenomena [...] the language of images and

likenesses is probably the only way of approaching the 'one' [the 'common good'] from more general domains. If the harmony in a society rests on a common interpretation of the 'one' [the 'common good'], the unitary principle behind the phenomena, then the language of poetry may be more important here than the language of science.[21]

Architecture as a humanistic discipline

From all that has been said so far, we can already draw a preliminary conclusion, that architecture is not in the first place a technical but a humanistic discipline. This must be clear to everyone who sees a distinction between means and goals, and agrees that the goal, the essence of architecture, its main purpose, is to situate our life in a particular place and create the right conditions for our existence and coexistence, not only with other people, but also with the given natural conditions and cultural circumstances. Skills, techniques and technologies are only means that can help us to fulfil this purpose and goal.

Unlike individual techniques and specialised sciences, architecture is faced with reality in its full given phenomenal presence. In any kind of design, we have to address a particular space in its totality. We can concentrate on particular aspects, such as light, structure, material, events, etc., but in the end, we can judge and appreciate the results only in the context of the space in its unity and as a whole. The unity of a space does not depend on the integrity of individual spatial aspects only, but also on their reciprocity with other meaningful phenomena—how changing light influences the materiality of the space, for instance. The possibility of grasping the space in its wholeness was, and to a great extent still is, a privilege of our imaginative abilities to hold together a coherent vision of space. However, under the pressure when experience is supposed to be presented in a form of explicit knowledge, an unanswered question opens: Where is the discipline that can grasp the full reality of space and elevate it to an explicit level of understanding? It is quite obvious that we don't have a science that can claim such ability. This is true not only for the specialised sciences but also for humanities as they are generally practiced today. The most likely discipline that can help us in the task of a better understanding of space is, as we have already seen, philosophy, particularly in its phenomenological and hermeneutical orientation.[22] This includes the possibility to use partial results of individual sciences and humanities subjected to a critical and creative interpretation.

To the results of science and the humanities we should add the contributions made by other areas of culture, such as painting, sculpture, literature, theatre, etc. Architecture is not only influenced by different areas of culture, but it is also created there, though only indirectly. The mediated, indirect contributions to the making of architecture increase the possibility that some aspects of architectural reality (space) are more clearly visible in the non-architectural areas of culture. The higher and more explicit level of articulation one finds in painting, sculpture, theatre and literature can tell us about the role of light, nature and the materiality of space, and about the role of particular events in the formation of space more than can isolated architectural studies on their own.

The final result and success of design depend on bridging the distance between the contribution of individual disciplines and the unifying philosophical understanding. The unifying understanding, we may already conclude, is an achievement of a humanistic approach; what makes this approach to design possible is not only the unifying nature of knowledge, but also the paradigmatic nature of typical human situations.

The paradigmatic nature of typical situations and identity or meaning

The term 'paradigmatic' refers to the power of typical situations to bring and hold together a vast richness of human experiences and give them relative stability. The stability of situations is revealed in habits, customs and traditions. It is a source of constant surprise to see to what extent our life is structured by the typicality of situations of our everyday life, such as eating, work, learning, and so on, situated in typical places. The process that constitutes and preserves the typicality of situations can be described as a continuity of reference to the ultimate source of stability in the given natural (cosmic) conditions of our world and its history.[23] However, if we want to appreciate the real nature of situations we must turn to a concrete example. If we look closely at a French café, for instance, it is obvious that its essential nature is only partly revealed in its visible appearance. For the most part, it is hidden in the field of references to the social and cultural life related to a particular place.

Any attempt to understand the character, identity or meaning of the situation and its spatial setting using conventional typologies is futile. The essential reality of the situation is not entirely revealed in its visible appearance. It cannot be observed or studied just on that level. Its representational structure can be grasped through a pre-understanding based on our familiarity with the situation and with the segment of world to which it belongs. Pre-understanding in this case is a sedimented experience of the world, acquired through our involvement in the events of everyday life. The identity of the French café is to a great extent defined by its institutional nature, rooted in the habits, customs and ritual aspects of French life. The formation of identity is a result of a long process in which the invisible aspects of culture and the way of life are embodied in the visible fabric of the café in a similar way as is language in the written text. The visible 'text' of the café reveals certain common, deep characteristics, such as its location, its relation to the life of the street, its transparency of enclosure and a certain degree of theatricality expressed in the need to see the life of the outside world, but also a need to be seen in it like an actor, the ambiguity of inside and outside expressed not only in the transparent enclosure but also in the choice of furniture etc. These are only some of the characteristics that contribute to the identity and meaning of the French café as a culturally distinct typical situation.

The task to grasp the essential nature and typicality of situations is critical not only for the making of architecture but also for its interpretation in reception and use. This brings us to the conclusion that we don't need to speak about the influence of the humanities on architecture or about a separate role of the humanities in design, because architecture itself is a humanistic discipline and should therefore be treated as such.

Notes

1 Charles Percy Snow, *The Two Cultures*, Cambridge: Cambridge University Press, 1993.
2 Hans-Georg Gadamer, 'Citizens of Two Worlds', in *On Education, Poetry and History: Applied Hermeneutics*, ed. Dieter Misgeld and Graeme Nicholson, trans. Lawrence Schmidt and Monica Reuss, Albany, NY: State University of New York Press, 1992, pp. 209–21.
3 Daniel Libeskind, *End Space*, London: Architectural Association, 1980, p. 20.
4 Daniel Libeskind, *Breaking Ground: The Journey from Poland to Ground Zero*, New York: Riverhead Trade, 2005, p. 230.
5 Nicholas Jardine, 'Epistemology and the Sciences', in *The Cambridge History of Renaissance Philosophy*, Cambridge: Cambridge University Press, 1988, pp. 694–96; Giovanni Crapulli, *Mathesis universalis: Genesi di un'idea nel XVI secolo*, Rome: Edizioni dell'Ateneo, 1969.

6   Charles H. Lohr, 'Metaphysics', *The Cambridge History of Renaissance Philosophy*, op. cit., pp. 616–20.

7   Alexandre Koyré, *Newtonian Studies*, London: Chapman & Hall, 1965, pp. 23–24.

8   Houdar de la Motte's commentary on Virgil's Ode, quoted in Paul Hazard, *The European Mind 1680–1715*, London: Penguin Books, 1953, p. 386.

9   Ibid., p. 387, citing Jean Le Clerc, *Parrhasiana ou, Pensées diverses sur des matiéres de critique, d'histoire, de morale et de politique*, Amsterdam, 1699.

10 Richard E. Palmer, *Hermeneutics: Interpretation Theory in Schleiermacher, Dilthey, Heidegger and Gadamer*, Evanston, IL: Northwestern University Press, 1969.

11 Hans-Georg Gadamer, 'Reply to Donald Philip Verene', in *The Philosophy of Hans-Georg Gadamer*, ed. Lewis E. Hahn, The Library of Living Philosophers, vol. XXIV, Chicago and La Salle, IL: Open Court, 1997, p. 154.

12 Hans-Georg Gadamer, *Truth and Method*, trans. William Glen-Doepel, ed. John Cumming and Garret Barden, London: Sheed and Ward, 1975, p. 22.

13 *The New Science of Giambattista Vico*, translation of the third edition (1744) by Thomas G. Bergin and Max H. Fisch, Ithaca, NJ: Cornell University Press, 1961, XI, 141, p. 63.

14 Ibid., XII, 142, p. 63.

15 Gadamer, 'Citizens', op. cit., p. 40.

16 Richard Avenarius' (1843–96) empirio-criticism, a radical version of late empiricism that can also be seen as a refined version of positivism, came close to a discovery of the phenomenal reality of the world as a common ground for all different interpretations of the world itself.

17 Richard Avenarius, *Der menschliche Weltbegriff*, Leipzig: O. R. Reisland, 1891.

18 Wilhelm Dilthey, *Poetry and Experience*, ed. Rudolf A. Makkreel and Frithjof Rodi, Selected Works vol. V, New Haven, NJ: Princeton University Press, 1985, p. 204.

19 Gadamer, 'Dilthey's entanglement in the impasses of historicism', in *Truth and Method*, op. cit., pp. 192–204.

20 Hans-Georg Gadamer, 'What is Practice? The Conditions of Social Reason', in *Reason in the Age of Science*, trans. Frederick G. Lawrence, Cambridge, MA: MIT Press, 1981, p. 82.

21 Werner Heisenberg, *Across the Frontiers*, trans. Peter Heath, New York: Harper & Row, 1974, pp. 120–21.

22 Hans-Georg Gadamer, 'The Universality of the Hermeneutical Problem', *Philosophical Hermeneutics*, trans. David E. Linge, Berkeley, CA: University of California Press, pp. 3–18.

23 Jan Patočka, 'Care and the Three Movements of Human Life', in *Body, Community, Language, World*, ed. James Dodd, trans. Erazim Kohák, Chicago and La Salle, IL: Open Court, 1998, pp. 143–51.

8 Elements of Architecture and Their Meaning

Is it possible to discuss architecture in terms of its elements, particularly when they appear so isolated and so archaic as do today the column, obelisk, pyramid or vase? It is certainly difficult to ignore the feeling that they should be discussed either as part of some larger configuration or as independent objects, perhaps like pieces of sculpture. Their architectural meaning is not immediately apparent and where we sense that there was one, we no longer seem to share it. Yet it is quite obvious that such elements as the column, for instance, belong to the very essence of architecture in a way that preserves its primary characteristics throughout architectural history. Is it not, then, possible that the column, obelisk or vase, despite their apparent isolation, represent some essential, timeless and universal aspects of architecture of which we are not fully aware?

Unfortunately, today we are not in a good position to answer such questions directly. To speak about eternal or universal meaning in a time when so much importance is given to change is problematic and makes us feel rather uncomfortable. And yet, dominated so much by change, our time is also haunted by the need for long-term cultural and personal identities. It is possible, however, and this will be my main argument, that the problem of identity and change belong together as a problem of situational integrity; that the universal meaning of the column, for instance, belongs to the changing nature of the overall structure of architecture and contributes to its deeper meaning. As a result, we may be able to see not only the meaning of particular elements but also how they belong together in a meaningful unity. A proper understanding of the deeper meaning of individual elements represents a context that I shall describe as situational. It is only by situating a particular element in the broader context of cultural circumstances that we can answer some of our questions.

DOI: 10.4324/9781003272090-9

Any contemporary attempt to understand the universal meaning of a particular architectural element and the source of its identity in the long span of history has to overcome certain obstacles. The traditional understanding of universality, always based on some form of reciprocity between the universal and particular, intelligible and sensible, was, in modern times, reduced to mathematical representation that claims for itself the monopoly of universality. What cannot be represented mathematically is seen as ambiguous and potentially chaotic. This state of affairs was obviously not accomplished overnight. Architectural reality and its power of representation were effected only in stages. What proved to be decisive in the development of architectural representation was the close link between the interpretation of architectural order and the order of reality as a whole (cosmos), and the growing mathematical understanding of the latter. The use of number and geometry allowed the formation of more complete and comprehensive cosmologies. As a result, architecture could be represented in a more universal manner that would give more defined and explicit meaning to the individual, very often primary, elements such as dome, wall, column, etc. This led inevitably to the early attempts to represent the whole body of architectural problems and, in the end, the overall order of architecture by geometry and number, and to articulate the resulting order in terms of mathematical proportions, symmetries and harmonies. The close relationship between architecture and cosmology culminated in the seventeenth century and is well-illustrated by the following statement:

> If we consider this beautiful machine of the world, with how many wonderful ornaments it is filled, and how the heavens, by their continual revolutions, change the seasons according as nature requires, and their motion preserves itself by the sweetest harmony of temperature; we cannot doubt, but that the little temples we make ought to resemble this very great one, which, by his immense goodness, was perfectly completed with one word of his ....[1]

Elements and situations

In contrast to architectural typology, the typicality of architectural elements and their situational structure is a historically evolved phenomenon that cannot be understood by reference to form alone. Embodied and sedimented meaning always precedes a particular form. Musical performance, for instance, is essential to the vision of the concert hall but always transcends it. The performance can take place elsewhere and can also exist without the hall. On the other hand, the concept of a concert hall without performance, audience and the concrete conditions of human presence is an empty concept. The concert hall seen as a type is not an original reference but is always preceded by the typicality of a particular situation.

The assertion of primary symbols in architectural tradition contributes decisively to the formation of typical (paradigmatic) situations and secondary symbols which, in turn, generate through further differentiation whole families of architectural forms and meanings. The hierarchy of the resulting forms and meanings is held together by the power of symbolic representation that allows us to move from one situation to another, as long as we understand their similarities, analogies and the poetics of their metamorphosis. It is in this framework that we may begin to understand better the nature of the universal meaning of a particular architectural element and of the situation to which it belongs.

In essence, universal meaning is never immanent in the element itself. It is, instead, a presence of identity mediated through a sequence of references towards a common ground, i.e., the natural or cosmic conditions represented by primary symbols. This understanding of universality may also explain why I have not used the term 'archetype'.[2] It is mostly because universal meanings are, in the modern understanding of archetype, reduced into their psychological equivalents that I have criticised the use of type. As a result, the ontological structure of meaning is reduced to an introverted epistemological concept.

The discipline that contributes in a decisive way to the mediation of reference towards a common ground is architecture itself. Whilst it is true that architecture was rarely seen as an explicitly imitative art—like painting for instance, mediating something clearly recognisable—it was always understood that architecture does imitate something. Such understanding was cultivated in the complex nature of particular paradigms most often without a clear or explicit knowledge. In the history of European architecture, we come across a number of such paradigms, each of them reflecting the overall order of reality as it was experienced, understood and represented in a particular epoch of history.

It is a generally accepted that the source of paradigms in European tradition can be found in the pre-history of the Mediterranean civilisations and particularly in the long period of transformation when the primary celestial and terrestrial symbols were formed among the Greeks and Romans. The key to the problem of paradigms is the mode of their representation. The creative imitation (*mimesis*) of primary symbols can be traced through the formation of such early paradigms as the cave or grotto and their re-presentation in early sanctuaries and archaic crypts. I have chosen the cave as a point of departure because it illustrates very clearly the formation of one of the paradigms in which the elementary meaning of column is articulated.

The cave of Amnissos, later known as the cave of Eileithyia, situated east of Herakleion on the north side of Crete, was in Minoan times the centre of the cult of a female deity.[3] In the depths of the long and narrow space of the cave several stalagmites are still visible today. One of them is shaped like a column, while two others resemble female figures that have been partly shaped by human hand. The stalagmites, with their ambiguous semi-figurative physiognomy, are most likely the aniconic epiphany of the great goddess of the island. This interpretation is strongly supported by the evidence of a large number of offerings in front of and around the stalagmite column that is further surrounded by a low rectangular wall, thus establishing a small *temenos* (Fig. 8.1). The cave was also used for sacrifices on

8.1 Cave of Eileithyia, Amnissos. Stalagmite with wall enclosure.

bench altars, for additional offerings in small pools of water and for other ritual ceremonies. The dark and misty atmosphere of the cave was a place where the numinous powers of the earth and the mystery of life and its renewal were manifested. A much later testimony, which may preserve a genuine memory of such a situation, describes the typical cave as 'a symbol of the cosmos, a symbol of generated and sensible nature, which the ancients also used as a symbol of all invisible powers, because caves are dark and the essence of these powers is indistinct.'[4] The verticality of the column is reinforced by its contrast with the horizontality of the ceiling and by the close affinity with the upright position of the human figure. It is well known that the Cretans recognised not only the numinosity of the earth, but also that of the sky. This is confirmed by the finds of offerings to the sky gods in the caves in the late Minoan period. The fact that the ceiling of the cave could be associated with the sky is demonstrated in the blue painted ceiling in the grotto sanctuary of the temple tomb in Gypsades outside Knossos.[5]

The space of the cave and its use can be seen as a paradigm of a natural sanctuary, in which the column plays a mediating role between the numinous powers sustaining the continuity of the life of nature, and the everyday existence of the people of the island. The development of the paradigm of the cave can be further illustrated by the transfer of meaning from the caves used originally as dwellings to those used later as tombs and finally to another group of caves used as sanctuaries.[6] The affinity between life, death and immortality became the decisive characteristic of the paradigm of the cave. This affinity was embodied in the stalagmite columns as an epiphany of the life-sustaining powers, which had their source not only in the chthonic depth of the cave but also in the celestial height of the sky. The earlier, compact symbolism of the column became more explicit in the mountain peak sanctuaries during the time of the great palaces in the middle Minoan period. The sanctuaries found on top of the more accessible mountains were dedicated to the deities of celestial phenomena, mostly of rain, wind, and lightning.[7] They were also the main source of the divine power of the king, as is illustrated on the seal impression from Knossos where the female deity standing on the mountain transfers a sceptre, the symbol of royal power, to the king[8] (Fig. 8.2 top).

The relationship between sanctuary, mountain and column is also demonstrated on the Sanctuary rhyton from Zakros, in a scene depicting the spatial arrangement and elevation of a fully developed

8.2 Two gold seals from Knossos, 14th c. BCE.

peak sanctuary. It is only the uppermost part of the scene that interests us here, particularly the central element representing a vertical sacred stone (*baetyl*) or mountain, guarded by two pairs of mountain goats. We know that mountain and column are very often used as aniconic representation of a deity whose presence is indicated by the pair of birds[9] (Fig. 8.3). The close relationship between the epiphany of the deity, the *baetyl* and the sanctuary is finally embodied in the syncretic meaning of the column. The complexity of this meaning is fully apparent in another golden seal from Knossos, where a

8.3 Detail from the Sanctuary rhyton, Zakros, ca. 1550 BCE.

freestanding column in the gate of a sanctuary represents both the deity and the inner world of the sanctuary. Here, the sky-oriented meaning of the column is reinforced by the presence of the pole in front of the sanctuary and by the sceptre of the young god appearing in the sky[10] (Fig. 8.2 bottom).

This abbreviated interpretation may already throw some light on the much debated meaning of freestanding columns guarded by a pair of animals, as they are found, for example, in the well-known Lion

Gate of the citadel of Mycenae. There is an obvious continuity in the use of this motif between the Minoan and Mycenaean epochs. In both cultures, the column does not necessarily represent the deity itself but rather the place of its epiphany that could be an open or closed sanctuary (cave, crypt) or sometimes the palace as a whole.[11] Freestanding columns can also be seen, though in an enigmatic manner, on seal cylinders from Mycenae[12] (Fig. 8.4).

We can perhaps draw a preliminary conclusion by saying, firstly, that the column plays an intricate mediating role between its object-like appearance and the space of meaning that it can represent or symbolise. Secondly, that it demonstrates most clearly the vertical organisation of the archaic culture where the high and low, divine and human, are related through a sequence of articulations and thus refer to the most important aspect of European culture as a whole.[13]

We have already seen that a typical spatial setting of an archaic situation is more like a space of a cave than a developed architectural space. This view is supported by the earliest available evidence, which speaks about archaic space as *chora*. *Chora* is not structured as an explicit space. It is more like a receptacle that allows everything to appear in it 'on pain of being itself nothing at all and serving only as a unity of place, ground of being and nurse of becoming.'[14] The quasi-mythical nature of *chora* is, to some extent, preserved in the later understanding of space as place (*topos*), which was seen as a vessel with content that could be replaced. This 'replacement seems at once to prove the independent existence of the place, from which, as if from a vessel, water, for instance, has gone out and into which air has come, and which some other body yet may occupy in its turn; for the place itself is thus revealed as something different from each and all of its changing contents. For "that wherein" air is, is identical with "that wherein" water was. So that the place (*topos*) or room (*chora*) into which each substance came or out of which it went, must all the time have been distinct from both of the substances alike.'[15]

The vision of a place as a vessel represents a symbolic understanding in which the space of the vessel is linked, in one sense, with the space of the cave, while in another sense, it is linked with any contained space. The most explicit example of such a contained space is the space of the 'vase', as described by Aristotle. There is a particularly clear affinity between the space of the cave, which was used as dwelling, tomb or sanctuary, and the space of the vase, used as a container for a burial or as an urn in the form of a dwelling or sanctuary (Fig. 8.5). In both cases, the nature of contained

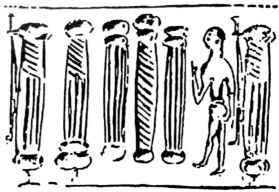

8.4 Tympanum relief of the Lion Gate (top), and cylinder seal (bottom); both Mycenae, 13th c. BCE.

space transcends the immediate purpose and finds its fulfilment in the domain of life, death and rebirth, as they are understood in the context of a particular culture. It is on that level that the space of a cave and the space of a vase share the essential characteristics of place, which is to contain and situate things. The reciprocity between situated things and place may help us to understand how it is possible that the column, as an isolated element always situated in a particular

8.5 Terracotta model of shrine or tomb containing a deity figure, Archanes, ca. 850 BCE.

place, can represent a complete hierarchy of places within a unified cosmic framework. 'If a thing is not separated from its embracing environment, but is undifferentiated from it, it is indeed "included in" it - not, however, as in its place, but only in the sense in which a part is said to be "included in" its whole.'[16] If the notion of reciprocity between places and things is valid, then places must be contained and situated in the same way as things are. Indeed, they are situated in the same hierarchy as things, which culminates in the unifying cosmic place. 'The centre of the universe and the inner surface of the revolving heavens constitute the supreme "below" and the supreme "above"; the former being absolutely stable, and the latter constant in its position as a whole.'[17]

There is a clear affinity between the hierarchical structure of space and the mediating role of the column. This affinity can help us understand the deeper meaning of the Minoan seal representation in

Fig. 8.2 (bottom), where, as we have seen, the freestanding column does not represent only the epiphany of the deity, but also the space of the sanctuary and its particular hierarchy. The unity of the epiphanic and spatial meaning of the column became the foundation of a development in which the column was seen mostly as a mediating link between the higher and lower levels of reality but could be also treated as a simple body or a simple spatial or structural element. The tension between the column seen as an autonomous element and as an element with a deeper situational meaning is revealed in the phenomenon of ornament and decoration. Both these terms are derived from the original Greek term for order (*kosmos*).[18] The fact that the column is the most exemplary mode of ornament was acknowledged many times, perhaps most clearly by Leon Battista Alberti in his well-known statement: 'In the whole art of building, the column is the principal ornament, without any doubt; it may be set in combination, to adorn a portico, wall, or other form of opening, nor is it unbecoming when standing alone. It may embellish crossroads, theatres, squares; it may support a trophy; or it may act as a monument.'[19] The relationship between ornament and order (*kosmos*) is not only metaphorical. Ornament should be seen literally as a creation or making of order—*kosmopoeisis*.[20]

It is true that the link between ornament and order is generally recognised, but this does not mean that it is always well understood. There is a tendency to see ornament as external to the primary nature of architecture, as something that can be added to the body of the building or taken away. Günter Bandmann probably came closer than many others to understanding the nature of ornament, when he spoke about its linguistic nature (*Sprachcharakter*), about its role to articulate our experience and vision of the world order, and about the possibility of ornament to become the abbreviation of the cosmos.[21]

The communicative power of ornament does not have its source in the ornament itself. It originates in the domain where ornament is situated, that is, in the reciprocity between the ideal, articulated, intelligible level of culture and its latent, silent, sensible ground. It is from within this domain that ornament is generated. The history of the column illustrates this very clearly. In the most characteristic arrangements, as part of a colonnade or arcade, as a freestanding support or as part of a wall, etc., the column tends to determine the primary spatial configuration of a building or a place, while at the same time it participates in the more differentiated and articulated areas of culture, which contribute decisively to the articulation of its own physiognomy and language. It is sufficient to recall here the appearance and the role of the column in the Christian *baldacchino* on the portal of High Gothic cathedrals, or, in the development of the post-Renaissance architectural orders, to appreciate not only the universality, but also the flexibility and creative role of the column in the formation of architectural language.

The question that cannot easily be ignored, is, what makes the column such a dominating element in the history of architecture? The most plausible answer, which may complement the convenient but inconclusive structural and functional explanations, is the proximity of the nature and meaning of the column to the central issues of European culture, its vertical structure and mediated unity. What makes the column particularly important in this context is the privileged role of human existence and the human body in the representation and understanding of reality, which has a long history in Europe. This is reflected most clearly in the deep affinity between the human body and the anthropomorphic character of the column[22] (Fig. 8.6). This affinity is reinforced by the fact that, in the same way as the animated human body is the medium through which the order of reality can be revealed, so is the column an element where the order of architecture is most often revealed and embodied. It is certainly characteristic that, in most cases, the proportional systems derive their unit of measurement (*module*) from the diameter of the column, which thus becomes the key reference for the structure and unity of the architectural order as a whole.

The extent to which the meaning of the column depends upon the presence of the articulated context becomes clear when we realise that any system of proportions, properly understood, represents an analogically structured world. In such a world, it is possible to move not only between different levels of reality but also between different areas of culture, such as architecture, sculpture, mythology, music, theatre and dance, and return back to architecture and its silent language informed by such a movement. In this context, the column is not only a structuring element but also a rhetorical one. It is an element open to rhetorical communication and language, which we are only slowly beginning to understand. In more recent literature, it is generally acknowledged that the column belongs to a more comprehensive order, which can be studied and understood only as part of an ensemble. Such ensembles (orders) are not determined by the strict rules of architecture but mostly by a broader sphere of culture that includes music and its *modi*, astronomy and its harmonics, ethics

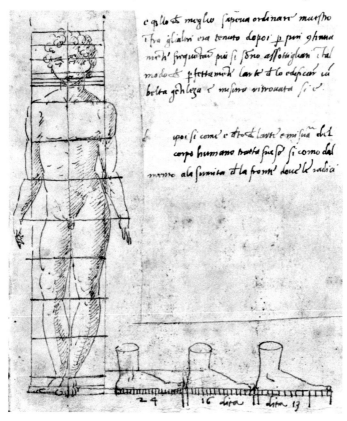

8.6 Francesco di Giorgio Martini, *Trattati di architettura ingegneria e arte militare*, 1476–77. Detail from marginal drawings showing proportions of the human figure in relation to the column.

and its decorum, the rules of rhetoric, etc.[23] We may understand some of the important aspects of the column in the history of a different kind of column, better known as the obelisk.

Obelisks, their nature and meaning

In the history of European architecture, the obelisk does not seem to play a very important role. Its appearance is more or less limited to the cultural territory of Rome and its influence on the rest of Europe. It is true that, on the whole, it is seen as an imported, alien and exotic element in a new setting. However, the more we understand the circumstances of its assimilation and its resonance within certain aspects of Classical culture, the more we can appreciate its unique power to represent some of the more essential aspects of architectural order and the process of its formation. In order to see the obelisk in such a light, we have to move away from interpretations in which it appears as an isolated, exotic object, towards a vision in which obelisk can be seen as part of a situational structure with corresponding situational meaning.

The first appearance of the obelisk in Rome in the first century BCE was preceded by a long tradition in which the role of the sun, related to the primary meaning of the obelisk, went through its own history on Italian soil. An early reference speaks about the Temple of the Sun God (*Sol indigenes*) on the Quirinal, already in the early years of the Republic.[24] In the same way as the Greek Helios, it is quite clear that, in those early stages, the Roman Sol was a rather secondary deity, merely a subordinated member of the pantheon of primary deities. This situation changed after the fourth century BCE in a transformation of the traditional Classical religion through a process that may be best described as 'cosmicisation'. We can find the first clearly articulated traces of this change in Plato. 'At this moment', he says in one of his later dialogues, 'all our Hellenic world as I may fairly say, habitually charges high gods sun and moon falsely. They are treated as planets and of secondary importance, while in fact they should be treated as deities.'[25]

The divine meaning of the perfect movement of the sun and its coincidence with the understanding of the animation of reality (soul) is summarised clearly in the following: 'The soul, moreover, whether it is by riding in the chariot of the Sun or from the outside, or otherwise, that it brings light to us all - every man is bound to regard as god. Is not that so?'[26] It is on that background that we can understand eventually the nature of Plato's new vision, and the nature of religion in his ideal state. 'Every year after the summer solstice the whole state must assemble at the common precincts of Helios and Apollo, there to present before the gods the names of three out of their number.'[27]

The change in the nature of religious beliefs in the post-Classical period shows a strong influence of philosophy, new political reality and the changing character of culture as a whole. There is no doubt that a distinct cult of celestial deities was a new and rather difficult achievement in such pluralistic cultures as were the Greek and the early Hellenistic. The long transformation of the original *Sol indigenes* into a fully developed, emancipated form of sun god

(*Sol invictus*) can be measured by the changes in the cult of Apollo. Apollo was not worshipped as an important deity in the Hellenistic period and in the early Roman Republic until the first century BCE. However, in a relatively short time, during the rule of Augustus, Apollo became the most important deity in the Roman pantheon.[28] In the well-known section of Virgil's *Eclogues*, Apollo is already associated with the end of one age and the beginning of another and is mainly for these reasons identified with the sun (*sol*).[29]

The evidence for the close association between Augustus, his role in the emerging new empire and the role of sun (Apollo) can be seen on the breastplate of the Augustus statue from the Prima Porta (Fig. 8.7). On the relief, inspired by the victory over the Parthians, the earth goddess with her chthonic attributes is situated at the bottom. At the top, on one side, the sun god in his chariot is situated above Apollo, and on the other side is Luna and the winged figure of

8.7 Statue of Augustus of Prima Porta, 1ˢᵗ c. BCE. Detail of breastplate.

Aurora situated above Diana. Between them is the figure of Caelus holding the canopy of the heavens uniting the whole scene.[30] The relief of the breastplate represents a world that is structured not only in terms of religious meaning but also in terms of its more specific philosophical, political and cultural meanings. The vision of the world is at that time already clearly differentiated into the zone of light (intelligibility), represented by the Sun and by Luna with a torch (*Luna lucifere*), while the zone of terrestrial embodiment is represented by the goddess of earth and her attributes. It is in the space between the zones that the drama of mediation between the celestial and terrestrial, between divine and human phenomena, and, on the whole, between the unity and diversity of culture is enacted. The enactment takes place on different levels: religious, philosophical, pictorial and literary. In the end, all of them are situated in the corporeality and spatiality of the contemporary everyday life.[31]

This is obviously no more than an outline of the situation under which the first obelisks were brought to Rome. This took place under Augustus after the annexation of Egypt (31 BCE), when the obelisk of Rameses (19th dynasty), originally erected in Heliopolis on the Nile delta, was transported with great difficulties to Rome and, eventually, was re-erected on the spina of the Circus Maximus (10 BCE). The original inscriptions of the obelisk, showing the Egyptian king making an offering to the solar gods, reinforced the overall dedication of the circus to the sun. It is very probable that the cult of the sun was linked with the meaning of the circus from the very beginning, that is, from the time of the Etruscan kings.[32]

What was, initially, most probably only an altar situated near the circus became, eventually, a proper temple incorporated in the structure of the arena itself.[33] It is interesting to note that the temple of the sun was situated on the finishing line, exactly opposite the *pulvinar*—the prominent seat of the emperor—treated itself as a shrine.[34] Apart from the sun, the circus was dedicated to a large number of other deities, mostly chthonic and local (Consus, Murcia, Ceres). The complex structure of the circus, its territory, as well as its immediate surroundings, was already in the pre-Augustan period becoming subordinated to the cult of the sun. Nothing was more logical, than to complete this subordination with the erection of the obelisk (Fig. 8.8). The inscription of the obelisk, which was added to the already existing one, says that 'Egypt had been brought back into the power of the Roman people', and that Augustus himself, 'had dedicated the obelisk to the sun as a gift'.[35]

8.8 Sarcophagus fragment, 1st–2nd c. CE, showing the Circus Maximus.

Isidore of Seville describes the obelisk as an arrow (*sagitta*) placed in the middle of the circus because the sun runs through the middle of the world, and that it signifies the peak and summit of the sky (*fastigium summitatemque caeli*).[36] The solar meaning of the obelisk was interpreted as the re-enactment of the movement of the celestial bodies of planets in the movement of the chariots around the spina of the circus. The *agon* of the circus was also often depicted on Etruscan cinerary urns as a representation of the cycle of human life. The movement of the chariots refers to the relation between divine and human temporal realities; and, in that sense, the agonic meaning of the circus recalls the cultic meaning of the cave.

The connection of the obelisk with the sun was clearly expressed in the shape of the obelisk. Ammianus Marcellinus speaks about this shape as 'little by little growing more slender to imitate a sunbeam'.[37] The most important part of the obelisk was its top—the pyramidion. The shaft was, in fact, only an extension bringing the pyramidion closer to the sun. The pyramidion of the obelisk brings forward the ambiguity but also the deep identity between obelisk and pyramid. The source of the identity must be traced back to the Egyptian origins of the obelisk (Fig. 8.9).

In the Heliopolitan cosmogony, the first god Atum (later identified as Re), born from the primeval waters, created a mound on which to stand. Adopting the form of the mythical bird (*Ben*), Atum illuminated the pillar that became associated with him. The conically shaped pillar, later known as Ben-ben, became the sacred symbol of

8.9 Pyramidion of the obelisk of Queen Ankhesenpepi II, Dahshur, ca. 2350 BCE (left); restored pyramidion of the pyramid of Pharaoh Snefru, Saqqara, ca. 2590 BCE.

the sun and served in Heliopolis as a cult object designating the place of creation. From the second dynasty onwards, the Kings adopted the title 'Son of Re' and, as a result, the sun temple became a religious and political institution. In Heliopolis, it consisted of a series of enclosures culminating in an open courtyard, where, in the middle, was a stone podium representing the original mound, on which was mounted a small conical obelisk.[38] The phenomenon of immortality was very closely linked with the unity of Egyptian culture and its continuity in time which, consequently, was closely associated with the cult of the sun. In a hierarchically structured society with very tight bonds, the continuity of the life of the community was dependent on the continuity of the life of its king. The first royal tombs were completed as mounds of sand or stones associated with the 'island of creation', where life came originally into existence.[39] This arrangement was also incorporated into the larger structures made from bricks and, later, from stone—such as the stepped pyramid of Saqqara—and, eventually, into a true pyramid, such as those of Gizeh. The Egyptian word for pyramid, *mer*, can be tentatively translated as the 'place of ascension', the place where the king can ascend to heaven and join his father in the eternal journey through the sky.

The meaning of the pyramidal tombs must be seen not only in terms of their relation to the creation cycle of birth and rebirth, but also in relation to their setting. In Saqqara, for instance, the pyramid was surrounded by a wall of white limestone imitating the wall of the royal palace, and by a large enclosure that included mortuary

8.10 Albert Fehrenbacher, *Modern Reconstruction of a New Kingdom Model of a Temple Gateway.*

temples, shrines, granaries, altars, courts and other tombs. The obelisks appeared very often in pairs before gates, whose significance is evident in the New Kingdom *Book of Gates*, which depicts the journey in the afterworld[40] (Fig. 8.10). The association of the pyramid and the obelisk with the sun, the latter understood not as an abstract entity but as a moving body and power, is clearly expressed in their shapes. The square base, in both pyramid and obelisk, is linked with the apex by four geometrical lines (edges) symbolising the four zones of the world through which the sun moves during the year. This point complements our attempt to see the pyramid and obelisk as situational structures and not as isolated objects. As situational structures they are engaged with their surroundings, which is manifested particularly in the movement of their shadows. The movement of light and shadow is the visible manifestation of their deepest meaning—the movement between life, death and rebirth.[41]

The situational character of the obelisk can be demonstrated beyond its original Egyptian context, several centuries later, in the development of the Campo Marzio in Rome, where Augustus built first his mausoleum and then the altar of peace (*Ara Pacis*). Both structures were linked by the large *gnomon* (*horologium*) where the second obelisk brought from Egypt was eventually situated.[42] The alignment of the mausoleum and Ara Pacis with the obelisk of the solarium, and the fact that on the birthday of Augustus the shadow of the obelisk pointed precisely towards the Ara Pacis, established a set of relationships where the cycle of life, death, and immortality was absorbed into the cycle of the birth of Augustus and the rebirth of the imperium (Fig. 8.11). In this context, it is also important that, in front of the mausoleum of Augustus, was eventually erected a pair of obelisks[43], in a similar manner as those in the temple of Isis, situated near the contemporary site of Santa Maria sopra Minerva.[44] The continuity between the primary meaning of the obelisks and their Christian meaning is clearly illustrated by the attempt of Constantine to erect an obelisk in the hippodrome of Constantinople. The attempt failed but another obelisk was eventually raised in the hippodrome by Theodosius in 390 CE.[45]

The continuity of the primary meaning of the obelisk was, to a great extent, sustained by the powerful presence of the cult of the sun and its ontological universality, but also by a culture where the tangible presence of the divine and its influence in terrestrial events played an important role.[46] For the later development of Christianity,

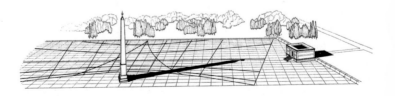

8.11 Diagram of Campo Marzio showing the gnomon and Ara Pacis *[Ed. more recent scholarship agrees that there was not a whole* horologium, *only a meridian line].*

during the Middle Ages, the tangible manifestation of the divine was not of primary importance. It is true that Christian theologians had, from the very beginning, used the sun to express the fundamental truth of revelation, but such expression was never direct or tangible; it was always mediated symbolically.[47] It was as a consequence of this change in European culture that obelisks lost their relevance and that they were forgotten for almost a millennium. The first serious interest in ancient culture and in obelisks began again in the fifteenth century, as a result of the changes effected in the context of Renaissance culture. This time, it was not the sun and its influence on terrestrial events that were of importance, but a more nuanced understanding of the mediating role of light, of which the sun was only a visible source. The development of Medieval philosophy of light reached, already in the thirteenth century, a point where it became a key discipline for the understanding of the mystery of creation and the structure of the world in its metaphysical and physical sense. The cosmic centrality of light found its natural place in the philosophy of Robert Grosseteste: 'It was a natural and evident consequence of his metaphysical use concerning light, one to which later humanists contributed nothing essentially new.'[48]

In the High Middle Ages, it was Grosseteste who took the initiative and stimulated what we may call a valuational heliocentrism, founded not merely upon symbolism, but upon the whole nature of reality as he portrayed it in his own metaphysical terms. The scholastic metaphysics of light, of which he was the best known exponent, was popularised by Pico della Mirandola, Marsilio Ficino, Pietro Pomponazzi and Francesco Patrizi, to find its way into the circles of thought out of which modern astronomy came forth.[49] The humanists did, nevertheless, contribute to the articulation of certain aspects of light as a source of intelligibility potentially present in the ancient texts, but most of all in the newly discovered hieroglyphs and in hermetic texts.[50]

The period from the fifteenth to the seventeenth century was dominated by an effort to reconcile the pagan and Christian traditions using a newly interpreted Egyptian tradition as a common ground. The result was a synthesis of impressive complexity, which influenced most areas of culture, including architecture.[51] The first clear manifestation of this synthesis in the domain of architecture was Pope Nicholas V's program for the rebuilding of Rome, particularly of the Borgo (*vicus curialis*) in the middle of the fifteenth century. The idea of the program was to create three parallel arcaded streets, culminating in the open square in front of the Vatican basil-ica. The critical part of the program was supposed to be the transfer of the Vatican obelisk, the only one still standing since Roman times, into the centre of the square.[52] It was one thing to erect an Egyptian obelisk in ancient Rome as the most typical monument of a con-quered country; it was very different to do the same thing more than a millennium later in the very centre of Christendom. Despite the numerous explanations available to us today, the meaning of such an act remains elusive. When Nicholas V himself discussed this, he used only a very general argument: 'We want you to know and to under-stand that there were two main reasons for our buildings. Only those who come to understand the Church's origin and growth from their knowledge of letters realise that the authority of the Roman Church is greatest and highest'.[53] The two reasons given by Nicholas V were the illiteracy of most Christians and the power of great buildings that appear to be 'made by God' to preserve and augment 'certain admira-ble devotions'.[54] The eventual transfer of the Vatican obelisk to its place in the Piazza San Pietro under Pope Sixtus V marked a new epoch, in which most of the obelisks visible today in Rome were raised again. The event also initiated a vast literary activity in which, alongside occasional poetry and religious pamphlets, a number of important archaeological and interpretative texts came into existence[55] (Fig. 8.12).

With those background conditions in mind, it would be most rewarding to look closely at one example, the obelisk Pamphili, which probably represents better than any other the synthesis of intentions behind the re-erection of obelisks in the Baroque era.[56] The area of the Piazza Navona was originally a stadium from the era of Domitian and not a circus, as was commonly thought in the sixteenth and sev-enteenth centuries[57] (Fig. 8.13). This impression, nevertheless, was what determined the choice of the obelisk and the fountain at its base[58] (Fig. 8.14).

The treatment of the fountain as a grotto surrounded by four river gods was a part of a complex program (*concetto*) conceived by Athanasius Kircher, who was appointed as the chief advisor, and by Gian Lorenzo Bernini, who was responsible for the architecture and the sculpture of the monument.[59] This arrangement illustrates the decisive role of solar symbolism in the meaning of the obelisks raised under Sixtus V as well as those raised later, in the seventeenth century.[60] The Christological meaning of the Vatican obelisk is rep-resented by the figure of Christ (*Sol invictus*) who, as the sun and the light of the Word, is present in the message radiated in the four

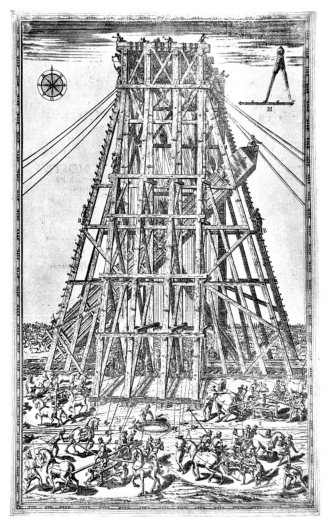

8.12 Domenico Fontana, *Della trasportatione dell'obelisco vaticano*, 1590.
Transportation of the Vatican obelisk.

directions of the world by the evangelists.[61] In the obelisk Pamphili,
the four parts of the world are interpreted as rivers. Their source is
in the grotto, treated as a fountain (*fons vitae et sapientiae*), with
an obvious reference to terrestrial paradise. The rivers of paradise
are replaced here by the rivers of the four continents, Ganges, Nile,

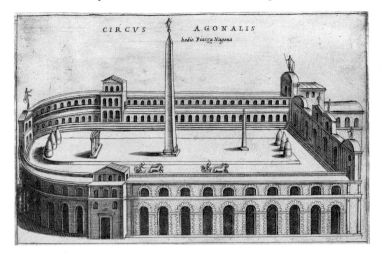

8.13 Giacomo Lauro, *Antiquae urbis splendor*, 1625. Circus agonalis.

Danube, and Rio della Plata, thus representing the world as a whole. In a similar way, the top of the obelisk is not dominated by the cross, as it likely would have been earlier, but by a more universal representation of light in the form of a dove, the symbol of divine love, spirit and the soul of the world; or in Kircher's own words, 'the generative force - *vis penetrativa universi*'.[62] The generative force is, at the same time, the source of intelligibility, identity and unity of the world, and penetrates into the world through participation and mediation. Kircher himself developed a very consistent philosophy of mediation based mostly on the neo-Platonic tradition. Its main characteristics do not differ as much as it is sometimes thought from the contemporary natural theology. Its main intention was to restore the unity of the Christian culture by restoring the relationship between divine and human, the intelligible and sensible realities through a more tangible articulation of the hierarchy of beings (*catena rerum*).[63] What makes this process of mediation specifically Baroque is the tendency to bring the individual steps as far as possible into visibility. Although the body of the obelisk was made of pink granite, it was interpreted by Kircher as a metamorphosis of light into terrestrial matter represented by four elements, corresponding analogically to the four main ingredients of 'porphyry'[64] (Fig. 8.15).

The generative force of light and the mystery of its impact is made visible in the movements and gestures of the river gods; for instance,

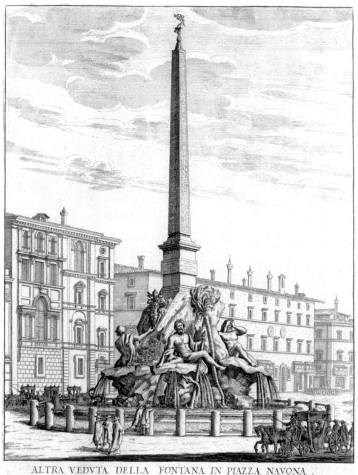

ALTRA VEDVTA DELLA FONTANA IN PIAZZA NAVONA ,
Architettura del Cau· Gio· Lorenzo Bernini .

G·B·Falda del·et inc·   G·Iac·Roßi le stampa in Roma alla Pace· cõ Priu del SP·

8.14 Giovanni Battista Falda, *Le fontane di Roma*, ca. 1691. The obelisk
and fountain at the Piazza Navona.

in the figure of the Nile, who is turning away from the light of the
obelisk, or the Rio de la Plata, who finds the light too painful to
look into and protects his eyes. The general meaning of the obelisk is
summarised by the palm tree at the base. Its symbolism refers to the
explicit form of life on earth and to the movement towards the sky. In a

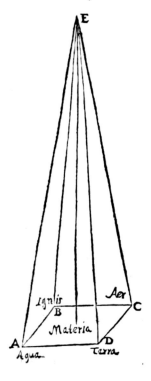

8.15 Athanasius Kircher, *Obeliscus Pamphilius*, 1650. Diagram of the change of light.

more articulated sense, the tree represents ascension, regeneration and immortality, linked to the mediating movement between the divine and the human, the sky and the earth, embodied in the obelisk. The nature of this type of representation is part of the general tendency of the seventeenth century to treat cultural reality in a more abstract (instrumental) sense. Under these conditions, the obelisks eventually became more independent and rather curious objects. However, before this happened, the obelisk was an important mediating element in the spatial order of the centrally articulated and structured world. It is important to notice the relationship between the changes in the meaning of the obelisk and the nature of cosmology.

In the geocentric situation, the spatial symbolism gives priority to the high and the low. The most excellent, the divine, is the most distant. 'In the supernatural or celestial order, the place of greatest dignity is not the most central but the highest.'[65] When the communicative space of the geocentric world was substituted by the geometrical coherence of the heliocentric system, the obelisk was destined to become a simple body in a homogenised space. The complex drama of a culture enacted, embodied and represented by the position of the obelisk in the articulated space, is for us today merely a curious aesthetic experience, in which the obelisk becomes a strange object situated in the void of its surroundings.

In conclusion, we may return to our initial question about the possibility of discussing architecture in terms of its elements. The question appears, no doubt, as a paradox in time when so much effort is invested in the restoration of the spatiality of architecture. And yet, in a space that is not structured by a unifying geometry or perspective but is organised as a configuration of places, there is always an implied reference to a sequence, hierarchy and mutual relationship between individual places (Fig. 8.16). Under such conditions, any place or element with a more explicit or important meaning can serve as a key to the overall spatial configuration. As a result, an important place or element can play the role of an integrating force, which can give the space not only its structure but also its meaning. We have seen a good example of that in the power of the Minoan column to represent a whole sacred precinct, or in the role of the obelisk to integrate and focus a relatively large and complex open space.

8.16 Sacred lake at the temple of Hathor, Dendera.

Notes

1 Andrea Palladio, *The Four Books of Architecture*, trans. Isaac Ware, New York: Dover Publications Inc., 1965, p. 79.

2 The problematic nature of archetype, particularly in the fields of the visual arts and religion was discussed by Jan Bialostocki, 'Die Rahmethemen und die archetypischen Bilder', in *Stil und Ikonographie*, Dresden: VEB Verlag der Kunst, 1966, pp. 144–73; and Henri Frankfort, 'The Archetype in Analytical Psychology and the History of Religion', in *Journal of the Warburg and Courtauld Institutes*, XXI, 1958, pp. 166–78.

3 Paul Faure, *Fonctions des cavernes crétoises*, Paris: Editions E. de Boccard, 1964, p. 21.

4 Porphyry, *The Cave of the Nymphs in the Odyssey*, trans. Seminar Classics 609, State University of New York, Buffalo, NY: Arethusa Monographs, 1969, p. 9.

5 Nanno Marinatos *Minoan Religion, Ritual, Image and Symbol*, Columbia, SC: University of South Carolina Press, 1993, p. 89.

6 There is no evidence that one particular cave was used for more than one purpose. The sequence of dwelling, burial place, sanctuary was nowhere clearly established, but this does not preclude a common meaning for these caves. See Walter Burkert, *Greek Religion*, trans. John Raffan, Oxford: Blackwell, 1985, p. 24.

7 Bogdan Rutkowski, *The Cult Places of the Aegean*, New Haven, NJ: Yale University Press, 1986, pp. 73–99.

8 Ibid., p. 87, Fig. 114; See also Martin P. Nilsson, *The Minoan-Mycenaean Religion and its Survival in Greek Religion*, Lund: C.W.K. Gleerup, 1968, p. 353, Fig. 162.

9 Nikolaos Platon, *Zakros: The Discovery of a Lost Palace of Ancient Crete*, New York: Scribner's, 1971, p. 167.

10 An insight first mooted by Arthur Evans, *The Mycenaean Tree and Pillar Cult*, London, 1901, p. 72.

11 Burkert, op. cit., p. 139.

12 Nilsson, op. cit., p. 257, Fig. 126.

13 I am referring to a structure that has archaic origins but was explicitly articulated in the Classical philosophy and cosmology of the Greeks as a structure of participation (*methexis*) of sensible reality in the intelligible world. In its more developed form, this structure of reality is better known as 'the Great Chain of Being' (*catena rerum*), which dominated European history until the eighteenth century.

14 Plato, *Timaeus*, 52b. [Ed. Vesely seems to have adapted the translation of this passage where most translators emphasise the modes of apprehension for which the description of *chora* is an example.]

15 Aristotle, *Physics*, trans. Philip H. Wicksteed and Francis M. Cornford, Loeb Classical Library, Cambridge, MA: Harvard University Press, 1937, 208b.

16 Ibid., 211a30.

17 Ibid., 212a20.

18 'The Greek word *kosmos* is primarily "order", whether with reference to the due order or arrangement of things, or to the world-order and

secondarily ornament. *Kosmema* is an ornament or decoration usually of dress.' Ananda K. Coomaraswamy, *Selected Papers*, Volume I, *Traditional Art and Symbolism*, ed. Robert E. Lipsey, Princeton, NJ: Princeton University Press, 1977, p. 249.

19 L. B. Alberti, *On the Art of Building in Ten Books*, trans. Joseph Rykwert et al., Cambridge, MA: MIT Press, 1988, p. 183.

20 'Kosmopoeisis is architectural ornament, hence our description of the Doric etc. "orders". Again, we see here the connection between an original "order" and a later "ornament."' Coomaraswamy, op. cit., p. 249.

21 Günter Bandmann, 'Ikonologie des Ornaments und Dekoration', in *Jahrbuch für Ästhetik und allgemeine Kunstwissenschaft*, Band 4, 1958–9, pp. 248–9.

22 The privileged role of human existence, and its symbolism of the body, in the interpretation of the world is closely linked with the anthropomorphic orientation of the Classical and Christian cultural traditions. This is very clearly documented in the history of macro/microcosmism. See George Perrigo Conger, *Theories of Macrocosms and Microcosms in the History of Philosophy*, New York: Columbia University Press, 1922; and Rudolf Allers, 'Microcosmus: from Anaximandros to Paracelsus', *Traditio* vol. 2, 1944, pp. 319–407.

23 Among the works that have made an important contribution to this kind of understanding should be mentioned: Erik Forssman, *Säule und Ornament*, Stockholm: Almqvist & Wiksell, 1956, and his *Dorisch, Ionisch, Korinthisch*, Akta Universitatis Stockhomiensis V, Uppsala, 1961; Günter Bandmann, 'Ikonologie der Architektur' in *Jahrbuch für Ästhetik und allgemeine Kunstwissenschaft*, Band 1, 1951, pp. 67–109; George Hersey, *The Lost Meaning of Classical Ornament*, Cambridge, MA: MIT Press, 1988; John Onians, *Bearers of Meaning*, Princeton, NJ: Princeton University Press, 1988; Joseph Rykwert, *The Dancing Column*, Cambridge, MA: MIT Press, 1996.

24 Kurt Latte, *Römische Religionsgeschichte*, Munich: C.H. Beck's Verlag, 1967, p. 44.

25 Plato, *Laws*, adapted from *Plato: The Collected Dialogues*, ed. Huntington Cairns and Edith Hamilton, trans. Alfred E. Taylor, Bollingen Series LXXI, Princeton, NJ: Princeton University Press, 1981, 821b.

26 Plato, *Laws*, trans. Robert G. Bury, Loeb Classical Library, Cambridge, MA: Harvard University Press, 1926, 899b.

27 Ibid., 945e.

28 It was probably Sulla who attempted for the first time to establish a special relationship with Apollo, claiming also that one of his ancestors created the *Ludi Apollinares* in 212 BCE. See Plutarch, *Sulla*, 29.11; and Stefan Weinstock, *Divus Julius*, Oxford: Clarendon Press, 1971, p. 13. However, it was only after the victory of Augustus at Philippi that Apollo received a permanent place in Roman religion. For further details, see Pierre Lambrechts, 'La politique "apollinienne" d'Auguste et le culte impérial,' in *La nouvelle Clio*, tome V, 1953, pp. 65–82.

29 'Born of Time, a great new cycle of centuries/ Begins. Justice returns to earth, the Golden Age/ Returns, and its first-born comes down

from heaven above./ Look kindly, chaste Lucina, upon this infant's birth,/ For with him shall hearts of iron cease, and hearts of gold/ Inherit the whole earth — yes, Apollo reigns now (*tuus iam regnat Apollo*).' Virgil, 'The Eclogues', IV, 5–10, in *The Eclogues and the Georgics*, trans. C.D. Lewis, Oxford: Oxford University Press, 1983.

30 For a more detailed interpretation see, Hans Jucker, 'Dokumentationen zur Augustusstatue von Primaporta', in *Hefte des Archäologischen Seminars der Universität* Bern, 3, 1977, pp. 16–37; and Klaus Fittschen, 'Zur Panzerstatue in Cherchel', in *Jahrbuch des Deutschen Archäologischen Instituts*, 91, 1976, p. 203.

31 In order to appreciate the complexity and the advanced nature of the problem of mediation, we also have to take into account the achievements of contemporary cosmology, theology and sciences as they were developed in Middle Platonism and Stoicism. The complexity of such mediation is well documented in André-Jean Festugière, *La révélation d'Hermès Trismégiste*, Paris: Les Belles Lettres, 1983.

32 For a more detailed discussion, see W. Quinn-Schofield, 'Sol in the Circus Maximus', in *Hommages à M. Renard*, vol. II, pp. 639–49, Brussels: Latomus, 1969.

33 In that shape, the temple appears on the denarius of Marcus Antonius dating to 42 BCE. See S. L. Cesano, 'M. Antonius Sol', in *Bollettino dell' Associazione Archaeologica Romana*, 1912, pp. 10–12.

34 The temple of the Sun was later dedicated to the Sun and Moon. See, 'Templum Solis et Lunae', in *Notitia*, Reg. XI, as cited in *Topographical Dictionary of Ancient Rome*, ed. Samuel Ball Platner and Thomas Ashby, Oxford: Oxford University Press, 1929, rubric 'Sol (et Luna) AEDES', p. 491.

35 *Corpus Inscriptionum Latinarum*, IV, 701 [trans. Vesely].

36 Isidore of Seville, *Etymologie*, Liber XVIII, 31, in his *Opera Omnia*, from Jacque-Paul Migne, *Patrologia Latina*, Vol. 82.

37 Ammianus Marcellinus, *History, Volume I: Books 14–19*, trans. John C. Rolfe, Loeb Classical Library, Cambridge, MA: Harvard University Press, 1950, 17.4.7.

38 Henri Frankfort, *Kingship and the Gods: A Study of Ancient Near Eastern Religion as the Integration of Society and Nature*, Chicago, IL: University of Chicago Press, 1948, pp. 151–54.

39 The meaning of the island of creation is discussed in E.A.E. Raymond, *The Mythical Origin of the Egyptian Temple*, Manchester: Manchester University Press, 1969, pp. 5–75.

40 The solar iconography of both pyramid and obelisk was observed by Ernesto Schiaparelli, *Il significato simbolico delle Piramide Egiziane*, Reale Academia dei Lincei, Rome, 1884. More recently, Alexander Badawy has called attention to the deities associated with the daily phases of the sun on the base of the dedication model of a temple portal fronted by two obelisks in the Brooklyn Museum (shown here in Fig. 8.10), in his *A Monumental Gateway to Sety I*, Brooklyn: The Brooklyn Museum, 1973.

41 In order to understand the original meaning of obelisks, we have to move away from the modern notion of the homogeneous perspectival

space and see the obelisk as part of a configuration of places structured almost like a narrative, in which temporal sequences constitute the order and not the simultaneity or the synchronicity of the appearance of the obelisk.

42 This obelisk, from the time of Psammetich II (26th Dynasty), was brought to Rome and erected as a gnomon in the solarium situated in the vicinity of the contemporary Palazzo Montecitorio, between 10 and 8 BCE. The obelisk was oriented 18″ 37′ away from the north-south axis in order to face the Ara Pacis (parallel with the Via Flaminia) and, at the same time, the Mausoleum. For the astronomical and symbolical aspects of the topography of the Solarium, and for the results of the recent excavations, see Edmund Buchner, *Die Sonnenuhr des Augustus*, Mainz-am-Rhein: Verlag Philip von Zabern, 1982.

43 The obelisks were erected before 98 CE. See Erik Iversen, *Obelisks in Exile*, Copenhagen: G.E.C. Gad Publishers, 1968, Vol. 1, p. 47.

44 Ibid., pp. 76–80. The attitude of the Romans to the cult of Isis is well documented in Plutarch, *Isis and Osiris, Moralia V*, and in Apuleius, *Metamorphoses*.

45 Both obelisks came from the Temple of Ammon in Karnak, where they were erected by Tuthmosis IV (fifteenth century BCE). The first caught the attention of Augustus but it was not moved, partly because people were 'overawed by the difficulties caused by its size' and partly because it was 'placed in the sacred part of the sumptuous temple which might not be profaned. There it towered aloft like the peak of the world' (Marcellinus, op. cit., 17.4.12). It was later moved to Alexandria, probably by Constantine the Great, and finally by his son Constantinus II to Rome, where it was erected in the Circus Maximus in 357. It was excavated in 1586 by Domenico Fontana and erected in the Piazza of San Giovanni in Laterano in the same year. The second obelisk was transported from Alexandria to Constantinople under Theodosius. It is still standing, though now isolated, in its original position on the spina of the Hippodrome. Iversen, op. cit., Vol. 2, p. 80.

46 *Sol Invictus* answered the need for such a tangible presence of the divine. Constantine required a symbol that would demonstrate the power he wielded. The parallel of *Sol* and emperor suggests that the imperial office is part of the world order and that 'the role of the emperor on earth corresponds to that of the Sun in heaven'. J.H.W.G. Liebeschuetz, *Continuity and Change in Roman Religion*, Oxford: Clarendon Press, 1979, p. 285.

47 A good example here are the writings of Lactantius, referred to by Liebescheutz, op. cit., p. 284. For a more complete discussion of the role of the sun in Christianity, see Hugo Rahner, 'The Christian Mystery of Sun and Moon', in his *Greek Myths and Christian Mystery*, trans. Brian Battershaw, New York: Biblo and Tannen, 1971, pp. 89–119.

48 James McEvoy, *The Philosophy of Robert Grosseteste*, Oxford: Clarendon Press, 1982, p. 201.

49 Ibid., p. 202.

50 Erik Iversen, *The Myth of Egypt and its Hieroglyphs in European Tradition*, Copenhagen: GEC Gad Publishers, 1961; and his 'Hieroglyphic

Tradition' in *Legacy of Egypt*, ed. J. Rendel Harries, Oxford: Clarendon Press, 1971; also, Frances Yates, *Giordano Bruno and the Hermetic Tradition*, New York: Vintage Books, 1969.

51 Rudolf Wittkower, 'Hieroglyphics in the Early Renaissance', in his *Allegory and the Migration of Symbols*, London: Thames and Hudson, 1977, pp. 113–29.

52 The Vatican Obelisk was originally in Heliopolis, but, as a cult obelisk, it was without inscriptions. It was transferred after 30 BCE to Alexandria and, finally, in 37 CE, under Caligula, it was moved to Rome and erected in the gardens of Agrippina, which eventually became the circus of Nero. It was on the north side of the circus that the Christian cemetery and the alleged tomb of St. Peter were situated. The obelisk was standing at the south apse of the old basilica until 1586, and was referred to as *Columna Petri*, but also as a sepulchre of Julius Ceasar, because of the alleged deposit of his ashes in the *guglia* (spire) of the obelisk. See Cesare D'Onofrio, *Gli obelischi di Roma*, Rome: Cassa di Risparmio di Roma, 1967, pp. 11–69.

53 Giannozzo Manetti, *Vita Nicolai V summi pontificis*, published in *Rerum Italicarum Scriptores*, ed. L.A. Muratori Milano, 1723–51, vol. 3.2, coll. 949–50 [trans. Vesely].

54 Ibid.

55 Among the texts related directly to the Vatican obelisk, the following are noteworthy: Petrus Angelicus Bargaeus, *Commentarius de obelisco*, 1586; Filippo Pigafetta, *Discorso d'intorno all'historia della aguglia*, 1586; and, by far the most important: Michele Mercati, *Degli obelischi di Roma*, 1589, which addresses the problem of obelisks in general, alongside their history, hieroglyphic aspects and meaning.

56 The obelisk was carved in Egypt, inscribed in hieroglyphics in Rome and dedicated to the Temple of Isis in the Campus Martius by Domitian, after 81 CE. In 309, it was transported and erected by Maxentius in his circus near the Via Appia. Under Innocent X, the obelisk was finally raised in the Piazza Navona in 1649 and consecrated in 1651. See D'Onofrio, op. cit., pp. 222–30; Iversen, op. cit., pp. 76–93; and Rudolf Preimesberger, 'Obeliscus Pamphilius: Beiträge zu Vorgeschichte und Ikonographie des Vierströmebrunnens auf Piazza Navona', in *Münchner Jahrbuch der Bildenden Kunst*, Band 25, 1974, pp. 77–162.

57 The reference to the piazza as *circus agonalis* decided the nature of archaeological reconstructions of the space by Pirro Ligorio (1553), Étienne Dupérac (1573) and Andrea Fulvio (1588). The most complete was the reconstruction made by Giacomo Lauro in his *Antiquae urbis splendor*, Rome, 1625, Plate 81 (shown here in Fig. 8.13).

58 In the Roman circus, the turning point (*meta*) in the shape of a pyramidal obelisk was frequently situated above a basin of water treated as a fountain. See John H. Humphrey, *Roman Circuses*, London: Batsford, 1986, pp. 55–58. The Obelisk Pamphili was regularly referred to as *meta*. See Preimesberger, op. cit., p. 97.

59 The background and specific theme of the programme are discussed in *Obeliscus Pamphilius*, Rome, 1650. It is interesting to note that, in

the programme of Pope Nicholas V, the Vatican obelisk was supposed to be supported by the four evangelists and dominated by the figure of Christ. See Carroll Westfall, *In This Most Perfect Paradise: Alberti, Nicholas V and the Invention of Conscious Urban Planning in Rome*, Pennsylvania: Pennsylvania State University Press, 1974, p. 113.

60 The Christian understanding of the primary meaning of the obelisk was perhaps most eloquently summarised by Torquato Tasso when he said [Ed. Vesely cites this in the original Italian, which we translated]: 'But this figure was deemed mysterious by the Egyptians and similar to that of the sun's rays; indeed, with this very name – that is, rays of the sun – they [the obelisks] used to be named by that nation, and by the king of Egypt they were consecrated to the sun, or to the son of the sun (which is how illustrious men were called in the following age). Now they are consecrated to the Cross, in which the intelligible Sun seemed to be eclipsed by the interposition of [Christ's] humanity'; [original text] cited in Preimesberger, op. cit., p. 109, n. 227.

61 This is clearly expressed in the following commentary: 'The four Evangelists, famous throughout the whole circle of the earth, and four [of them], perhaps since there are four parts of the earth through the entirety of which they were to spread the church of Christ ...' [Ed. Vesely gives this in the original Latin, which we translated; he cites Ernst Schlee, *Die Ikonographie der Paradiesesflüsse*, Leipzig, 1937, p. 33, who, however, misattributed the passage to St. Jerome, when in fact it is from St. Augustine, *De consensu evangelistarum*, Bk. I.2.3 (thanks to Fabio Barry for pointing this out)].

62 Athanasius Kircher, *Ad Alexandrum VII Pont. Max. Obelisci Aegyptiaci*, Rome, 1666, p. 11–19. In the same text, Kircher also speaks about the analogy of the Christian notion of spirit and the *anima mundi*, understood more in a metaphysical, rather than the traditional theological sense.

63 Thomas Leinkauf, 'Catena Rerum; ein Grundmotiv barocker Kosmologie', in his *Mundus combinatus*, Berlin: Akademie Verlag, 1993, pp. 110–22.

64 [Ed. Vesely cites this in the original Latin, which we translated] 'The Sun indeed extends its dominion principally into the four elements of the world, they [the Egyptians] specified this dominion of the Sun through Obelisks [...], which we have said they called *fingers of the Sun*; just as without doubt the four elements through the quadruple mixture ...'; Athanasius Kircher, *Obeliscus Pamphilius*, Rome, 1650, p. 50.

65 Giovanni Battista Riccioli, *Almagestum novum*; Bologna, 1651, Vol. 2, p. 469 [trans. Vesely].

9 *Mathesis Universalis* in the Jesuit Tradition

The decisive transformation of the nature of knowledge in the Baroque age is traditionally associated with the origins of modern science. We still hear, even today, that modern forms of knowledge were formed in conflict with Aristotelian scholasticism, traditional cosmology and generally with the inherited humanistic culture. In this conventional understanding, what is meant by science usually connotes its later forms of fully emancipated knowledge, seen as a source of truth contradicting not only the whole body of traditional truth, but most of all the truth of theology. This understanding obscures the fact that the new knowledge has its origins in the universalistic tendencies of the Baroque, manifested in the affinity of theology, metaphysics (*prima philosophia*) and universal mathematics (*mathesis universalis*). It was in this context that the main characteristic of the new knowledge, the mathematisation of reality and in particular the mathematisation of movement were born. Some of the first, most important contributions to this development were made by religious institutions and clerics, mainly members of the Jesuit order. Apart from the main centre of the new type of studies in the Collegio Romano[1], some provincial centres such as the Jesuit colleges in Coimbra, Louvain, Antwerp, Vienna and Prague among others played a very important role in the new development.

Scepticism and mathematical reaction

The beginning of the development of this type of new knowledge was a response to the prevailing scepticism, religious polarisation and fragmentation of sixteenth-century culture, manifested most clearly in probabilism and pyrrhonism. The first step in this development was the debate about the scientific nature of mathematics

DOI: 10.4324/9781003272090-10

in the Collegio Romano. The sceptical position was summarised by Paulus Valla-Carbone SJ (1561–1622) in his *Dubitationes quaedam circa scientias mathematicas* where it was claimed that mathematical sciences were not sciences, because they did not fulfil the criteria of demonstration.[2] On the other side of the debate were Christopher Clavius SJ (1538–1612) and his followers, who believed that mathematics should be a standard part of a university curriculum and saw the need to train instructors of mathematics. In his 'Modus quo disciplinæ mathematicæ' Clavius writes: 'Since the mathematical disciplines in fact require, delight in, and honour truth, there can be no doubt that they must be conceded the first place among all the other sciences.'[3] Clavius was the sole teacher of mathematics in the Collegio Romano in the years between 1564 and 1595. In the first edition of the Jesuit *Ratio studiorum* (1586), it was proposed that Clavius should give private lessons in mathematics to eight or ten Jesuits, selected from all the different provinces of the order, to furnish the provinces with teachers of mathematics.[4] The next published edition of the *Ratio* (1591) suggested that in addition to this private academia, the most gifted students could continue their mathematical studies. The two primary documents written by Clavius for that purpose were *Modus quo disciplinæ mathematicæ in scholis Societatis possent promoveri* (1582) and *De re mathematica instructio* (1593).[5]

    The decisive step in the elevation of mathematics into a primary discipline (science) was the contribution of Josephus Blancanus SJ (1566–1624), the disciple and younger colleague of Clavius. He dismissed the critical objections of Alessandro Piccolomini and Benedict Pereira (his colleagues from the Collegio Romano), and the Jesuits of Coimbra, all of whom claimed that mathematical disciplines were not true sciences, because they lacked causal demonstrations, abstracting quantity from sensible matter.[6] In an ingenious interpretation of the old notion of 'intelligible matter' (*materia intelligibilis*), Blancanus showed that not only formal but also material causality functions in the mathematical demonstrations (*demonstratio potissima*) and that mathematics could be thus elevated to the status of a proper science.[7] He had no difficulty admitting that mathematical entities did not exist in the world with the perfection they had in the intellect; but he observed that this did not alter the fact that they were realised in sensible matter, even though imperfectly. Mathematical entities could be seen in his view as forms of things corresponding to ideas in the mind of God. On the whole, Blancanus believed that mathematical entities are not merely figments of the intellect associable with physical objects but archetypes in the mind of God, and that they find realisation, however imperfect, in sensible matter. The historical importance of this step is reflected in the development of Galilean science, Cartesian philosophy, the formation of the *mathesis* and *characteristica universalis* and, indirectly, in the development of modern, natural sciences up our time. In order to understand not just the importance but also the true nature of this development, we must look more closely at the circumstances under which such a development became possible.

Existence, essence and number

The critical element in the development of modern knowledge was the new interpretation of the relation of the essence of things to their existence. In the nominalistic orientation of the second scholastic, manifested most clearly in the philosophy of Francisco Suarez SJ (1548–1617), the relation of essence and existence was reduced to the primacy of essence, while existence was seen merely as an actualisation of essence. In Suarez's view, essence exists out of itself, but owes its existence to the divine act of creation. This is not far from Blancanus's understanding of mathematical entities seen as ideas or archetypes in the mind of God. In such an understanding, all actual beings are simply many fully actualised essences, while existences are more or less their appendix; and, as Etienne Gilson says, 'this is why Suarez does not know existence when he sees it'.[8] Having identified existences with actual essences, Suarez's disciples could be forgiven for ruling existence out of metaphysics altogether. Joseph Kleutgen, a Jesuit writer, makes this very clear in his *La philosophie scolastique* (1868). In reference to Suarez, he writes: 'When we conceive of being as real, we do not think of it as merely possible by excluding existence, nor do we think of it as existing, but we leave existence out of consideration. Thus, and only thus, can those finite and created things, to which existence is not essential, become objects of science.'[9]

The affinity between the new metaphysics and mathematics (*mathesis*) becomes more comprehensible if we take into account similar developments in contemporary mathematics, particularly in the newly revived discipline of algebra. Algebra is not only a mathematical discipline, as is often believed, but also a new way of thinking. Letters, replacing traditional numbers, when introduced, 'were just representations of numbers and so could be treated as such. The more complicated algebraic technique seemed justified either by geometrical arguments such as Cardan used, or by sheer induction in specific cases. Of course, none of these procedures were logically satisfactory.'[10] Leibniz characterised the work in algebra as a 'melange of good fortune and chance'.[11] In algebra the number is removed from the continuum of the articulated world into an imaginary world, where number as structure (*arithmos*), becomes an abstract symbol, an entity. This is well illustrated by the thoughts of a contemporary mathematician: 'The numbers with which we work, are so, as it were, swallowed up into that new [algebra] which is brought forth, that they quite vanish, not leaving any print or footstep of themselves behind them.'[12]

With that step, the Classical science of the ancients was replaced by a symbolic discipline whose ontological presuppositions were left unclarified; and yet, it is in this discipline that the things of this world are no longer understood as countable beings, but as lawfully ordered course of events. The very nature of one's understanding of the world is henceforth governed by the symbolic 'number' concept, which determines the modern idea of science in general. In the development of algebra, the notion of universal science (*scientia universalis*) culminates in the formation of universal mathematics (*mathesis universalis*).

Mathesis universalis became the mathematical equivalent of traditional logic. Because universal mathematics operates with the pure essences of things, which are taken for simple magnitudes, the formal essence becomes identical with pure mathematical essence-magnitude.[13] Under these conditions, universal mathematics (*mathesis universalis*) could lay claim to cover the same area of knowledge as traditional logic—in other words, the area of all possible knowledge. The new idea of all possible knowledge is very different from traditional dialectical or demonstrative knowledge. It aims to explain things only in terms of order and measure, regardless of their material and qualitative nature. Because of the universality of such a claim, universal mathematics had already earned the title of the 'queen of sciences' (*regina scientiarum*) in the sixteenth century, sometimes elevated to terms such as *ars magna, scientia divina* or *ars divina*.

However, these lofty names could not convince without supporting evidence from the physical world. As in mathematics, the development of knowledge in late sixteenth-century physics also went through a radical change. The traditional distinction between divine and human knowledge was weakened to such an extent that it became possible to speak of physics and metaphysics in the same terms. Once theological problems could be treated as metaphysical and eventually as physical, they could be, in the end, expressed in the language of natural theology.[14] Newton's circle, for instance, developed what came to be known as *physica sacra*, a study of the history of creation as presented in Genesis and in the works of Newton, showing line by line the perfect harmony between them.[15] In his time, Herder still refers to fifty systems of physical theology (*Physik-Theologie*), all of them claiming that God's actions follow mathematical laws.[16]

The affinity between the metaphysical interpretation of physics and universal mathematics was reflected in the new understanding of astronomy, optics, music and, in particular, of mechanics. All these disciplines were known since the Middle Ages as *scientiae mediae*, or physico-mathematical disciplines. Like universal mathematics, the new metaphysics (*prima philosophia* or the science of Being) refers ultimately to the principles of non-contradiction and of sufficient reason. The new algebra of a meta-mathematical kind and physics of a metaphysical kind found in the principle of non-contradiction their common roots and foundation. The sharing of the common foundations brought metaphysical essences and mathematical entities—numbers—close together.

In the *L'impiété des Deistes* (1624) Marin Mersenne describes their link and proximity: 'If you want to compare all the diverse kinds (species) to diverse numbers, which conserve themselves by the indivisibility of their differences, like the essence of things, you will see that unity produces diverse kinds.'[17] Creatures draw their perfections from God just as numbers draw theirs from unity, 'to which they add nothing new'.[18] As the being of creatures represents participation in the divine being, so the numerality of numbers represents the participation in unity 'on which they depend, such that it is impossible that they exist without It'.[19] The production of diverse creatures from an absolutely simple Creator depended on the existence of the divine intellect. Similarly, the production of numbers from unity depended on an intellect, be it human or divine; without it, the potentiality of number contained in unity could not be actualised (the principle of *arithmos* represents the unity in plurality as one and many). This brings the argument to a possible conclusion: 'essences are just like numbers' (*essentiae sunt sicut numeri*).[20]

Mathematisation of the creative movement

The possibility to see essences as numbers was one of the most important contributions to the formation of Galilean science and Cartesian philosophy, two different, but complementary attempts to grasp the

mystery of creation manifested most explicitly in the creative movement. Mathematical representation of movement, based on the deep
metaphysical faith in the mathematical nature of reality, sanctioned
by divine presence did not, in the end, grasp the mystery of creation,
but it did lay the foundations for modern natural science. The new
science was motivated by an ambition to be nothing less than *creatio
ex nihilo*, traditionally linked only with divine creativity. However,
what was traditionally true for the divine became now considered
to be also true, or at least possible, for humans. In other words, we
may know and can create as God knows and creates. This is clearly
expressed by Descartes when he writes: 'For a short time, allow your
thought to leave this world in order to come to see a wholly new one,
which I shall cause to be born in the presence of your thought in
imaginary spaces'.[21]

We can appreciate the unique place of movement in the formation
of the new science by comparison with the meaning of movement
in the Baroque period (the time of the emergence of mechanics).
Movement represents most clearly what is new and what defines the
nature of Baroque culture. The understanding and representation
of the divine, structured in the past around the power of the word
(*verbum Dei*), around epiphanic images and later around the philosophy and theology of light, was, during the Baroque era, transformed
into a representation structured around the phenomena of movement, infinity and universality. We may begin with the reference
to movement that we find in the writings of Johannes Kepler who
writes: 'The sun, located in the middle of the moving planets, itself
at rest, yet a source of motion, carries the image of God the Father
as Creator. For what creation is to God, motion is to the sun and the
rest of the world.'[22] (Fig. 9.1).

The continuity of movement between the celestial and terrestrial
domains already played a critical role in Aristotelianism and later in
the scholastic metaphysics. Both played a decisive role in the formation
of modern mechanics. Only with great effort can we now comprehend the complexity and importance of movement in the seventeenth-
century vision of reality. The enigma of creation, the manifestation
of the divine order in the terrestrial world, and the continuity of this
order, were all related to the phenomenon of movement. Movement
was seen not only as a universal principle of reality but also as the efficient cause of everything persisting in life. The divine origin of movement was not yet in doubt, nor was the tradition in which divine reality
manifested itself as an eternal truth. It is characteristic that Leibniz,

9.1 Andreas Cellarius, *Atlas coelestis*, 1660. Diagram of the
Copernican system.

the most representative thinker of the Baroque era, held firmly against
Descartes that motion and not extension (*res extensa*) defines physical
bodies and the reality of the created world.[23]

In his *Lexicon mathematicum*, the first encyclopaedia of mathematical disciplines, Girolamo Vitale (1624–1682) writes: 'Nature
may be defined as the totality of things which have a source of *motion*
internal to themselves and of the constituent parts of such things'.
Vitale defines motion as simultaneity of 'passion, and the property
of the celestial bodies'.[24] Life is for him the 'intrinsic principle of

self-motion'.[25] To the 'three-fold ratio' of animation—vegetative, sensitive and local motion, based on *de Anima* of Aristotle—he adds the 'intellective' motion, which represents the 'life of the world'. Vitale secures the 'life of the world' as the order of things such as the proper movement of the elements 'filling in the vacuum, conserving the connection of things, which equally sustains life in the soul, as any discontinuity of parts would induce danger of life, and even death'.[26]

Guarini and intellective movement

The 'life of the world' understood as intellective motion can be best illustrated by examples from the development of Baroque architecture, which shows very clearly the role of intellective motion, seen as light, in addressing the problem of actual infinity. The problem of actual infinity became a logical product of the mathematical interpretation of divine reality. While in the human world there is room only for potential infinity, in mathematical speculations one can speak about infinity as actual. Because the new mathematical interpretation of divine order includes the human world, the problem of actual infinity could not remain unaddressed. I am using as an example Guarino Guarini's upper dome of Sacra Sindone (chapel of the Holy Shroud) in Turin, which is a result of movement through a pyramid of light representing the attempt to resolve the problem of actual infinity (Fig. 9.2). Guarini (1624–83) was convinced that light in its essential sense has an intrinsic incorruptibility and, therefore, given perfect conditions, can progress to infinity (*posse progredi in infinitum*). The perfect conditions would be the perfect diaphaneity (*diaphanum subjectum*).[27]

With the notion of perfect conditions, we move into an imaginary world of supra sensible, intelligible light (analogy of intelligible matter). Guarini 'sees' light on that level literally as the shining (*relucere*) of divine ideas in human intellect. The light that comes into visibility is inseparably connected with the receding configuration of the hexagons in the dome. The important step in Guarini's thinking is the contemplation of the possibility of approaching the problem of infinity through the continuous progression, i.e., movement of proportions (*ratios*) in asymptotic approximation. The pyramidal stacking of the hexagons follows the rule of gnomonic difference of surfaces, which is a proportional difference between the surfaces of individual figures. For this step Guarini found a precedent in the diagram

9.2 Guarino Guarini, chapel of the Holy Shroud,
Turin, 1610–80. View of the upper dome.

illustrating the geometrical progress to infinity in Gregory of
St. Vincent's *Opus geometricum quadraturae circuli* (Fig. 9.3 top).
The key to the construction of the upper dome is a relatively little-
known drawing (preserved in the Archivio di Stato in Torino)
showing the stereographic pyramidal projection of the triangular
elements of the dome (Fig. 9.3 bottom). It is through a simple transformation that triangles create a hexagon and finally the twelve rays
of light of the sun in the lantern.

Guarini's orientation to intellective movement and, as a result, on
reality perceptible only to the intellect may explain the transparent
nature of the upper dome and its meaning, which cannot be grasped
through direct observation but only through intellectual vision. The
source of the radiation of light and vision is not the human eye but the
absolute and ineffable God-like eye. The attempt to resolve the problem of infinity by the intellective movement of ratios—in other words
through a gradual approximation—is described in Guarini's own
words: 'The boundary of progression is the end of a series to which no

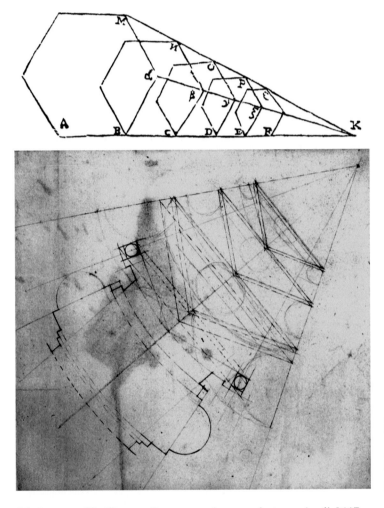

9.3 Gregory of St. Vincent, *Opus geometricum quadraturae circuli*, 1647.
Hexagonal diagram (top); Guarino Guarini, original drawing for the structure of the upper dome of the chapel of the Holy Shroud, ca. 1667.

progression can approach, even if it is contained in infinity [...] but it
approaches it in perpetuity (*sed ei perpetuo accedet*)'[28] (Fig. 9.4).

This conclusion shows that such transformational thinking is
more far reaching. It transforms not only local phenomena one into
another, but, in the works of Guarini, it also transforms the spatial

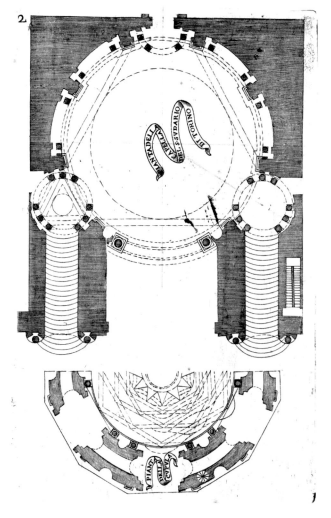

9.4 Guarino Guarini, *Disegni di architettura civile ed ecclesiastica*, 1737.
Plan for the chapel of the Holy Shroud.

infinity of the universe into a temporal one. Such a possibility coincides with the changes in Baroque culture in which the traditional
cosmological structures are gradually replaced by structures generated by movement in time, in a process of generation. The process of
generation is described by Benedict Pereira where he writes: 'As the
prior is joined with the posterior through the present, now; thus, it

can be said to be a perpetual generation not because any generation is perpetual, but because one succession of generation after another is perpetual, and is never interrupted.'[29] The most important contribution to Guarini's interpretation of actual infinity was made by the optical studies of Francois d'Aguilon and the geometrical studies of Gregory of St Vincent, to whom Guarini regularly refers and whom he follows very closely.

François d'Aguilon SJ (1546–1617), born in Brussels, studied under Christopher Clavius (mentioned earlier) in Rome, and in 1611 founded a school for mathematics in Antwerp where many new talented students were educated, and where he was joined in 1617 by Gregory of St. Vincent. Aguilon's main contribution was in the area of optics. His *Opticorum libri sex* was the most complete synthesis of the optical knowledge of the time and was used as a textbook in most Jesuit colleges[30] (Fig. 9.5). Aguilon's optical interpretation of motion anticipated Vitale's understanding of intellective motion. According to Aguilon, there is an ascending motion from the perception of things through the incarnate, unborn (*innata*) light of the Sun, to the Creator. This is a motion that reflects the very dynamics of the Trinity and Incarnation. The ascending motion coincides with the descent of light, understood by us humans only imperfectly. It is in this context that Aguilon employs the expression *pyramis luminosa*, which entirely coincides with the visual pyramid (*pyramis optica*).

Gregory of St. Vincent SJ (1584–1667), born in Bruges, became a close collaborator of Aguilon, whom he replaced as head of the mathematical school in Antwerp in 1617 after Aguilon's death. In 1628 Gregory was sent to Prague, where he stayed until 1632 and met his great supporter Rodrigo de Arriaga SJ (1592–1667). Arriaga was intellectually to Gregory what Suarez was to Clavius.[31] It was in Prague that Gregory completed (as much as was eventually published) his major work *Opus geometricum quadraturae circuli et sectionum coni* (Fig. 9.6). The manuscript was saved by Arriaga during the Swedish invasion of Prague and published only much later in Antwerp.[32] The philosophy, including metaphysics, available at that time in the Clementinum was an important framework for the development of the more advanced mathematical ideas that, in turn, influenced the nature of the college curriculum.[33] Gregory's *Opus geometricum* is praised even today as a fundamental contribution to the development of modern analytical and projective geometry, the theory of exhaustion and

9.5 François d'Aguilon, *Opticorum libri sex*, 1613. Frontispiece, engraving
by Theodore Galle after a drawing by Peter Paul Rubens.

infinitesimal calculus. Gregory was classed already by Leibniz
alongside Fermat and Descartes as one of the founders of modern
geometry.

The works of Gregory and Arriaga accomplished in the Prague
Clementinum bring us back to Guarini. His *Placita philosophica*

9.6 Gregory of St. Vincent, *Opus geometricum quadraturae circuli*, 1647.
Frontispiece, engraving by Cornelis Galle II after a drawing by Abraham
Diepenbeeck.

was, as already mentioned, organised almost entirely like Arriaga's
Cursus philosophicus, not only in its structure but to some extent
also in its content. Guarini's achievement in addressing the problem of actual infinity was directly inspired and informed by the
work of Gregory of St. Vincent. Is it a historical coincidence, or is

there some deeper reason which we don't fully understand yet, that Guarini's architecture had such a decisive influence in the formation of the radical Baroque in central Europe? Is it not possible that there is a certain resonance between Guarini's thinking and that of the Jesuits in the sphere of philosophy, theology and mathematics? Textual comparison shows sufficient evidence of such a resonance, but our question would have to be answered on the level of architecture (Fig. 9.7). Assuming that Guarini's influence was not only

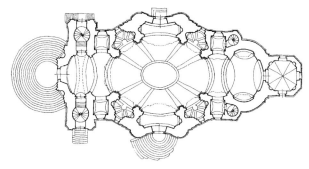

9.7 K. I. Dietzenhofer, church of Mary Magdalene, 1737, Karlovy Vary. Plan and interior view.

formal, it would be necessary to identify and understand not only the presence but also the meaning of Guarini's main architectural intentions and principles, such as his understanding of corporeal transparency, resulting in the penetration of volumes; of projective transformations of conic sections, resulting in the desired configuration of space; and of generative sequences of the individual parts of the building, resulting in a convincing unity of space. These rather difficult questions are still widely open and remain as a challenge for the future.

Notes

1 Philip Caraman, *University of the Nations: The Story of the Gregorian University with its Associated Institutes, the Biblical and Oriental, 1551–1962*, Ramsey, NJ: Paulist Press, 1981; Adriano Carugo and Alistaire C. Crombie, 'The Jesuits and Galileo's Ideas of Science and Nature', *Annali dell'istituto e museo di storia della scienza di Firenze* 8, no. 2, 1983, 3–68; Alistair C. Crombie, 'Sources of Galileo's Early Natural Philosophy', in *Reason, Experiment, and Mysticism in the Scientific Revolution*, ed. Maria Luisa Righini Bonelli and William R. Shea, New York: Science History Publications, 1975, pp. 157–75; D'Elia Pasquale, *Galileo in China: Relations through the Roman College between Galileo and the Jesuit Scientist-Missionaries (1610–1640)*, trans. R. Suter and M. Sciascia, Cambridge, MA: Harvard University Press, 1960; William A. Wallace, *Galileo and his Sources: The Heritage of the Collegio Romano in Galileo's Science*, Princeton, NJ: Princeton University Press, 1984; James M. Lattis, *Between Copernicus and Galileo: Christoph Clavius and the Collapse of Ptolemaic Cosmology*, Chicago, IL: University of Chicago Press, 1994.
2 Paulus Valla-Carbone, 'Dubitationes quaedam circa scientias mathematicas' in *Introductione in universam philosophiam*, Venice: Apud Marcum Antonium Zalterium, 1599, pp. 288–302.
3 Christopher Clavius, 'Modus quo disciplinæ mathematicæ' in *Euclidis Elementorum*, Rome: Apud Bartholomaeum Grassium, 1589, pp. 14–17 [trans. Vesely].
4 Christopher Clavius was born in Bamberg, Germany in 1538. In 1555 he travelled to Rome to join the Society of Jesus. Nine years later, in 1564, he was ordained a priest while finishing his theological studies at the Jesuit-run Collegio Romano. He began teaching mathematical subjects on a regular basis at the Collegio Romano around 1564. Clavius taught for more than 45 years in Rome, until his death in 1612.
5 Other major works of Clavius include *In sphæram Ioannis de Sacro Bosco commentarii*, (1581), *Epitome arithmeticæ practicæ* (1583), *Astrolabium* (1593), *Geometria practica* (1604), *Algebra* (1608) and *Triangula sphærica* (1611). These well-written texts were reprinted numerous times and widely used in Jesuit schools. They were also used

by such mathematicians as Leibniz and Descartes (Descartes studied at the Jesuit college of La Flèche). Matteo Ricci translated Clavius's *Elements of Euclid* into Chinese. Clavius's greatest practical achievement was the reformation of the Gregorian calendar.

6 The most important arguments and summary of Blancanus's teaching were published as 'De mathematicarum natura dissertatio', in his *Aristotelis Loca Mathematica*, Bologna, 1615; and in his *Apparatus ad mathematicas addiscendas et promovendas*, Bologna, 1620.

7 The concept of 'intelligible matter' was known and discussed already by Aristotle in his *Metaphysics* VII.x.18, VIII.vi.6, XI.i.7., in relation to the matter of mathematical entities.

8 Etienne Gilson, *Being and Some Philosophers*, Toronto: Pontifical Institute of Medieval Studies, 1952, p. 105.

9 Ibid., pp. 105–6.

10 Morris Kline, *Mathematics: The Loss of Certainty*, Oxford: Oxford University Press, 1980, p. 125.

11 Ibid.

12 William Oughtred, *Clavis mathematicæ*, Oxford, 1631, p. 4.

13 Giovanni Crapulli, *Mathesis universalis: Genesi di un'idea nel XVI secolo*, Rome: Edizioni dell'Ateneo, 1969, pp. 145–55.

14 Amos Funkenstein, *Theology and the Scientific Imagination*, Princeton, NJ: Princeton University Press, 1986, pp. 243–71.

15 Frank E. Manuel, *The Religion of Newton*, Oxford: Clarendon Press, 1974, p. 37.

16 Johann Gottfried Herder, *Älteste Urkunde des Menschengeschlechts, Sämtliche Werke*, ed. Bernhard Suphan, Berlin: Weidmann, 1877–1913, Vol. VI, p. 202.

17 Marin Mersenne, *L' impiété des déistes*, Paris: L. Billaine, 1624, vol. I., pp. 425–6 [trans. Vesely].

18 Ibid., p. 424.

19 Ibid., p. 427.

20 Ibid., p. 426.

21 René Descartes, *The Philosophical Works of Descartes*, trans. E.S. Haldane and G.R.T. Ross, Cambridge: Cambridge University Press, 1982, p. 107.

22 Johannes Kepler, *Gesammelte Werke*, ed. Walther von Dyck and Max Caspar, Munich: C.H. Beck Verlag, 1937, vol. 13, p. 35 [trans. Vesely].

23 Martial Gueroult, *Leibniz: Dynamique et métaphysique*, Paris: Aubier-Montaigne, 1967, pp. 155–86.

24 Girolamo Vitale, *Lexicon mathematicum*, Paris: L. Billaine, 1668, p. 297 [trans. Vesely].

25 Ibid., pp. 307–8.

26 Ibid., p. 308.

27 Guarino Guarini, *Placita philosophica*, Paris, 1665, p. 859. *Placita philosophica* was published during Guarini's sojourn in Paris where he was a professor of sacred theology (1662–1666). The work consisted of eight books, of which the most important, from our point of view, are Book IV, on light and Book VIII on metaphysics. The structure

of the *Placita* is based on the standard *cursus philosophicus* of the seventeenth century, most clearly exemplified in Rodrigo d' Arriaga's *Cursus philosophicus*, written in Prague and published in Antwerp in 1632. Guarini's second most important text is *Euclides adauctus et methodicus mathematicaq(ue)universalis*, Turin, 1671. The text is divided into 35 *tractati* devoted mostly to the problems of continuous quantity, proportions, conic sections, proportional progressions, the problems of surface and solid geometry.

28 Guarini, *Euclides adauctus*, op. cit., p. 256 [trans. Vesely].

29 Benedict Pereira, *De communibus omnium rerum naturalium principiis et affectionibus*, Rome, 1616, lib. 12. cap. 1 [trans. Vesely].

30 François d'Aguilon, *Opticorum libri sex philosophis juxta ac mathematicis utiles*, Antwerp, 1613.

31 The motto 'Videre Pragam et audire Arriagam', illustrates the level of prestige Arriaga acquired on the international scene. He came to Prague in 1626 and stayed to the end of his life. In his major work, *Cursus philosophicus*, Antwerp, 1632, he writes: 'the nominalistic teaching, which some years ago nobody followed, contemporary philosophers defend' [trans. Vesely]. His second most important publication was *Cursus theologicus (Disputationes theologicae)*, Antwerp, 1643–1649. In his philosophy, which can be best described as critical nominalism, Arriaga refuses analogical reasoning and concepts. His main form of reasoning is based on the principles of *preciosis formalis*—knowledge of the individuals extended into the formation of universal ideas through similarities between things (individuals). His *conceptus univocus* leaves no room for participation; reality is homogenous and structured in our mind. This is very close to Galileo's understanding of primary and secondary qualities. Arriaga writes: 'My kind reader, don't be frightened by the novelty of my arguments (opinions), in this book. I am dealing not with theological problems but with questions, raised during the investigations of the natural world around us.' (*Cursus philosophicus*, introduction [trans. Vesely]; for a further reference see Stanislav Sousedík, *Filosofie v českých zemích*, Prague, 1997, pp. 101–2).

32 Gregory of St. Vincent, *Opus geometricum quadraturae circuli et sectionum coni*, Antwerp, 1647.

33 [Ed.] The Clementinum was an important Jesuit college between 1556 and 1773. It merged with Charles University in 1654, absorbing its library eight years later. It is now the National Library.

10 Surrealism and the Latent World of Creativity

It was the belief shared by all Surrealists that the truth of dreams, myth and marvels stands above the truth of contemporary logic, which can be applied only to the resolution of problems of secondary interest. This was the point of departure for the development of a different understanding of truth and creativity that addresses the dormant (latent) sphere of reality accessible through pre-reflective experience. The most popular and best-known Surrealist creative tool, which was key to the dream-like state of mind, had been discovered in direct inspiration from a psychoanalytical method of free association and became known as 'pure psychic automatism', rooted in the life of dreams. Dreams have all the qualities that the Surrealists were searching for. They have the inexhaustible richness of spontaneous associations and the ability to transform conventional reality into fantastic reality, but most of all dreams are infinitely poetic. At the beginning, it was not yet realised that dreams also have the authenticity of an encounter with the great cosmic symbols, sky, earth, water, trees, stones, and with the origins and ends of things, which are the same as myths. The world of dreams was for the Surrealists a true substitute for the whole outside world.

However, the Surrealists soon discovered that the long practice of automatism led to problematic states of hypnosis; the text tended to be meaningless, or, to use the expression of Michel Leiris, 'inorganic'. It also became clear that the quality of the results did not depend so much on the technique as it did on the power of imagination and the gift of expression of the author. André Breton himself never expressed scepticism about automatism. Nevertheless, in later formulations he changed substantially its original meaning. 'It is possible for automatism', he writes in 1934, 'to enter into the composition of a painting or a poem with a certain degree of pre-meditation.'[1] The reference to pre-meditation

DOI: 10.4324/9781003272090-11

indicates a new stage in the development of the Surrealists' understanding of creativity. This new stage is usually described as a stage of surreal encounters, or 'objective chance' (*objet trouvé*).[2] Objective chance is initiated by the projection of desire into a phantom-like image. The result depends on the circumstances. In the surreal encounter ordinary objects, and, on a larger scale, whole streets, squares and houses become a 'forest of indices', capable of producing an unlimited number of metaphors. However, only those chance encounters that set off a spark with the phantom-like image, in other words those that come to resonate with our desire, turn into true surreal encounters. Objective chance, unlike pure automatism, is always more than just a personal experience. It is a medium or tool, capable of producing new realities and works of art.

In the mature phase of the movement (after the late 1930s), which Breton describes as the reasoning epoch, the Surrealist interest shifted from preoccupations with dream, automatism and objective chance to a new type of exploration, which was more rational and systematic. The motivations for the shift were mainly internal—the recognised inadequacy of dream interpretation, automatism and objective chance in its early form. It was objective chance, interpreted later more systematically, that initiated the culminating epoch of Surrealism.

The tool that dominated this epoch was analogy. The analogical image that illuminates partial similarities cannot be seen as a simple equation; it moves and mediates between two different realities present in a way that is never reversible (Fig. 10.1). 'The greater and truer the distance between two juxtaposed realities, the stronger will be the image and the greater will be its emotive power and reality.'[3] In the introduction to Max Ernst's exhibition of collages Breton has this to say: 'The marvellous faculty of reaching two distant realities without leaving the field of our experience and their coming together, of drawing out a spark, of putting within reach of our senses figures carrying the same intensity, the same relief as the other figures, and in depriving ourselves of a system of reference, of displacing ourselves in our own memory—that is what provisionally holds us.'[4]

However, it was only in the narrative journeys through Paris that the poetic experience of particular places opened up a full sequence of analogical readings that led eventually to the formation of a coherent poetics of analogies. It is important to note that the coherence of analogies is not a result of personal imagination but has its roots in the coherence of the experienced world. Analogies are always potentially present in the world, constituted in our earlier experience. The world of the Surrealists is, despite its coherence and reference to the

10.1 André Breton, Jacqueline Lamba, Yves Tanguy, *Exquisite Corpse*, 1938.

everyday reality, a world that preserves the nature of a dream. Its main characteristics are the introverted nature of experience, immanent representation of transcendental phenomena and the intimate nature of the space in which the world of the Surrealists is situated. The space itself can be visualised as a private domain of a house.

The development of European culture in the twentieth century reached a point where the vision of reality and creativity became radically introverted.[5] In such a situation, culture became personal and its embodiment found its most adequate place in the domain of intimate familiarity exemplified in the paradigm of the house. However, what is true for culture as a whole was, in Surrealism, developed much further. The house became a symbol of the unconscious (latent) experience and a metaphor for creativity.

The key to understanding the role of the house in the Surrealist movement can be found in the private apartment of Sigmund Freud.[6] In the main rooms of the apartment are books not only on medicine, but also on general history and cultural history, which includes, among other things, religion and mythology. The historical and cultural part of the library is complemented by a vast collection of small-sized sculptures. The collection is situated in the working parts of the apartment in such a way that the result appears to be an intimate domestic museum. The meaning of this extraordinary collection is closely linked with the phenomenon of representation. What is represented in the collection is the history of culture and its transformation in time. The transformation that interests us can be traced back to the sixteenth century, when for the first time European culture began to be radically introverted.[7] This took place in the formation of the late Renaissance villa, an idealised substitute for the existing urban culture, in the formation of a private study known as *studiolo*, representing the available knowledge of the world, and in the creation of large collections of minerals, plants, works of art, etc., representing physically the knowledge of the world and known better as cabinets of curiosities, the origin of future museums.[8] The first signs of the transformation were expressed already in the Renaissance, saying that the house is a small city and the city a large house.[9] This rather problematic reduction of the complex reality of a city to the scale of a house illustrates a process that culminates in a general 'domestication' of culture and in the formation of the modern museum. In a later development, the museum entered the private dwelling where museum rooms and objects were intertwined with objects and spaces of everyday life. A very good example is Sir John Soane's Museum in London.[10]

10.2 Sigmund Freud's desk, reconstruction in the Freud Museum, London.

In the apartment of Sigmund Freud, this development reached its most radical point. On his desk, which occupies a corner of his study, we can see a row of statuettes behind a portfolio with Freud's manuscripts (Fig. 10.2). This juxtaposition illustrates the representation of a long historical tradition and its transformation into memory of that tradition, treated as a subject of psychoanalysis. The history of the tragic Oedipus myth, to use one example, is transformed into a well-known 'Freudian' complex'.[11] With this step, the process of domestication reached the boundary of the conscious and unconscious (latent) reality. It was this boundary that became the point of departure for the understanding of the nature and role of the house as a paradigm in the poetics of Surrealism. In a less known poem, *La maison d'Yves*, André Breton refers to the house (*maison*) as a place of synthesis of all the main creative principles of Surrealism.[12] He sees the structure of the house as labyrinthine, symbolising the structure of the unconscious (latent) world. In Breton's poem, the house is entered by night with a lantern, like through a dream. The lantern represents here the possibility of the Surrealist vision to penetrate and make transparent the perilous domain of the unknown and dreams. The movement through the labyrinth follows a line, which appears to be infinite but becomes finite in the enclosing space of the labyrinth. The infinite line refers to the infinite combinations available in the journey and in our imagination, but also to the solving of the problem of the labyrinth enigma (the thread of Ariadne). Referring to the enigmatic landscapes of Yves Tanguy, Breton speaks about the tension between the inner, furnished space and the landscape (*pays*) outside. Both these spaces are contained in the maze, which represents the house as labyrinth. Breton uses the vision of a house primarily as a paradigm of the constructive role of the imagination in the Surrealist creative process. It is mainly for that reason that he refers to the mythical origins of the labyrinth, animated by the figures of Theseus, Minotaur and Ariadne. The main actor is Theseus, the embodiment of the Surrealist artist, who must confront the Minotaur, a symbol of the unconscious, the unknown, the dreamt.[13] The house-labyrinth, seen as a metaphor of creativity, was closely associated with poetic intuition, which, 'finally unleashed by Surrealism, seeks not only to assimilate all known forms, but also boldly to create new forms—that is to say, to be in a position to embrace all the structures of the world, manifested or not. It alone provides the thread that can put us back on the road of gnosis as knowledge of the suprasensible reality, invisibly visible in an eternal mystery.'[14]

The mystery, which coincides with the main goal of Surrealism to reconcile the world of dreams and reality, is described well in Breton's seminal work *Communicating Vessels*: 'Surrealism, as many of us had conceived of it for years [...] I hope will be considered as having tried nothing better than to cast a conduction wire between the far too distant worlds of waking and sleep, exterior and interior reality, reason and madness, the assurance of knowledge and love, of life for life and the revolution, and so on.'[15] This effort, motivated by the intention to reconcile the world of dreams with that of reality, led to the discovery of the unique role of dreams (oneiric world) in everyday life and in creative work.

However, it is very important to see what dreams, as they become available to us, really are.[16] We have no access to dreams as dreamt, but only as they are remembered. In other words, the remembered dream is only accessible in the waking state, by which it is influenced and transformed. The transformation of a dream encompasses the distance between the reality of the dream and the waking reality, a distance that is difficult to determine, as the Surrealists themselves discovered. In the reference to a dream, we grasp not only something of the dream itself, but also of the world, always present in our waking state. The reality that is opened up by dreams should therefore not be sought in the isolated depths of our personal life, but in the depths of experience and reality spontaneously acquired in our being in the world. The deeper, hidden strata of our world, which may be described as latent, are the domain of which dreams are a testimony. The most suitable place for understanding the nature of dreams is therefore the border area between sleeping and waking.[17]

This is an area that we can describe as the twilight or oneiric zone. It is here that we first encounter our dreams. What makes the oneiric zone (world) a unique field for the discovery of 'the marvellous', 'convulsive beauty', the realisation of desire, etc., are the temporality and spatiality of dreams. In dreams, time melts away; dreams take place repeatedly in the present, without any possibility of determining past or future.[18] Space in dreams does not have any perspective and is indeterminate in its extent, because it does not have definable borders. Nor does it have any distances that can be measured; they change according to the motivation and nature of the situation.[19] This understanding of the nature of the oneiric world differs from the pure memory of dreams.[20] In his discussion of the nature of the oneiric house, Gaston Bachelard comes to a similar conclusion:

> When one knows how to grant to all things their exact dream potential, one lives more fully in the oneiric house than in the house of memories. The oneiric house is a deeper theme than that of the house of our birth, it corresponds to a more profound need [...] With the cellar as its root, with the nest on its roof, the complete oneiric house constitutes one of the vertical schemes of human psychology [...] There is no true oneiric house which is not vertically organised; its cellar firmly rooted in the earth, the ground floor for daily life, the upper floor for sleeping, and the attic near the roof. Such a house has everything necessary to symbolise the deep fears, the banality of daily life at ground level, and sublimations at the upper levels.[21]

It is important to remember that the introverted nature and apparent intimacy of the oneiric house would be misleading if we did not take into account what is, in the end, revealed in the house: not only the world but also a cosmic image of the house. 'Through the cosmicity of an image, we receive an experience of the world; cosmic reverie causes us to inhabit a world. It gives the dreamer the impression of a home (*chez soi*) in the imagined universe. The imagined world gives us an expanding home, the reverse of the home of the bedroom.'[22] At this point, it may be interesting to see what Breton's own image of an ideal house was. 'For today', Breton writes, 'I think of a castle, half of it is not necessarily in ruins. This castle belongs to me, I picture it in a rustic setting, not far from Paris.'[23] To which he adds, elsewhere, that 'the human psyche, in its most universal form, found in the gothic castle and its accessories a point of fixation so precise that it would become essential to discover what would be the equivalent of such a place for our own period.'[24] Breton's own answer? 'I myself shall continue living in my glass house where you can always see who comes to call; where everything hanging from the ceiling and on the walls stays where it is as if by magic, where I sleep nights in a glass bed, under glass sheets, where *who I am* will sooner or later appear etched by a diamond.'[25]

The Surrealist house is not in the first place the one in which we live or work, but rather a vision, a metaphor and a paradigm, situated in the world of dreams and fantasy. Breton himself makes this clear: 'Is it certain that this castle into which I cordially invite you is an image? What if this castle really existed? [...] We live by our fantasies when we give *free rein to them* [emphasis original].'[26] To live in a glass house, where one's identity sooner or later appears as if etched by a diamond, can be seen as a product of an unlimited fantasy without any particular meaning, but also as a metaphor for the creativity associated by the Surrealists with the transparency of glass, closely linked with the nature of the crystal (Fig. 10.3). '[...] I have never stopped', writes Breton, 'advocating creation, spontaneous action, insofar as the crystal, non-perfectible by definition, is

10.3 Brassaï, *La maison que j'habite*, ca. 1932.

10.4 Coop Himmelblau, conversion of attic space, Falkestrasse, Vienna, 1989.

the perfect example of it.'[27] The crystal became for the Surrealists a supreme metaphor, not only for creativity but also for spontaneity and imagination. It also became a principle of order more primordial than the order of reason.

It is perhaps not necessary to argue any further that only by interpreting the house as a metaphor or paradigm is it possible to understand its presence and role in painting, film and other media. The same is true for the link of Surrealism and architecture, where the vision of the house played a role of implicit paradigm and not a role of a principle of explicit creativity. This may explain why the relation of the Surrealists to architecture, was limited almost exclusively to the discovery of buildings and places appreciated as a result of objective chance (*object trouvé*). The typical examples usually discussed are the architecture of Antonio Gaudi, the *Palais idéal* of Ferdinand Cheval and places and ruins of Mexico.[28] It is true that it is possible to find exceptions in the installations of Marcel Duchamp or in the *Endless House* of Friedrich Kiesler, for instance, but in a more critical view it becomes clear that their involvement with mainstream Surrealism was limited in time and rather tangential. This brings us to the conclusion that the role of the house in Surrealism was critical and deep as an intrinsic paradigm of artistic creativity, but in the sphere of architecture it never became a paradigm of explicit or positive creation. These limitations did not reduce the influence of some aspects of Surrealism on architecture of different orientations. Out of many possible examples we can choose two as illustrations.

The first is the work of the contemporary Viennese group Coop Himmelblau, whose creative process is very close to the nature of Surrealist automatism (Fig. 10.4). The main precondition of their approach is full emancipation from conscious and logical precedents. In the authors' own words:

> We conceive of architecture which would engage complicated human procedures and psyches, and which would represent a personal statement, with all the attendant strengths and weaknesses implied — not unlike the way art is made [...] our approach is a kind of release from fixed ideas [...] and for that reason we never talk about architecture for fear that inhibitions about what is possible functionally or what others have done before us in similar circumstances will creep in [...] We have to be self-monitoring, or else we could get side-tracked. We avoid analysis but remain aware of our bodies and our hearts.[29]

The second example, used very often as an illustration of genuine Surrealist architecture, is Le Corbusier's interpretation of the solarium on the roof terrace of the Beistegui apartment on the Champs Elysées in Paris. The solarium is treated simultaneously as an open space and a closed interior. The carpet of grass on the ground and the openness of the space to the sky refer to the first, while the furniture and fireplace in the back wall refer to the second. The setting is open to a series of analogical readings in which individual elements play the role of metaphorical fragments, revealing an open set of poetic analogies. The carpet of grass on the floor of the solarium and the low walls, which are too high to be a parapet but too low to be a proper wall, are metaphors of inside and outside, respectively; the fireplace in its relation to the partly visible Arc de Triomphe is a metaphor of monumentalised domesticity and domesticated monumentality, the fire of the living room against the fire of war. The relationship of the fireplace to the meaning of the solarium is also a metaphor for the sun and light, and so on. The spatial configuration of the solarium follows very closely the principles of Surrealist poetics of analogies (Fig. 10.5).

10.5 Le Corbusier, solarium in the apartment of Charles de Beistegui, Paris, 1929–31.

For the Surrealists, 'the tool that permits us to move through the forest of symbols and indices is analogy. Analogy can reveal the deep relation between distant realities which the logical functioning of our mind cannot link together'[30]. In the exploration of analogies, the Surrealists discovered the richness of spontaneous creativity, and also, without being fully aware of it, the latent world where our imagination and its organising power have their source. The poetic experience of particular places opens a sequence of analogical readings that eventually lead to the formation of a coherent poetics of analogies. The apparent proximity of Le Corbusier's approach and Surrealism reveals, nevertheless, a fundamental difference. There is a difference between creativity based on explicit, conscious use of analogies and creativity based on dream-inspired oneiric analogies, that 'reveal the deep relation between distant realities which the logical functioning of our mind cannot link together'.[31] It is for this reason that works such as Le Corbusier's Beistegui apartment or, even more so, the work of Coop Himmelblau cannot be described as Surrealist architecture, but only as architecture that came into existence under the influence or in the shadow of Surrealism.

This brings us to a final conclusion, that architecture never became an integral part of Surrealist thought or endeavour in the same way as painting, sculpture, Surrealist objects, theatre or film. Architecture has a different, much closer link with reality, and, as is well known, the 'principle of reality' was always a bitter encounter for the Surrealists. Their admiration of architecture was limited mostly to that already existing, experienced as 'discovered' architecture in a similar way as *objet trouvé*. It is interesting that Duchamp and Kiesler, who probably contributed more than anybody else to Surrealist 'architectural' activities, were not happy to be described as Surrealists. The difference between genuine and peripheral Surrealist architecture can perhaps be best judged by the nature and creative implications of the 'oneiric house', the paradigm of Surrealist creativity.

Notes

1 André Breton, *What is Surrealism*, trans. David Gascoyne, London: Faber and Faber, 1936, p. 126. *What is Surrealism* was the title of a lecture given by Breton in Brussels on 1 June 1934 at a public meeting organised by the Belgian Surrealists and published as a pamphlet immediately afterwards. A slightly abridged English translation was published in 1936.

2 Christian Kellerer, *Objet trouvé und Surrealismus: Zur Psychologie der modernen Kunst*, Hamburg: Rowohlt Verlag, 1968.

3 Paul Reverdy, 'L'image', *Nord-Sud*, 13 March 1918; reprinted in his *Oeuvres complètes*, Paris: Flammarion, 1975, p. 73 [trans. Vesely].

4 Breton quoted in Max Ernst, *Beyond Painting*, trans. Dorothea Tanning, *The Documents of Modern Art* vol. 7, New York: Wittenborn Schultz, 1948, p. 13.

5 Charles Taylor, *Sources of the Self: The Making of the Modern Identity*, Cambridge, MA: Harvard University Press, 1989, pp. 127–59; Paul Ricoeur, *Oneself as Another*, trans. Kathleen Blamey, Chicago, IL: University of Chicago Press, 1992.

6 Breton had taken an interest in psychoanalysis as early as 1919, at the time his first articles were published in the magazine *Littérature*. In 1921 Breton visited Freud in Vienna. The meeting, however, resulted largely in disappointment. In Freud's view, the Surrealistic conception of dreams was completely different from the psychoanalytical one.

Freud was convinced that 'a collection of dreams without taking into account of their associations, without any knowledge of the circumstances in which the dreams came into being, tells us nothing, and I find it difficult to imagine what they may have to say to anybody at all.' (Sigmund Freud, a letter published in Andre Breton ed., *Trajectoire du rêve*, Paris, 1938, p. 62.) Whereas the Surrealists were interested in the freedom of imagination that dreams offer, Freud was interested solely in the therapeutic role of dreams. This difference emerged clearly during Salvador Dali's visit to Freud in London, less than a year before Freud's death. Freud did not take the Surrealists seriously and, in a letter to Stefan Zweig, he even described them as fools. (Sigmund Freud, letter to Stefan Zweig, cited in Dawn Ades, *Dali*, London: Thames and Hudson, 1982, p. 82.) Nevertheless, Freud took an interest in Dali after the visit. His comments on Dali's pictures are very interesting: 'It is not the unconscious that I look for in your pictures, but the conscious, whereas in the works of old masters, which are full of hidden mystery, I look for the unconscious. In your pictures, what is mysterious and hidden is expressed directly; it is in fact the theme of the pictures.' (Ibid., p. 74; also, Salvador Dali, *The Secret Life of Salvador Dali*, London, 1976, p. 397.) For the photo-documentation of Freud's apartment before his departure to London, see Edmund Engelmann, *Berggasse 19: Sigmund Freud's Home and Offices, Vienna 1938*, Chicago, IL: Chicago University Press, 1976.

7 Ernst Cassirer, *The Individual and the Cosmos in Renaissance Philosophy*, trans. Mario Domandi, New York: Harper & Row, 1963; Miguel Benasayag, *Le mythe de l'individu*, Paris: La Découverte, 1998.

8 Reinhard Bentmann and Michael Müller, *The Villa as Hegemonic Architecture*, trans. Tim Spence and David Craven, Atlantic Highlands, NJ: Humanities Press International Inc., 1992; Paula Findlen, *Possessing Nature: Collecting and Scientific Culture in Early Modern Italy*, Berkeley, CA: University of California Press, 1994.

9 Leon Battista Alberti, *On the Art of Building in Ten Books*, trans. Joseph Rykwert et al., Cambridge, MA: MIT Press, 1988, pp. 91–4.

10 Susan Feinberg Millenson, *Sir John Soane's Museum*, Ann Arbor, MI: UMI Research Press, 1987.

11 See Paul Ricoeur's discussion of the Oedipus complex in his *Freud and Philosophy: An Essay on Interpretation*, trans. Denis Savage, New Haven: Yale University Press, 1970, pp. 188–201 and 515–8.

12 Andre Breton, *La maison d'Yves*, in his *Poèmes*, Paris: Gallimard, 1948, p. 139; Hans Hollander, 'Ars inveniendi et investigandi: Zur surrealistischen Methode', *Wallraf-Richartz-Jahrbuch* XXXII, 1970, pp. 222–30; John Zuern, 'The Communicating Labyrinth: Breton's *La Maison d'Yves* as a Micro-Manifeste', in *André Breton Today*, ed. Anna Balakian and Rudolf E. Kuenzli, New York: Wills Locker & Owens, 1989, pp. 111–21.

13 *Minotaure*, the longest running Surrealist journal (1933–1939), illustrates that the Minotaur was a compelling figure in the late history of Surrealism.

14 André Breton, 'Manifesto of Surrealism (1924)', in André Breton, *The Manifestoes of Surrealism*, trans. Richard Seaver and Helen R. Lane, Ann Arbor, MI: University of Michigan Press, 1974, p. 304.
15 André Breton, *Communicating Vessels*, trans. Mary Ann Caws and Geoffrey T. Harris, Lincoln, NE: University of Nebraska Press, 1990, p. 86.
16 Dalibor Vesely, 'Surrealism and the Latent Reality of Dreams', *Umení* LVI, 2008, pp. 325–33.
17 Erwin W. Straus, *Phenomenological Psychology*, London: Tavistock, 1966, pp. 101–18.
18 It is true that in our dreams we do move in time, but that time is deter- mined only by a series of events that sometimes gives us the impression of freedom, the feeling of moving into another time, the negation of tem- poral circumstances, and so on. We become most clearly aware of the nature of time in dreams at the moment we wake up and we ask: what time is it? The answer includes not only a particular time, but also morn- ing, evening, a certain day, the month, etc. Dreams do not contain this possibility. From the point of view of time it is also interesting that we are clearly aware of waking up, but not of falling asleep. In the first case, time has a structure and a clear awareness of the present, while in the second, when falling asleep, awareness of time merges with the present.
19 The indeterminate character of space is not always a limitation but can also be the source of unusual possibilities for movement and new, inventive spatial configurations.
20 The difference between the oneiric world and memory of dreams stems from the fact that memory is situated on the level of personal experience, which points to its source in the oneiric world. To remem- ber is a result of conscious effort, it is what comes to visibility from the reference to the latent (oneiric) world. The relation between the oneiric world and memory is analogical to the relation between world and our experience.
21 Gaston Bachelard, *On Poetic Imagination and Reverie: Selection form the Works of Gaston Bachelard*, ed. and trans. Colette Godin, Indian- apolis, IN: Bobbs-Merrill, 1971, pp. 98–9.)
22 Gaston Bachelard, *The Poetics of Reverie: Childhood, Language and the Cosmos*, trans. Daniel Russell, Boston, MA: Beacon Press, 1969, p. 177.
23 Breton, *Manifesto of Surrealism*, op. cit., p. 16.
24 André Breton, *Free Rein (La clé des champs)*, trans. Michel Parmentier and Jacqueline d'Amboise, Lincoln, NE: University of Nebraska Press, 1995, p. 16.
25 Andre Breton, *Nadja*, trans. Richard Howard, New York: Grove Press, 1960, p. 18.
26 Breton, *Manifesto of Surrealism*, op. cit. p. 18.
27 André Breton, *Mad Love*, trans. Mary Ann Caws, Lincoln, NE: Uni- versity of Nebraska Press, 1987, p. 11.
28 The case of Mexico is particularly illustrative. Breton visited Mexico in 1938 and was intrigued not only by the ruined architecture but also by the nature of its cities (Tenochtitlan, Cuernavaca, Malinal), and by the country as a whole, which he described as a 'Surrealist land'. See his

account 'Souvenir du Mexique', in *Minotaure*, no. 12–13, May 1939, pp. 31–51.

29 Conversation between Alvin Boyarsky and the members of the Coop partnership, Wolf Prix and Helmut Swiczinsky, *Blau Box: Coop Himmelblau*, London: Architectural Association, 1988, p. 16.

30 André Breton and Gérard Legrand, *L'art magique*, Paris: Club Français du Livre, 1957, p. 93 [trans. Vesely].

31 Ibid.

11 Czech New Architecture and Cubism

The relatively short period in the development of Czech architecture at the beginning of the twentieth century, referred to even today as 'Cubist', was a movement that was, strangely enough, related to the mainstream of international Cubism only to a limited extent. It is true that, on the surface, it may appear that such architecture has something in common with the nature of Cubist painting and sculpture. However, to draw from that a conclusion about the nature of a whole movement would be very misleading. Appearance is not a direct manifestation of the movement's nature, essence and meaning. We have to look more closely at the historical conditions and real intentions that brought the so-called Cubist architecture to existence, in order to understand better the meaning of the term. The main characteristics of this movement point to deeper tendencies in European culture at the beginning of the twentieth century.

It is perhaps understandable that the close links between architecture and painting at that time, together with the general tendency to see Paris rather than Vienna as the main centre of European art, created the illusion that French Cubism represented all that was modern. The problem with the apparent hegemony of this movement, much debated and very often rejected by the 'Cubist' artists themselves, is the tendency to reduce the broader and more relevant context of architecture and visual arts to the narrower context of mainstream Cubism.[1] Once the horizon of reference is reduced, the meaning of Czech Cubism, its cultural identity and specificity, are lost to a great extent, and a false image is created about its true nature and place in relation to other European avant-gardes. The term 'Cubism' refers overwhelmingly to its origins in France and, taking into account the distinction made there between its inventors and followers, the

DOI: 10.4324/9781003272090-12

reference tends to be reduced to the works of the main protagonists: Pablo Picasso, Georges Braque, Juan Gris, Fernand Léger and very few others. This small circle of protagonists becomes a problematic reference for the assessment of the creative possibilities and contributions made outside the Parisian cultural scene. The use of the term 'Czech Cubism' leads inevitably, even today, to its secondary place in relation to its French counterpart; and no amount of explanatory or critical argument seems to change the feeling that the Czech version of Cubism is only an interesting, sometimes rather exotic imitation of the French precedent. This conclusion misses many of its original and creative characteristics, which have their source elsewhere, and as a result, situates the Czech movement on the periphery of mainstream European culture as a short historical episode. The notion 'Czech Cubism' can be defined, I believe, only in the dialectics of the broad sphere of non-Cubist art and mainstream Cubism. The openness to the first changes the meaning of the second and vice versa. Looking at the art of the early twentieth-century avant-gardes in this way would not only give Czech art a more central position, but would also help us to see that there is a common, deeper level of creativity behind most of the period's movements, including Cubism. On this level, we can see a common orientation moving away from perspectival illusionism, a clear tendency to search for the more essential representation of reality, a new creative freedom and new creative principles of art.

The primary mode of creativity

It is interesting to see how much the search for new generative principles of art at the beginning of the twentieth century was influenced by the Romantic and Symbolist notions of creativity, manifested in the paradigm of the crystal[2] (Fig. 11.1). Following the idealistic vision of creativity, the Viennese art historian Alois Riegl writes: 'All artistic creation is thus essentially nothing other than a competition with nature [...] And the fundamental law according to which nature forms dead matter is that of crystallisation.'[3] Crystallisation is seen by Riegl as a cosmic principle that brings together nature and art.

In the opening ceremony of the exhibition *Ein Dokument deutscher Kunst*, in the Mathildenhöhe in Darmstadt (1901), a 'prophet' exhibiting a large crystal, recited: 'This is the symbol of a new life, in this sign it is disclosed, young souls, young year, the time has arrived, you have not waited in vain.'[4] The symbol of the crystal in the early

11.1 Wenzel August Hablik, *Crystal Castle in the Sea*, 1914.

twentieth century plays the role of mediator in the battle against historicism; it is a symbolic transmitter in the move towards abstraction as the revelation of absolute truth. In that sense, it is also a symbolic form of creation in the era of modernity. This conclusion may bring us one step closer to understanding the crystalline nature of Czech 'Cubist' architecture. In the retrospective assessment of the early avant-garde, influenced very strongly by French Cubism, Amédée Ozenfant writes:

> On the whole and in spite of personal coefficients one can detect a tendency which might be described metaphorically as a

tendency towards the crystal. The crystal in nature is one of the phenomena that touch us most, because it clearly exemplifies its movement towards geometrical organisation. Nature sometimes reveals to us how its forms are built up by the interplay of internal and external forces. The crystal grows and stops growing, in accordance with the theoretical forms of geometry; man takes delight in these forms because he finds in them what seems to be a confirmation for his abstract geometrical concepts. Nature and the human mind find common ground in the crystal as they do in the cell, and as they do wherever order is so perceptible to the human senses that it confirms those laws which human reason loves to propound in order to explain nature. In genuine cubism there is something organic, which proceeds outwards from within [...].[5] (Fig. 5.1)

The organic aspect of Cubism points to a domain of primary creativity as it is manifested in the anonymous creative processes of nature and in the conscious creativity of a genius. In the Romantic understanding, later taken up by the Cubists and Expressionists, 'the creativity which brought forth independent and organically evolved works of art was given to the artist by great creative nature, the productive force or originating spirit at the centre of life. The artist could create like nature, because, being a force of this creative nature, he possessed in his soul an unconscious formative power, which enabled him to identify himself with the formative energies of the world.'[6] This rather unreal sense of creative freedom may explain the ease with which artists saw the possibility to create a new style of architecture from their own resources. What may appear to us today as a purely utopian endeavour became possible in a culture where art was dominated by aestheticism and the understanding of history by historicism. In such a culture, the work of art became a world in itself, virtually removed from all connection with practical reality, and it was to be experienced only as a beautiful form. Through this 'aesthetic differentiation', the work of art loses its place in the world to which it belongs in so far as it belongs to aesthetic consciousness. On the other hand, this is paralleled by the artists also losing their place in the world. Secondly, in the aesthetic experience nothing is known about the objects that are judged as beautiful. The nature and meaning of the object do not affect the essence of aesthetic judgement. As a consequence, the work of art has nothing to do with truth. The work of art is only a beautiful form, a 'mere nodal point in the possible variety of aesthetic experiences.'[7]

The loss of art's place in the world is compensated for by the self-sufficiency of the artist, who feels 'self-sufficient like God'.[8] To be self-sufficient means to be able to appropriate the whole of history and culture and make them part of one's own world, and to remain open to unlimited inventiveness—in other words to be a true genius. The concept of genius represents a transition from a long tradition of creative imitation to self-expression. In this transition, the unity of representation, sustained by the communicative space of culture, was replaced by fragmentary individual achievements appearing to represent the world in its wholeness. This corresponds to a new sense of the present and its history known as historicism. The growth of historicism was initiated by a desire for autonomy, independent judgement and an analytical approach to the past. The problem of architectural historicism coincides with the problem of style. Style represents a conflict between the normative idea and historicity, between the idea as an ahistorical element of tradition and the individuality and wholeness of an epoch. The only way historicism could resolve this conflict was by eliminating the normative idea altogether and proclaiming its own historical relativity as the norm. In such a situation, the architect alone becomes the source of reference, of continuity and meaning, in fact the sole legislator of his art. Paul Klee made it plain, that 'genius cannot be taught because it is not a norm but an exception [...] It has no other law than itself.'[9] As a result, the law of genius was seen as the law of creation.[10]

Mainstream Cubism

The attempt to grasp the most elementary mode of creativity, manifested in the process of crystallisation, constitutes a common ground for most of the avant-garde movements, most explicitly for Expressionism, Cubism and Futurism. Each of them represents a particular articulation (crystallisation) of similar problems, mainly the emancipation from the illusionistic perspectival representation, the overcoming of historicism and aestheticism, and the more tangible grasp of the 'truth' of reality. The sharing of the common ground, represented by the process of crystallisation, may explain their occasional overlap, expressed sometimes in not very helpful terms such as 'Cubo-Expressionism' or 'Cubo-Futurism'. In order to avoid such awkward hybrids, it seems to me crucial to preserve the cultural integrity and identity of individual movements and their regional characteristics. In our case, it is most important to ask what is the cultural integrity of Cubism when we speak of Czech 'Cubist' architecture. Here, we have no choice but to turn to the place of its origin in France between 1909 and 1911.

Our attempt to understand the movement labelled rather accidentally as Cubism must begin with Cézanne and his effort to restore the communicative power of the fragment. 'If the painter is to express the world,' Cézanne claimed, 'the arrangement of his individual colours must carry with it this indivisible whole, or else his picture will only hint at things and will not give them the unity, the presence, the unsurpassable plenitude which is for us the definition of the real.'[11] For this reason, each separate brush stroke (fragment) satisfies a number of conditions. It must contain 'the air, the light, the object, the composition, the character, the outline and the style'.[12] The fragmented patches of colour, across which the receding perspective, the outlines, angles and curves are inscribed like lines of force, create a spatial structure that vibrates as it is formed. We can see objects in the state of appearing and organising themselves before our eyes. What motivated Cézanne was not perspective space, geometry, or laws governing colour, but the subject, the still life, portrait, or landscape in their totality. This is what Cézanne himself referred to as 'motif' (Fig. 11.2). The organising power of the motif is not always apparent and can be easily confused with the purely formal configuration of a painting. This occurs not only in the interpretations of Cézanne but also in the interpretation of Cubism, where the formal problems of space, volume and the fragmentation of objects into geometric elements are considered to be the main characteristics of the movement. The standard belief that contents can be identified only with the advent of Synthetic Cubism is not really true; it clearly originates in Analytical Cubism. The replacement of traditional perspective by a notion of space that was, as a rule, more complex and abstract may appear as a formal endeavour, but the configuration of geometrical lines and fragments characteristic of the early period of Cubism was only a transition to a stage in which a new world was slowly revealed in the process of construction, resulting in a new symbolic representation of reality.

The dissolution of the object in Analytical Cubism created an ambiguous situation in which fragments always preserved some reference to the original objects. In the new structure of space, objects lost their rigid definition and became part of the newly articulated

11.2 Paul Cézanne, *L'Estaque, the Village and the Sea*, 1882.

world. Braque describes this phenomenon very clearly when he notes: 'It seems to me just as difficult to paint the spaces "between" as the things themselves. The space "between" seems to me to be as essential an element as what they call the object. The subject matter consists precisely of the relationship between these objects and between the object and the intervening spaces. How can I say what the picture is of when relationships are always things that change? What counts is this transformation.'[13] (Fig. 11.3) The relationship between objects (fragments) and the intervening spaces is not formal, as we have already said. It is always rooted in the context of a particular setting. The nature of the relationship is thus determined by

11.3 Georges Braque, *Violin and Clarinet on a Table*, 1912.

the content of the situation and the meaning of individual elements. 'The subject, for instance a lemon next to an orange, ceases to be a lemon and an orange – they become fruit.'[14] What we see at work here is a metaphor, which has the capacity to establish the similarity between different fragments, and, as a consequence, the capacity to reveal on a deeper level what is common to them. The metaphorical vision of the given reality depends on the productive imagination and on the existence of a world, which is always present as a latent world waiting for articulation.[15] In other words, behind each fragment is always present a potential object like a shadow.

In its most abstract, so-called hermetic phase, the structure of the Cubist painting was reduced to a relatively homogenous grid organising individual fragments with the help of light. The single source of illumination was replaced by the alternation of light and dark fragmented planes. Their luminous values gave the fragments their relative positions. Objects represented by their most evocative fragments are drained of their substance and become immaterial and transparent, which means that it is possible to see through them into another layer of the pictorial space. The true purpose of the Cubist painting is to represent objects as they really are in the phenomenal world; that is to say, differently from the way we see them in superficial perception. Perspective and natural lighting used to alter objects and dissimulate their true form. The knowledge we have of an object is a complex sum of perceptions and memories.[16] The main achievements of Cubist art, mostly painting, were the transformation of the perspectival into a non-perspectival space leading to the restoration of the concrete spatiality of the real phenomenal world, the restoration of the true richness of objects and the freedom to explore their most characteristic qualities accessible through the artist's imagination.

Although there is reasonable agreement about the nature of French Cubism, Maurice Raynal, one of its most reliable witnesses, wrote already in 1912: 'The term "cubism" is day by day losing its significance, if it ever had a definite one.'[17] This degree of ambiguity and doubt should certainly apply to the interpretations of Cubism outside France, particularly in the Expressionist circles in Germany, where the role of Cubism was taken very seriously, but in a fundamentally different way. While in France the goal of Cubism was the mundane reality of everyday objects and life, exemplified in the genre of still-life, in Germany, Cubism was elevated into a transcendental phenomenon of almost cosmic proportions. This is quite clearly apparent in the writings of Adolf Behne, the most eloquent voice of the Expressionist movement. Behne introduced the question of 'Cubism' in his writings already in 1911 and discussed it first in terms of its *Architektonik*. Later he goes on to speak of the mission of Cubism as the guide to the future. He refers to the 'architectonic' quality of the new Cubist art as the 'disguised aspiration of all art towards unity' (i.e., the *Gesamtkunstwerk*), with architecture itself as the leader towards this unity.[18] He differentiates, nevertheless, between Richard Wagner's vision of the *Gesamtkunstwerk* and his own: 'If we wish to call our aim a *Gesamtkunstwerk*, we see this as an ideal, which will only be fulfilled completely from inside and with total necessity once the arts are leaning towards each other on their own accord [...] We wish for an inner transformation of all Art.'[19] Behne's syncretic and rather grandiose vision of Cubism is quite obvious when he writes: 'In Cubism we find the great will which opens up the world and which erects forms of a transhuman kind that create a world-body.'[20] It is interesting to see Behne write often about Cubism in a similar way as he does about Expressionism, emphasising the flexible representation of objects, the growth and the genesis of forms and other mutual characteristics. Cubism is for him the vehicle of an order that can help us to grasp the essence of our experience and the relations between things revealing the cosmic sense and order of the world. 'The term Cubism,' he writes, 'means that there are elements of painting that Cubism can, using the geometrical means and the process of crystallisation, bring to an expression.' In Behne's own summary: 'Expressionism is the goal, modern art is the art of expression and Cubism is the language that many, but not all, Expressionists use.'[21] The reception of Cubism in Germany shows quite clearly how different the perception of Cubism in art was outside France and, therefore, how difficult it is to identify its nature and role if we limit our focus to the French milieu. This situation leads to the most difficult question that we have to address here: what is the relation of Cubist painting as a European phenomenon to architecture, or more precisely, can Cubism proper, which originated in painting, also be identified in architecture?

The relation of Cubist art and architecture

The difficulty of this question is reflected in the fact that, despite the large amount of literature devoted to the subject, the question is still hotly debated today and remains unanswered. The debate oscillates between the position of those who don't see any relation between Cubist painting and architecture, and those who don't have any difficulty to transfer, mostly naively, the achievements of Cubist painting directly to architecture.[22] An appropriate point of departure for furthering this debate would be the *Maison Cubiste* at the *Salon d'Automne* of 1912, which is frequently used as an example of the most explicit link between Cubism and architecture (Fig. 11.4). It was designed by André Mare, interior and furniture designer, in

11.4 Raymond Duchamp-Villon, *Maison Cubiste*, 1912.

collaboration with the sculptor Raymond Duchamp-Villon as an entry into the exhibition, which contained the first substantial collection of Cubist paintings.[23] In order to understand the nature of the *Maison Cubiste*, it is necessary to consider the situation and circumstances of its genesis.

In the period preceding the 1912 exhibition, one of the most discussed issues in official cultural circles in France was the status of the French decorative arts in relation to the rest of Europe, and particularly Germany.[24] André Mare, who was mostly responsible for the programme and character of the *Maison Cubiste* was deeply committed to raising the standard of French decorative arts. In a letter to his friend Marinot in February 1912, Mare spelled out what he intended the *Maison Cubiste* to be: 'something very French, traditional, looking to motifs typical of French decoration from the Renaissance to Louis Philippe, its innovations rooted in these'.[25] By innovations he meant the inspiration that can be taken from Cubism. Because Cubism was seen as a great innovation in painting, what was now needed was an innovation in the decorative arts. The link between decorative art and high art had in France a long tradition, which goes back to *la peinture décorative* at the end of the nineteenth century (Gauguin, the Nabis) and extends to the Art Deco of the second decade of the twentieth century (Delaunay). In conclusion, it is possible to say that 'where there was an evident congruence between Mare's project and some Cubist paintings, it was in terms of the provincial classicist affiliations and in the ambivalence that these imply toward the process of modernisation'.[26]

Among the different attempts to understand the relation of Cubism and architecture, the most convincing so far is the notion of phenomenal transparency as a mediating link.[27] This link may not be the only or final answer, but it is still closest to grasping the main achievements of Cubist painting—the articulation and structure of non-perspectival space in a way that is compatible with the similar effort in architecture. The question of the compatibility of pictorial and architectural space is the key to any serious attempt to define the nature of their possible relationship. It is perhaps not surprising that in the French milieu the clearest example of understanding and developing the non-perspectival architectural space was the work of Le Corbusier. Despite an apparent move away from Cubism in his polemical treatise 'After Cubism' and the investigations of the new configuration of space in his Purist paintings, he uses in the first generation of his buildings principles sufficiently compatible with those used in Cubist paintings. What are these principles?

The individual elements of the Cubist work of art are endowed with transparency, which means, 'they are able to interpenetrate without an optical destruction of each other. Transparency, however, implies more than optical characteristics, it implies a broader spatial order. Transparency means a simultaneous perception of different spatial locations. Space not only recedes but fluctuates in a continuous activity.'[28] Transparency is closely linked with the formation of the relief space built up as layering of planes, but in such a way that there is a visible communication between them. This leads away from the homogenous illusionistic space to the new type of space that may be best described as a configuration of places. The change in the nature of space restores the sense of place as a primary mode of spatiality of the visible world.

This new organisation of space is well demonstrated in Le Corbusier's villa Stein-de Monzie at Garches, for instance (Fig. 11.5). The face of the building cannot be identified with one particular plane. It is stratified into a series of planes and fragmentary slots. The play of shallow and deep space creates a complex three-dimensional configuration that changes as we move around and through the building. Because the individual fragmentary elements represent

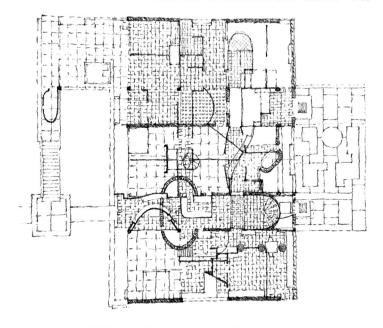

11.5 Le Corbusier, villa Stein-de Monzie, Garches, 1926–8.
Superimposed plans of all levels.

the habitable (living) parts of the house, the play is not formal but thematic, in the same way as it is in the transformation and metaphorical role of fragments in Synthetic Cubism. As an example, at Garches the journey of transformation begins in the north-oriented and thus dimly lit entrance vestibule, follows the main stair into the salon, and ends up in the open-air restatement of the whole house in the form of the suspended terrace garden.

The transformation of individual elements and the overlapping of planes discussed so far in terms of phenomenal transparency can be understood even better in terms of the metaphorical power of fragments. Each fragment is like a potential whole to which it may belong and contribute thus to the richness of the building as a whole. There is a close analogy between the role of the fragment in architecture and painting, where fragments represent actual or potential objects in their situational configuration. The key to the analogy is the structure of situational configurations (settings) of our life world, which cannot be reduced to visual perception, but can be visualised. It was this rather difficult shift in modern experience that motivated the effort to create a non-perspectival, Cubist space. It is interesting to note that Corbusier compares the process involved in the creation of the new type of space with the process of crystallisation and the result, the villa in this case, to a crystal. The villa, he writes, 'the pure solution, compressed by constraints, appears as a concentrate, as a crystal'.[29]

The nature of Czech 'Cubist' architecture

The decisive change leading to the formation of Czech 'Cubist' architecture took place in the year 1910 and can be associated with an important article 'From Modern Architecture to Architecture' by Pavel Janák, in which he distances himself and part of his generation from the legacy of the Viennese rationalism of Otto Wagner and his school.[30] Janák (1882–1956) studied at the Czech Technical University (1899–1906) and later at the Vienna Academy with Otto Wagner (1906–08). After his return to Prague, he worked in the office of Jan Kotěra, also a former student of Wagner. Here, he met with Josef Gočár, his future companion in the effort to create a new architecture. One of the most important platforms for this effort was the foundation of the magazine *Umělecký měsíčník* (*Arts Monthly*) of which Janák became the main editor.[31] Janák's own work, his publications and personal influence made him a pivotal figure in the movement associated with the Group of Visual Artists (*Skupina výtvarných umělců*).

Janák's vision of the new architecture was based on certain art and architectural precedents (such as Gothic and Baroque, the projects and drawings of Wenzel Hablik and Josip Plečnik, etc.) but most of all on an impressive body of knowledge derived mainly from Viennese art history (Alois Riegl, Max Dvořák) and idealistic German philosophy and aesthetics (Adolf von Hildebrand, Theodor Lipps, Wilhelm Worringer et al.). It is almost impossible to tell what made Janák and his generation adopt, in a relatively short time, such a radically new attitude to design, which they themselves described as 'new', and which was labelled only later as 'Cubist'. The unusual and, in many ways, provocatively unique treatment of architectural volume and space, the use of crystalline forms, the geometrical articulation of surfaces and the attempt to reduce spatial problems to the problems of plane or relief, cannot be traced to one single source of inspiration. It is partly for this reason that the old argument about the influence of Cubist painting on Czech 'new' architecture is rather futile (Fig. 11.6).

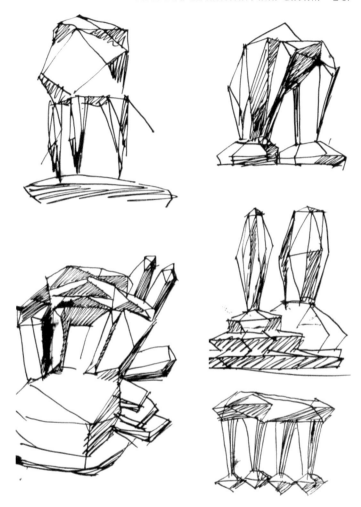

11.6 Pavel Janák, *Four Architectural Studies*, 1912.

On the deepest level, the 'new' Czech architecture belongs to a modern gnostic dream about cultural emancipation, the possibility to appropriate the whole of culture and history, and about the universality of one's individual creative contribution, with the hope that art, more than anything else, could change the world.[32] This rather unreal sense of creative freedom was anticipated and expressed very clearly in a seminal gnostic dream already at the beginning of

the modern age. 'For a short time', writes a well-known philosopher, 'allow your thought to leave this world in order to come to
see a wholly new one, which I shall cause to be born in the presence of your thought in imaginary spaces.'[33] By the end of the
nineteenth century, this thought had become a reality, supported by
a curious combination of positivistic instrumentality and Romantic
idealism. It is important to realise that it was in this atmosphere of
imaginary space, dominated by aestheticism and historicism, that
modern art history, philosophy of art and criticism came to existence.
With this in mind, we may understand better the sources, the language and the intentions of Janák's generation, and be fair to them
rather than overly critical or dismissive of their contributions.

In his main programmatic text, the 'The Prism and the Pyramid',
Janák outlined the main principles of the new architecture.[34] The
outline should be read as a theoretical programme articulated in
the 'imaginary space' of the current culture and not as a recipe for
design. The text is based on the assumption, taken mostly from
Wilhelm Worringer, that European architecture is defined by two
traditions, one Classical, in the south, represented by the horizontality and verticality exemplified by the prism, and the other Christian,
in the north, represented by forces that challenge the inertia of matter and are exemplified most clearly in Gothic and Baroque art.[35]
The best example of forces that move matter beyond its natural state
is crystallisation, which is not influenced by gravity that represents
the natural world of matter and materialism in general. The oblique,
diamond-like planes of the crystal represent a movement, which
transforms the passive natural reality into an animated, more abstract
and thus a spiritual reality. The highest form of spiritually abstracted
matter is the pyramid (Fig. 11.7 top).

The spiritual meaning associated with the pyramid is not Janák's invention. It was discussed already by Adolf von Hildebrand in his *Problem
der Form* (1893), later by Alois Riegl in his *Spätrömische Kunstindustrie*
(1901)[36] and finally by Wilhelm Worringer (1908), who writes:

> Our reasons for terming the pyramid the perfect example of all
> abstract tendencies are evident. It gives the purest expression to
> them. In so far as the cubic can be transmuted into abstraction,
> it has been done here. Lucid rendering of material individual-
> ity, severely geometric regularity, transformation of the cubic
> into surface impressions: all the dictates of an extreme urge to
> abstraction are here fulfilled.[37]

11.7 Pavel Janák, *Design for a Façade*, 1912 (top); and *Façade Study*, 1918.

Architecture in Janák's definition is 'in contrast to the natural form of building a higher activity, it brings together two activities: the satisfaction of basic human needs and artistic expression, i.e., the abstraction of matter. It is for that reason that it brings together also two systems of creation: technical prismatic building in two planes and abstract transformation of matter in three planes (pyramid) either in the linear or curved manner (system)'.[38] The distinction between natural and spiritual creativity is, again, not Janák's invention, but has its origins in Riegl's distinction between the *Naturwerk* and *Kunstwerk*, both mutually independent.[39]

Spiritual creativity, dependent to a great extent on the basic natural requirements and purpose of the task, was otherwise free to follow the possibilities of imagination along the line of the already mentioned principles of the new architecture. In Janák's own words: 'Everywhere where the spirit is active, the surface is transformed, moved, as if there was in its folds and waves a mixture of matter, we don't see individual materials (their qualities, the colour of stones, the shine of metals or glass) we see in all of them only matter.'[40] We can understand even better Janák's intentions from certain passages in his unpublished journals.[41] In one of them, he talks about the nature of drapery, which seems to be the best illustration of his understanding of spiritual creativity. He writes:

> Drapery is something very interesting and suggestive. Drapery for us is something more than inert material spread out [before us]. If something happens with the material, if we move it, gather it, it becomes drapery. Drapery is material visually transformed by movement into which action has been integrated. The same amount, the same surface of material is contained in the drapery, but what is visible for us are only the parts and folds which are essential and which carry action. Drapery represents the most dynamic possibility of material, the degree to which the material can be imbued with life [...] We know now how to acknowledge and accept the surface as draped—in contrast to our earlier understanding of the surface as inanimate.[42]

The reference to drapery illustrates how Janák saw, most personally, the treatment of the surfaces of his buildings. At the same time, his language shows that the alleged spiritual creativity is probably not, in the end, as spiritual as it may appear. It has lost most of its transcendence and has become closely linked with personal will, as we can read in the following journal entry: 'The modern form in general is transformed into a bearer of will, it is not something independent, it is where I want it in the way I want it, it is a relief generated by my will.'[43] This degree of freedom can explain the innovative character of the new architecture, but also the difficulty of creating a new style from one's own resources and purely by will (Fig. 11.7 bottom).

'The word "style"', wrote Kurt Schwitters, 'is worn out but it still signifies better than anything else the type of artistic striving that is characteristic of our age.'[44] The concentration of the creative effort on style creates a situation in which style becomes superior to truth and, as a result, carries within itself the proof of its own sufficiency. This attitude seems to be based on the belief 'that in the cultivation of a new style is concealed the only sublime possibility of making life bearable'.[45] The urgent need to overcome the stylistic vacuum and cultural anxiety was characteristic for the whole of Janák's generation. In such a situation, it is understandable that even an imaginary solution of the problem of style was better than none. The following two journal entries seem to say just that: 'More beautiful than a castle really built is a castle in the mind. More beautiful than a tower one can touch, an impossible one, so conceived that it cannot be constructed, that it would not stand.'[46] And, 'perhaps this sounds strange but I would invent a table or another body, formed in such a way that its volume would be substituted by others, half rotated against each other, antipodal but connected only by the structure, around which they would be spiritually organised.'[47] Under such conditions, in the words of André Breton, the object of design 'ceases to be fixed permanently on the near side of thought and recreates itself on the further side as far as the eye can reach'.[48]

Despite all the effort to justify the new architecture by elaborate theoretical arguments the *praxis* was usually intuitive, full of searching improvisations and dominated almost entirely by optical criteria.[49] This is clearly articulated in the following statements by Janák: 'If I say that the mass of the prism has been pushed out into the pyramid through internal expansion or because of the eye, in both cases it happened in the same way, through movement. What if I said the following: the eye sees the expansion. That the eye is a causal organ is evident: the mass would not boil over; it erupts under the hand commanded by the eye.'[50] And, later: 'Higher degrees of real things, statues, columns always appear where in or out of them and on them a relief begins. Relief is a reduction of reality for the eye, whereas reality has yet to be transposed into relief. Relief exists only in relation to our eye.'[51] The notion of relief brings us to the most frequently raised comments and criticism of the new architecture, its sole concentration on the surface and façades of buildings. Janák, who wrote a strong defence of the façade in his article 'Renewal of the Façade', does not advocate a return to the perspective of the plane or wall but, instead, to a strong faith in the 'spiritual' dimension of architecture and its association with the notion of relief.[52]

Again, this was not Janák's own idea—it was shared across his generation. Adolf von Hildebrand wrote in his *Problem of Form* already in 1893:

> As long as a sculptural figure makes itself felt primarily as a cube it is still in the initial stage of configuration; only when it creates an impression of flatness, although it is cubic, does it acquire artistic form. Only through the consistent implementation of this relief interpretation of our cubic impressions does the representation gain its sacred fire, and the mysterious blessing that we receive from the work of art rests upon it alone.[53]

If we look more closely at one of Janák's best achievements, the Fára house in Pelhřimov, dominated by a triangular gable, it is impossible not to see the close affinity between the highly sophisticated shallow relief of this gable and Otto Gutfreund's sculptural reliefs of the same time (Fig. 11.8).

The link between the new architecture and sculpture was very close and was supported from both sides. Janák writes:

> Sculpture, in spite of its three dimensions, should be abstracted into surface vision and appearance. In the same way, drama, which is always three-dimensional in life, is abstracted into the limited plane of the stage, defined as a picture frame. Then there is the same effort as in visual art: to place every essential thing in an essential ratio sequentially next to, or rather behind each other, so that everything would be visible. Dramatic is that which stands out of it all.[54]

Gutfreund, a very close friend of Janák, with whom he shared many conversations and correspondence, states in his seminal text 'Plane and Space': 'The contemporary sculptor substitutes volume with an illusory volume – a plane. The moving plane creates a volume, which as a new form cannot be measured anymore by intellect.'

11.8 Pavel Janák, Fará House, Pelhřimov, 1913–4.

The sculpture is no longer a solid volume, it is a 'continuous vibration of planes, illusion of volumes, a vibration, which as a stream destroys the boundaries defining the space, a vibration with whirls which indicate on the plane the depth and reflect like streams without interruption, the fragments of reality'[55] (Fig. 11.9).

Janák's Fára house also illustrates well the often-mentioned affinity between the new architecture and Gothic and Baroque art. Speaking not only for himself but for his whole generation, Janák writes: 'They [the Gothic and Baroque] appeal to us by the power of

11.9 Otto Gutfreund, *Portrait of the Father IV*, 1911.

their spirit that penetrates matter, and by the dramatic quality of the expressive means that have given birth to their forms […] they have become the essence of what enriches our feelings.'[56] The reference to the Baroque in particular oscillates between the optical analogies of the movement of animated surfaces and a deeper 'spiritual' affinity of the Baroque and the new architecture.

A similar affinity with the local historical context and, mostly, Baroque tradition is addressed in Gočár's House at the Black Madonna in Prague[57] (Fig. 11.10). It would be very interesting to see to what extent the acknowledged success of the building depends on its new architectural characteristics, rather than on the sensitive adaptation to the character of the place and to the surrounding buildings. As a whole, the building is probably more modern than 'new'. What can be characterised as 'new' is limited to the secondary

11.10 Josef Gočár, House (now Museum) at the Black Madonna, Prague, 1911–12.

architectural elements and details, such as the entry and the balcony above, the internal staircase, the dormer windows in the mansard roof, and the capitals on the pillars between windows.

This is even more apparent in the Spa building in Bohdaneč, designed for a long-distance view in a classic symmetrical manner (Fig. 11.11). Again, it is only on the level of secondary architectural elements—the projecting entry hall, the gable above and the windows on the ground level—that it is possible to see some characteristic features of the new architecture. The nearest to the declared intentions of the latter is the treatment of the ground floor windows and doors. The oblique arrangement of the mullions simulates a volume projected onto a plane, which is itself part of the prismatic treatment of the window and door as a whole, situated in real space.

Gočár's use of prismatic elements, the commitment to the material qualities of construction, to volume and space, and his openness to modern architecture, were all characteristics that Janák would have resisted, at least theoretically, before the war. The distance that separates Janák's Fára house and Gočár's Bohdaneč Spa building illustrates the spectrum of creative achievements in which most of the

11.11 Josef Gočár, Bohdaneč Spa, 1912–13.

new architecture oscillated. However, this spectrum is sometimes represented almost as a whole in the works of one person, if we consider the character of his realised buildings together with the character of his exploratory drawings and other works. Such an exception is the life achievement of Vlastislav Hofman, who was an architect, but also an interior, stage set and graphic designer, as well as an accomplished writer. In his early works and early writings, he shares to a great extent Janák's vision of the new style. However, despite a similarity of vision, Hofman's understanding of the role of the artist and creativity in general is fundamentally different. The difference is partly related to the development of his personal style of work, but this is not as important as the deeper identities of his philosophy and work.

Hofman explained his position most clearly in 'The New Principle in Architecture' (1913). He differs from the prevailing doctrine of the new architecture by questioning the role of surface, matter and space (Fig. 11.12 top). He writes:

> Modern architecture does not require surface forms, which is why we dislike contaminating form with detail. The basic form is that which evolved from the inherent potential of matter;

11.12 Vlastislav Hofman, *Detail of a Façade*, 1914 (top); and *Garden Pavilion*, 1914.

this potential is caused by the vision of a space and its interior. Architecture organises technical expression by rhythmic form, thereby creating its own original principal relationships of spaces. These are the property of art; they belong to the principles of architecture. The principle of 'space in matter' seems to dispense entirely with the need for decoration.[58]

By questioning some of the main elements of the established doctrine of the new architecture, Hofman leaves behind the duality of matter and form, the passivity of matter and the association of space with materialism. He believes strongly in the creative role of the cultural environment and tradition and the intrinsic creativity of matter.[59] This reduces the unlimited freedom of the individual in favour of the creative principles and laws that remain relatively stable in time. He shares the belief in the dematerialisation of the new architecture, but accepts the contribution of new materials and techniques to this process. 'As an example', he writes, 'it is enough to mention construction made out of concrete, which by its courage and thinness represents a new process of dematerialization.'[60] Hofman's ideas and intentions are, in many ways, alien to the intentions of the first protagonists of the new architecture. And yet he very often shares these intentions, contradicting thus his own view, sometimes even in the same text. However, the contradictions may not be just personal, but may reflect the disagreements and contradictions in the movement as a whole. This may altogether coincide with the uncertainties about the nature of the new architecture and the oscillations in the spectrum of possible creative achievements, mentioned earlier. Hofman himself acknowledged that 'each new idea of a project brings with it the need of a new type of construction and use of materials. However, there is no answer yet to the question as to what character modern forms should have; so far we can only guess their outline and specific taste, hidden in the depth of modern life'.[61] In Hofman's view architects and artists are not inventing their forms, but discover them partly in history and partly as hidden principles in nature, in a process that can be best described as 'cultural crystallisation'. The complexity and the inconclusive nature of this process can be illustrated by two very different drawings from the same year (1914) (Fig. 11.12 bottom).

The study of the façade of a garden pavilion explores the possibilities to create a transparent wall using cylindrical, conical and small relief elements in a configuration that can be seen as an imaginative transformation of human figures into abstract caryatids. This

11.13 Vlastislav Hofman, *Ďáblice cemetery*, Prague 1912.

organic, rather irregular anthropomorphic result stands in sharp contrast to the study of the façade of a prismatic building treated in a rigid geometrical manner, resembling the crystalline architecture of the early years of the movement. The latter drawing continues the earlier thinking in the only project Hofman ever realised, the cemetery in Ďáblice (Fig. 11.13). What was finally built is only a torso of the original project, but it still shows quite clearly the thinking of the architect, who was at that time preoccupied with grasping the essential form of the programme, using the most elementary crystalline forms and simple planes. In his view:

> The forms of matter, manifested as planes, express not only the content but also the movement related to the essence of the object (building). For those reasons the plane can have two meanings: either a constructed one or fulfilling optical interest. In the case of moving planes, the factual purpose can be expressed by their own movement corresponding to their form and character, which determine their overall expression. The expression may result in a system of scanted [oblique] planes executed in correspondence with optical experience.[62]

In the completed part of the Ďáblice cemetery, which includes an entry with two octagonal pavilions and the surrounding wall, Hofman attempted to grasp the most essential form of each element by reducing them to their skeletal substance, expressing their primary purpose and by treating the remaining body of the elements using pure moving planes.

To what extent the result can be associated with Cubism, Hofman discussed in a very interesting review of the *Maison Cubiste* at the *Salon d'Automne* (1912).[63] In this review, he addressed mainly the question of the relation between Cubist painting and architecture in the contribution of Duchamp-Villon:

> Villon's solution shows the use of the pictorial creative means, the discoveries of the Cubists. However, there is a question to what extent the achievements and means of painting can be the sole and true source; in architecture and in sculpture they can fail in a collision with the intrinsic law essential to architecture [...] If architecture understands its formal sense only from painting and applies it only on the surface, it does not fulfil its original and last task: to create a new conceptual vision, a new essential understanding of space and a new concept of mastering the plasticity of matter in its appropriate possibilities and abilities [...] Where the painting on canvas is transferred to the corporeal reality of sculpture or architecture there is a beginning of a danger: the loss of understanding the nature of one's own creative task. The pictorial means, acquired in the attempt to create a representation of space on the surface cannot be fully transferred into a full volume, they remain only on the surface.[64]

The genuine movement of matter, the very essence of new sculpture and architecture, is not taking place on the surface, 'it is a formal construction that penetrates matter'.[65] This view was, to a great extent, shared by Josef Chochol, a close friend of Hofman. Most of Chochol's architectural realisations were in the citadel of Vyšehrad, an area in Prague associated with its earliest history and legend, which became, in modern times, a pantheon and monument of Czech cultural identity. Chochol shows in his plans that the whole area of the citadel would be left almost untouched and surrounded by a park with low buildings situated against the background of the large surfaces of the brick fortification walls.[66] This vision is reflected in the treatment of the villas and apartment block he built around

11.14 Josef Chochol, villa in Libušina Street, Vyšehrad, Prague 1912.

the citadel between 1912 and 1914 (Figs. 11.14 and 11.15). In all of them, the crystalline detail coincides with the surface and structure of the walls to such an extent that they appear as one continuous body in movement. As he himself states: 'We are not interested any-more in the small architectural details and don't believe in them. We are attracted to exciting and lively forms, global and summary, affecting us in their wholeness and instantly. In the same way as we obtain an unusually dense and synthetic image of a landscape thanks to the means of modern technology, we would like to achieve the sense of speed, in fact a lightning speed, through the synthetic qual-ities of the work.'[67]

The nature of the 'new' architecture began to change after 1915, when it acquired qualities fundamentally different from the quali-ties of the earlier period. The character of the change became clear after the war, in a period described variously as decorative, as Czech Art Deco or as a style named 'Rondocubism'. This last term illus-trates very clearly the degree of confusion and misunderstanding that dominates the interpretation of the new architecture to this

11.15 Josef Chochol, apartment Block in Vyšehrad, Prague, 1913–14.

day. What makes the term problematic and rather absurd, is the assumption that post-war architecture, exemplified in Gocár's Bank of the Czechoslovak Legion for instance, may have still something in common with Cubism (Fig. 11.16). There is a continuity, no doubt, between the new decorative style and the pre-war architecture.

A clear example of the continuity is the privileged role assigned to the surface and its articulation, which we already saw expressed by

11.16 Josef Chochol, Bank of the Czechoslovak Legion, Prague, 1921–23.

Janák in his reference to surface as drapery, a 'material visually transformed by movement into which action has been integrated'; and by Hofman's concept of 'mastering the plasticity of matter in its appropriate possibilities and abilities'. However, it is quite clear that the integration of action and mastering the plasticity of matter follows in the post-war period very different rules from the earlier ones (Fig. 11.17). The new rules, exemplified in the artificially constructed 'national' decor, were motivated by the political and cultural imperative to help the formation of the new national identity and by the radicalised will of the artists to create a new unifying style. Here we can repeat with Schwitters, that 'in the cultivation of a new style is concealed the only sublime possibility of making life bearable'.

The search for national identity and style is a characteristic of a culture dominated by aestheticism and historicism. It is quite astonishing to see how long this old Romantic idea survived as a dream

11.17 Pavel Janák, *Façade Study*, 1921.

without clear substance. It presumed to possess a past and believed in its future; out of both it attempted to construct what it was lacking: substance.

From 'Cubist' to 'new' architecture

We have reached the point where it may be possible to answer better our initial question about the relation between the new Czech architecture and Cubism. The buildings, drawings and texts of the main protagonists of the movement show some affinities with French Cubist painting, but they also do so with the symbolism of the Secession, with Expressionist art and, to some extent, even with Futurism. And yet, on the whole, they represent a unique phenomenon in the context of European culture. The animating spirit behind the new architecture was not new, its origins go back to late Symbolism and the Secession. It is perhaps not a coincidence that the art historical, philosophical and aesthetic texts, which had such influence on the birth of the new architecture, were published mostly in that period.

In a short essay, published in 1913, Hofman acknowledged, that 'the Secession was the first modern phase of the architecture of the new age' and that some of the principles of the new architecture were anticipated already in Secessionist art.[68] The relative autonomy of the new architecture was very clearly revealed in the critical assessment of the influential contemporary movements. Expressionism was seen as too ambiguous with too many naturalistic elements and without any particular sense of order, and therefore, rather arbitrary. Futurism was criticised for its one-sided preoccupation with the superficial aspects of modern life and technology expressed in the obsessive representation of material movement. 'The Futurists try to create a style of move-ment,' writes Vincenc Beneš, however, 'style is only a result of a great vision. Only the great issues of human life can be the source of vision, but not movement.' The attitude to Cubism was, as we have already seen, more complicated and controversial. The same author writes:

> The Cubists, which means those who adopted this label, under-stand the nature of the new art only insufficiently. The term originated in front of Picasso's paintings as an indication of their 'cubic' character, but for those who are using this term in their theoretical writings it is typical to emphasise a second term, *kubus*, which sounds similar, believing that it is characteristic for addressing the problem of space.[69]

Among many other commentaries on the link between the new art and Cubism, one of the most explicit is that of Bohumil Kubišta, who states quite categorically:

> The condition and requirement of the new art is not inevitably Cubism, it could be any other movement, and I am convinced that if something else would appear rather than Cubism, spring-ing out of our spiritual situation, it would be equally modern. Modernity does not coincide with Cubism. Therefore, to consider Cubism or Picassism as the only dogma of salvation is a terrible error and nonsense [...] Cubism does not cover all the modern issues and does not, therefore, have a universal legitimacy.[70]

It is in the background of these critical assessments that we can grasp and understand better the specificity and identity of the new

Czech architecture. Its main characteristic, as we have seen, was its theoretical nature. History does not know many examples when a philosophy and theoretical thinking would succeed to create an imaginary cultural space as a plausible and convincing mode of cultural reality and creativity. It was in such an imaginary space that the new Czech architecture established its main principles, elements and physiognomy. Today it is difficult for us to understand how a theoretical doctrine could influence a whole generation of creative artists and give them the confidence that they could create a universal style of the future, which could change the real world itself.

Some explanation for that can be found in the already mentioned radical aestheticisation and historicisation of culture at the turn of the century, and in the vacuum left behind the disintegrating and disappearing order of traditional architecture. However, on a deeper level we can find an even more convincing explanation in the resonance between the abstract nature of theoretical thinking and the abstraction of architectural forms seen as a road to spirituality.

The identification of the spiritual with abstraction was the most fatal development in the culture of the twentieth century.[71] In the case of the Czech new architecture, the process of abstraction led to the use of primary crystalline forms, triangles for planes and pyramidal forms for three dimensional bodies. The critical problem was how to reconcile the abstracted forms with the concreteness of architectural tasks. This was an undefined territory, open to the imaginative interpretation of individual authors, resulting in great differences between them. If we look at all the results, it is quite clear that in most cases the process of reconciliation was not entirely successful. In too many cases, despite the large variety and flexibility of the invented architectural elements, the result remains abstract and unconvincing. The abstract nature of the results has, no doubt, much to do with the aim to see the style of the new architecture as a universal one. Because of its universality the style was supposed to apply to all arts, including furniture and the decorative arts. It is probably not an accident that not only architects but also painters and other artists were involved in a broadly oriented creativity, which was supposed to contribute to the unity of culture as a *Gesamtkunstwerk*. However, it is very often forgotten that the possibility to speak about the *Gesamtkunstwerk* depends entirely on the existence of a modern aesthetic culture, and that under such conditions it is only a substitute of the lost cultural unity. In the artificial nature of the

Gesamtkunstwerk, 'art has preserved the utopia that fled religion, the aesthetic replaced the religious experience of unity'.[72]

The problem of the *Gesamtkunstwerk* is its search for wholeness as an organic totality, but one treated as a construct and system. This led eventually to its failure. The failure of the *Gesamtkunstwerk* to reach wholeness, which became so explicit in the twentieth century, was caused mainly by the fact that it became an aesthetic utopia and dream, 'a dream without substance and presence'.[73] The lack of presence is grounded in the impossibility of substituting a system or style for the unity of culture, which is always situational and depends on the continuity of communication with reality as a whole, including its past, and not only on a communication with other arts in their present form.

The dream to restore the unity of culture opens still another, very much debated question about the nature of the new architecture: its relation to the local tradition of the Gothic and the Baroque. Both periods are often seen as the movement's most important source of inspiration, and its reference to them is taken as an argument supporting the correspondence between the nature of the new architecture and the historical context of these periods.[74] There may be some truth in this argument, but only as far as the optical experience is concerned. The new architecture does not refer to the original Gothic or Baroque, but to the Gothic and Baroque of the dead God, where transcendence is absorbed in the immanence of direct perception. It is on that level that we can, in the end, not only experience, but also appreciate or judge the new architecture. It is perhaps no longer necessary to emphasise that the term 'new' does not stand for 'Cubist', but for a much broader effort and uniqueness of the Czech contribution to the formation of European architecture of the twentieth century.

Notes

1　Vincenc Kramář, *Kubismus*, Brno: Morav. Slezské Revue, 1921; Marie Benešová, O kubismu v české architektuře, *Architektura ČSR* XXV, 1966, pp. 171–4; Miloš Pistorius, 'Kubistická architektura v Praze', *Staletá Praha* IV, 1969, pp. 139–54; Friedrich Czagan, 'Kubistische Architektur in Böhmen', *Werk* XVI, 2/50, 1969, pp. 75–79; Robert Rosenblum, *Cubism and Twentieth-Century Art*, New York: Prentice Hall/Abrams, 1976; François Burkhardt and Milena Lamarová, *Cubismo cecoslovacco: Architetture e interni*, Milan: Electa, 1982; Miroslav Lamač, *Osma a Skupina výtvarných umělců*, Prague: Odeon, 1988; Patricia Leighten, *Re-Ordering the Universe, Picasso and Anarchism*

268   *Czech New Architecture and Cubism*

1897–1914, Princeton, NJ: Princeton University Press, 1989; Tomáš Vlček, 'Český kubismus', in *Český kubismus 1909–1925*, ed. Jiří Švestka and Tomáš Vlček, Prague: Modernista i3 CZ, 2006, pp. 22–26; Alexander von Vegesack, ed., *Czech Cubism: Architecture, Furniture and Decorative Arts 1910–1925*, Princeton Architectural Press and Vitra Design Museum, 1992; Jiří Padrta and Miroslav Lamač, eds., *Osma a Skupina výtvarných umělců 1907–1917: Teorie, kritika, polemika*, Prague: Odepn, 1992; Lynn Zelevansky, ed., *Picasso and Braque: A Symposium*, New York: The Museum of Modern Art, 1992; Eve Blau and Nancy J. Troy, eds., *Architecture and Cubism*, Cambridge, MA: MIT Press, 2002.

2 Regine Prange, *Das Kristalline als Kunstsymbol*, Hildesheim: Olms Verlag, 1991; Rosemarie Haag Bletter, 'Expressionist Architecture and the Crystal Metaphor', *Journal of the Society of Architectural Historians*, XL, 1981, pp. 21–43.

3 Alois Riegl, *Historische Grammatik der bildenden Künste*, ed. Karl M. Swoboda and Otto Pächt, Graz: Böhlau, 1966, p. 22 [trans. Vesely].

4 Georg Fuchs, 'Das Zeichen', in: *Ein Dokument deutscher Kunst: Die Ausstellung der Künstler-Kolonie in Darmstadt 1901: Festschrift*, Munich: Bruckmann Verlag, 1901 [trans. Vesely].

5 Amédée Ozenfant and Charles-Edouard Jeanneret, *La peinture moderne*, Paris: Éditions Crès, 1925, pp. 137–8 [trans. Vesely].

6 August K. Wiedmann, *Romantic Roots in Modern Art: Romanticism and Expressionism*, Oxford: Gresham Books, 1979, p. 155.

7 Hans Georg Gadamer, *Truth and Method*, trans. William Glen-Doepel, ed. John Cumming and Garret Barden, London: Sheed and Ward, 1975, p. 75.

8 Jean-Jacques Rousseau, *Reveries of the Solitary Walker*, trans. Peter France, London: Penguin, 1979, pp. 82, 89.

9 Paul Klee, *Notebooks Vol. 1: The Thinking Eye*, trans. Ralph Manheim, London: Lund Humphries & Co., 1961, p. 70.

10 There is a close relationship between the narrow formal notion of style and the formation of the modern history of art and architecture. This is reflected in most of the discussions of Cubism, pervaded even today by the stifling influence of stylistic thinking. How stifling this influence is, we can see in the obsession with a personal or national style as a possible substitute for the richness and complexity of the cultural tradition.

11 Maurice Merleau-Ponty, 'Cézanne's Doubt', in his *Sense and Non-Sense*, trans. Hubert L. Dreyfus and Patricia Allen Dreyfus, Evanston, IL: Northwestern University Press, 1964, p. 15. For a more detailed discussion of the nature and positive role of the fragment see Chapter 5 in this book.

12 Émile Bernard, 'Souvenirs sur Paul Cézanne et Lettres Inédites', in *Conversations avec Cézanne*, ed. P. Michael Doran, Paris: Éditions Macula, 1978, p. 158 [trans. Vesely].

13 Georges Charbonnier, *Le Monologue du Peintre: Entretiens avec Braque*, Paris: R. Julliard, 1959, pp. 10–11 [trans. Vesely].

14 Ibid., p. 13.

15 The term 'latent world' is understood and used here as a totality of references in which we are always involved, and which are most conspicuously articulated in language. This understanding follows the tradition formed by the work of Edmund Husserl and Martin Heidegger, which has been enriched more recently by modern hermeneutics. See Edmund Husserl, *The Crisis of European Sciences and Transcendental Phenomenology*, trans. David Carr, Evanston, IL: Northwestern University Press, 1970; Martin Heidegger, *Being and Time*, trans. John Macquarrie and Edward Robinson, Oxford: Blackwell, 1967, pp. 102–22; Walter Biemel, *Le concept de monde chez Heidegger*; Paris: Vrin, 1950.

16 Jacques Rivière, 'Sur les tendances actuelles de la peinture', *Revue d' Europe et d' Amérique*, Paris, 1 March 1912, p. 386.

17 Maurice Raynal, in the exhibition catalogue *L'exposition de la 'Section d'Or'*, Paris, 9 October 1912, p. 2 [trans. Vesely].

18 Adolf Behne, *Die Wiederkehr der Kunst*, Leipzig: Kurt Wolff Verlag, 1919, p. 22.

19 Ibid., p. 40.

20 Prange, op. cit. (note 2), p. 173 [trans. Vesely].

21 Adolf Behne, 'Deutsche Expressionisten', *Der Sturm*, V, No. 17/18, December 1914, pp. 114–5 [trans. Vesely].

22 Beatriz Colomina, 'Where are we?', in Blau and Troy, op. cit. (note 1), pp. 141–66.

23 David Cottington, 'The *Maison Cubiste* and the Meaning of Modernism in pre-1914 France', in Blau and Troy, op. cit. (note 1), pp. 17–41.

24 Nancy J. Troy, *Modernism and the Decorative Art in France: Art Nouveau to Le Corbusier*, New Haven, NJ: Yale University Press, 1991.

25 Cottington, op. cit. (note 23), p. 27.

26 Ibid., p. 29; See also Vlastislav Hofman's review of the 1912 Salon d'Automne: Vlastislav Hofman, 'K podstatě architektury, poznámky k podzimnímu salonu, Paříž 1912', *Volné směry* XVII, 1913, pp. 53–56.

27 Colin Rowe and Robert Slutzky, 'Transparency: Literal and Phenomenal', in Colin Rowe, *The Mathematics of the Ideal Villa and Other Essays*, Cambridge, MA: MIT Press, 1976, pp. 159–85; Zelevansky, op. cit. (note 1).

28 Rowe and Slutzky, op. cit. (note 27), p. 161. For a discussion of the positive role of fragment see the reference in note 11.

29 Le Corbusier, *Une maison, un palais*, Paris, 1929, pp. 71–2 [trans. Vesely].

30 Pavel Janák, 'Od moderní architektury - k architektuře', *Styl*, II, 1910, pp. 105–09.

31 *Umělecký měsíčník* was founded in 1911 as a platform of the Group of Visual Artists established in the same year. All the main protagonists of the 'new architecture', Pavel Janák, Josef Gočár, Josef Chochol and Vlastislav Hofman were, at the beginning, members of the Group.

32 Erich Voegelin, 'Science, Politics and Gnosticism: Two essays', in *The Collected Works of Erich Voegelin*, vol. V, Columbia, MO: University of Missouri Press, 2000, pp. 243–315.

33 René Descartes, 'Le monde', in *Oeuvres*, vol. XI, ed. Charles Adam and Paul Tannery, Paris, 1974, p. 31 [trans. Vesely].

34 Pavel Janák, 'Hranol a pyramida', *Umělecký měsíčník*, I, 1911–12, pp. 162–70.

35 Wilhelm Worringer, *Abstraction and Empathy*, transl. Michael Bullock, London, 1963.

36 Adolf von Hildebrand, *Das Problem der Form in der bildenden Kunst*, Strassburg: Heitz, 1893; Alois Riegl, *Die Spätrömische Kunstindustrie*, Wien, 1901, p. 36, p. 42.

37 Worringer, op. cit. (note 35), p. 91.

38 Janák, 'Hranol a pyramida', op. cit. (note 34), p. 168 [trans. Vesely].

39 Alois Riegl, *Gesammelte Aufsätze*, Berlin, 1995, pp. 51–64.

40 Pavel Janák, 'O nábytku a jiném', *Umělecký měsíčník* II, 1912–1913, p. 28 [trans. Vesely].

41 Irena Žantovská-Murray, *Sources of Cubist Architecture in Bohemia: The Theories of Pavel Janák*, MA dissertation, unpublished, McGill University, Montreal, 1990. The dissertation is based on a systematic interpretation of Janák's unpublished journals, and includes the English translation of the text, which I have used with her kind permission, in my own references to the journals (J 1...etc. refers to the pages in the original, followed by the date of the entry).

42 Ibid., J 15, 8 April 1912.

43 Ibid., J 85–86, 29 July 1914.

44 Kurt Schwitters, *Das literarische Werk*, vol. V, ed. Friedhelm Lach, Cologne: DuMont Verlag, 1973–1981, p. 168 [trans. Vesely].

45 Ernst Jünger, *Strahlungen*, Tübingen: Heliopolis, 1949, p. 16 [trans. Vesely].

46 Žantovská-Murray, op. cit. (note 41), J 43, 3 August 1912.

47 Ibid., J 82, 20 July 1913.

48 André Breton, *Surrealism and Painting*, trans. Simon Watson Taylor, New York: Harper & Row, 1972, p. 277.

49 The background to this doctrine is Riegl's hypothesis of the transition from haptic to optical stage in his developmental vision of art.

50 Žantovská-Murray, op. cit. (note 41), J 23, 6 June 1912.

51 Ibid., J 51, 4 October 1912.

52 Pavel Janák, 'Obnova průčelí', *Umělecký měsíčník*, II, 1912–13, p. 86.

53 Worringer, op. cit. (note 35), p. 90.

54 Žantovská-Murray, op. cit. (note 41), J 12–13, 20 March 1912.

55 Otto Gutfreund, 'Plocha a prostor', *Umělecký měsíčník*, II, 1912–13, pp. 240–3.

56 Janák, 'Hranol a pyramida', op. cit. (note 34), p. 165.

57 Rostislav Švácha, 'Josef Gočár', in Švestka and Vlček, op. cit. (note 1), pp. 222–32.

58 Vlastislav Hofman, 'Nový princip v architektuře', *Styl*, V, 1913, pp. 13–24 [trans. Vesely].

59 This links Hofman's position with Alois Riegl; see Riegl, *Historische Grammatik*, op. cit. (note 3).

60 Vlastislav Hofman, 'Duch moderní tvorby v architektuře', *Umělecký měsíčník*, I, 1911–12, p. 133 [trans. Vesely].

61 Ibid., p. 132.

62 Vlastislav Hofman, 'Příspěvek k charakteru moderní architekury', *Umělecký měsíčník*, I, 1911–12, p. 230 [trans. vesely].

63 Hofman, review of the 1912 *Salon d'Automne*, op. cit. (note 26).

64 Ibid., p. 54.

65 Ibid., p. 55.

66 Josef Chochol, 'Velkoměsto', *Umělecký měsíčník* I, 1911–12, pp. 54–56; Rostislav Švácha, Hofmanův Vyšehrad, *Výtvarná kultura*, VIII, 1984, No. 6, pp. 30–23.

67 Josef Chochol, 'K funkci architektonického článku', *Styl*, V, 1913, pp. 93–94.

68 Pavel Liška, 'Symbolistický kubismus', in: Švestka and Vlček, op. cit. (note 1), pp. 360–78; Vlastislav Hofman, O secessi, *Styl*, V, 1913, pp. 118–20.

69 Vincenc Beneš, Nové umění, *Umělecký měsíčník*, vol. 2, no. 7, 1913, pp. 152. [Ed. The term *kubus* in the sense here is obscure to Czech speakers, and seems to mean something like 'massiveness'. In the same article cited by Vesely, Beneš clarifies: 'Real materiality, *kubus* (a word often used today in art theory) thus requires…stasis/stability.' Ibid., p. 152 (with thanks to Dagmar Motycka-Weston for finding and translating this)].

70 Bohumil Kubišta in a letter to Jan Zrzavý, 10/2/1914 [trans. Vesely].

71 Kathleen J. Regier, ed., *The Spiritual Image in Modern Art*, Wheaton, IL: Theosophical Publishing House, 1987; Edward Weisberger, ed., *The Spiritual in Art: Abstract Painting 1890–1985*, New York: Abbeville Press, 1986.

72 Helmut Jensen, 'Theodor W. Adorno', in *Klassiker der Kunstsoziologie*, ed. Alphons Silbermann, Munich: Beck Verlag, 1979, p. 214 [trans. Vesely].

73 Wieland Schmied, 'Notizen zum Gesamtkunstwerk', in *Der Hang zum Gesamtkunstwerk: Europäische Utopien seit 1800*, ed. Harald Szeemann et al., Aarau and Frankfurt: Sauerländer Verlag, 1983, p. 7 [trans. Vesely].

74 For a discussion of the relation between new architecture, Gothic and Baroque, see Gutfreund, 'Plocha a prostor', op. cit. (note 55).

12 Spatiality, Simulation and the Limits of the Technological Imagination

It is one of the paradoxes of our time that a large number of architects ascend the steps to the zone of purer technological possibilities, meeting on the same steps a large number of engineers moving in the opposite direction in order to grasp the deeper ground and broader context of their own field and operations. It is perhaps not a coincidence that many architects are proud to operate like engineers, while many engineers would like to call themselves architects. We have reached the point where it probably does not matter what we call ourselves and who does what, as long as we understand that the higher we want to build, the deeper must be the foundations. It is clear that the notion of technological autonomy is an illusion and that coming to terms with technology is possible only by accepting the conditions of our earth-bound existence. This understanding will be particularly important in the coming years which are likely to be dominated by the new generation of dreams of emancipation from everyday reality, boosted to a great extent by the current digital revolution.

The digital revolution offers new possibilities of representation, where not only the formal structures, but also the physiognomy of architecture can be manipulated within a simulated environment to a much greater degree. The new simulations are believed to be an adequate representation of reality, following the assumption that the more 'realistic' an image is, the more adequate it must be as a representation. With the new techniques, the traditional relation of representation and what is represented is no longer seen as a dialectical process of disclosure, but as a 'direct presence' of reality. This is a logical outcome of the experimental productive mentality, based on the assumption that we can understand only what we can make, and only what we can make is real.[1]

DOI: 10.4324/9781003272090-13

Telepresence

Against this background we can better understand the visions of the immediate future, produced today not by the writers of science fiction, but by the researchers from the most respectable and influential institutions in the architectural profession. The following argument is a good example of such visions:

> We are entering an era of electronically extended bodies living at the intersection points of the physical and virtual worlds, of occupation and interaction through telepresence as well as through physical presence of mutant architectural forms that emerge from telecommunication-induced fragmentation and re-combination of traditional architectural types and of new, soft cities that parallel, complement and sometimes compete with our existing urban concentration of brick, concrete and steel.[2]

The critical term in this vision of architectural reality is 'telepresence', which, understood ontologically, represents a transformation of the traditional fabric of architecture, including our own corporeal involvement into a 'new' kind of reality structured by electronic media, in which, as it is envisaged, 'computers will weld seamlessly into the fabric of buildings and buildings themselves will become computers—the outcome of a long evolution. It will become meaningless to ask where the smart electronics end and the dumb construction begins. Architects will increasingly confront practical choices between providing for bodily presence and relying on telepresence.'[3]

Corporeal involvement

It is perhaps not necessary to take such vision word for word and too seriously, but at the same time it would be naïve to ignore it. Regardless of the nature of possible results and consequences in the future, this newest form of instrumental representation plays already a very important role in current design and planning. The question, which is not very easy to answer, is how the new electronic representations differ from the traditional ones, and to what extent they are only more sophisticated tools or something altogether different. There is no doubt that even the most advanced forms of representation are, in the last instance, only tools, because they contribute to the representation of reality and only indirectly to its transformation.

They are certainly not independent or self-sufficient. However, those who believe that corporeal involvement can be substituted by involvement in a virtual reality through skilful imitation of our intellectual abilities, assume that it is merely a matter of the degree of knowledge and technology we acquire to make such an imitation possible.

This brings the assumptions of instrumental representation and, indirectly, that of technology to a real test. The critical understanding of these assumptions has its own tradition and history, particularly in the domain of philosophy, but, so far, this seems to be ignored by the protagonists of digital representation. In the domain of productive knowledge, philosophical understanding usually does not count for very much. The only convincing argument seems to be an experimental demonstration, but, so far, this did not prove to be very successful. Unsuccessful results became nevertheless useful in showing how intricate human perception, orientation in space and intelligence are. We can see it in our own field, mainly in the attempts to design intelligent buildings and in the experiments with the virtual reality of space. Virtual reality in its more ambitious forms follows the principles of artificial intelligence and, to that extent, also shares its limits. The possibility of producing a complete and authentic simulation of human perception, recognition of meaning, orientation in space in general and adequate knowledge of the world, proves to be more difficult than it was originally envisaged. The main source of the difficulty is the discrepancy between natural human knowledge of reality, which is mostly implicit, and its explicit representation.[4]

Simulation of knowledge and space

In digital simulation, it is quite common to represent with great accuracy discrete data or complete data structures, simulated perspective, colour, texture, edge quality, illumination, light, haze or movement, integrated in a programme structured by explicit rules. What has proved so far impossible to simulate is the context in which the defined data and elements are situated. This is well reflected in the impossibility to represent space just by the means of geometry, on which all these context-free elements depend.

On April 9, 1830, Carl Friedrich Gauss, the famous German mathematician, wrote to his friend Friedrich Bessel:

> According to my most sincere conviction the theory of space has an entirely different place in knowledge from that occupied by

pure mathematics. There is lacking throughout our knowledge of space the complete persuasion of necessity, which is common to mathematics; and so we must add, in humility, that if geometry and number are exclusively the product of our mind, space has a reality outside our mind and we cannot completely prescribe its laws.[5]

In other words, space has a nature *sui generis*, that is, of its own. A very good example, illustrating the generic nature and structure of space, is an experiment, using spectacles, in which vision is inverted, while the rest of experience remains unchanged.[6] On the first day of the experiment everything in the visual field appears upside down, but the original orientation, manifested most clearly through the sense of touch, remains intact. The arms and legs are localised in a dual manner. The body is generally experienced as upright, the space around as upside down. Everything that is touched provokes the old visual image, while the scene, seen directly, is inverted. The whole experience is accompanied by a feeling of dizziness and nausea. In the following days the conflict between the old and the new localisations becomes less explicit and unpleasant. But even on the sixth day there is still a great discrepancy between the original and the new situations. A pendulum for instance, which appears at first to be upside down, appears upright if we suspend it from our hand. When the index fingers are brought into the visual field, the right being where the left was in the old situation, a touch could be felt in either of them, sometimes in both. It is usually around the eighth day that the visual and tactile fields of experience are more or less reconciled, though even then never completely. The parts of our body which are not directly visible remain permanently in the old orientation. After the removal of the spectacles at the end of the experiment, the visual world becomes straight again, almost immediately, but it takes one or two days more before it becomes entirely normal.

The logic of the transformation is still a mystery that resists clear description. A similar situation, which illustrates even better the generic nature of space, is the recovery of sight after a successful operation, showing that the recovery of the retinal image is not a sufficient condition of a proper vision and sense of space. Proper vision can be acquired only through a process of adaptation in which visual, kinaesthetic and tactile experiences are co-ordinated in a long and very often painful process of learning.[7] This explains the depth and plasticity of normal vision, and its fundamental difference from the visual experience in virtual reality, which consists of context-free information and images produced in accordance with the principles of retinal photo-images. In order to be plausible, the simulated experience of reality must be initiated and completed in the domain of a situated human experience and existence. These are the conditions that any electronic device will have to meet in order to achieve full autonomy. The electronic device would have to be 'a learning device that shares human concerns and human structure to learn, to generalise the way human beings do. And as improbable as it was that one could build a device that could capture our humanity in a physical symbol system, it seems at least as unlikely that one could build a device sufficiently like us to act and learn in our world.'[8]

Embodied knowledge

To perceive, to move and to learn is possible only due to a corporeal involvement. The disembodied nature of computer programmes is the main reason for their inability to match human intelligence. This is acknowledged, though only indirectly, in the failed attempts to digitally simulate larger segments of environment. Because 'it turned out to be very difficult to reproduce in an internal representation for a computer the necessary richness of environment', the researchers at Stanford University came to the conclusion that 'it is easier and cheaper to build a hardware robot to extract what information it needs from the real world than to organise and store a useful model.'[9] This leads inevitably to the conclusion 'that the most economic and efficient store of information about the real world is the real world itself'.[10] Despite its problematic and limited relevance, artificial intelligence is important as a critical turning point in the development of modern technology. It is the last sphere of reality where technology finds its ideal fulfilment but also its limits. 'The recent difficulties in artificial intelligence', writes one of the critics, 'rather than reflecting technological limitations, may reveal the limitations of technology'.[11]

This conclusion reflects an awareness which so far is rather rare. The current situation is dominated by the faith in the unlimited possibilities of technology, including artificial intelligence. The current monopoly of the computer paradigm represents a seminal danger of dogmatism and naïve optimism, as did the Newtonian paradigm at the beginning of the eighteenth century. In both cases, the one-sided and over-optimistic expectations tend to suppress any other access to truth, and this leads to similar consequences—a painful weakening and impoverishment of culture. In other words, 'if a computer paradigm becomes so strong that people begin to think of themselves as digital devices on the model of work in artificial intelligence, then, since machines cannot be like human beings, human beings may become progressively like machines. Our risk is not the advent of super-intelligent computers, but of sub-intelligent human beings.'[12] This danger is potentially present in all areas of modem technology, though sometimes in a less explicit and less conclusive form. Most often, it manifests itself as a monologue of instrumental thinking, accepted as a universal approach to all possible questions and problems that may be encountered.

Originality and competition

Belief in the universal power of instrumental reasoning is reinforced by the search for originality and by the competitive advantages of new inventions. In these tendencies, it is taken for granted that what is new and original must be the best and most appropriate. This creates a strange situation, particularly in fields like architecture, where only certain areas are susceptible to radical technological innovation and change, while other areas remain relatively stable. Technology tends to develop in areas that can be more easily rationalised, are technically more interesting and where the market offers a better return. Architecture has only a very limited influence on what is produced. This is a paradox in view of the difficulties and the time it takes to make new materials and new structures architecturally relevant.

How difficult, intricate and controversial this process of transformation and adaptation is, can be illustrated by the phenomenon of transparency. Since the first decades of the last century, transparency was hailed as one of the main achievements and characteristics of truly modern buildings. However, it is doubtful that architectural conditions or requirements played any important role at the beginning of a development that was determined by the new ways of using concrete and steel in frame structures, by the redundancy of load-bearing walls and by the growing indifference to the physiognomy of buildings. From an architectural point of view, transparency is welcome where unobstructed visibility or light is required, but this is not everywhere. In many parts of buildings, larger surface areas and solid enclosures are equally required as desirable. However, once the process of making, determined by material and structural reasons, is established, transparency is a predictable outcome. It mostly does not follow architectural requirements and does not discriminate between what is and what is not desirable. It becomes merely an aspect of a value-free style and, eventually, an emancipated symbolic representation of modernity.

The current tendency to use ingenious and complex structures to perform relatively banal tasks, or to use elaborate lightweight structures in circumstances where there is no place or need for them, cannot be explained by reference to technical or architectural reasons, but only by reference to some deeper reasons and motives. Some of the deep motives, I believe, are the desire for emancipation and autonomy that we mentioned earlier. The emancipation from history and from the unquantifiable conditions of design finds its fulfilment in the transformation of buildings into structures representing the transparency of pure concepts. The transparency of concepts expresses the will to eliminate everything from design that cannot be calculated or controlled. This brings us to one of the most enigmatic characteristics of contemporary architecture: the fascination with the aspects of design that can be treated like a disengaged problem of construction and the urge to suppress everything that is beyond our control, namely the material and spatial reality of the intended results.

Simulated space and its limits

It is interesting to compare the tendency towards idealisation and disembodiment in contemporary architecture and design with the most recent developments in artificial intelligence, and the attempts of contemporary technology to simulate the conditions of embodiment in a form of imaginary reality. In these simulations of embodied experience, the dialogue with phenomenal reality is replaced by a monologue of conceptual imagination. Under such conditions 'the illusion of seeing is, therefore, much less the presentation of an illusory object than the spread and, so to speak, running wild of a visual power which has lost any sensory counterpart'.[13] This loss is the main characteristic of a situation that leads to hallucinations, 'because through the phenomenal body we are in constant relationship with an environment into which that body is projected, and because, when divorced from its actual environment, the body remains able to summon up, by means of its own settings, the pseudo-presence of that environment'.[14]

The space of virtual reality can be considered as a consciously structured and controlled hallucinatory world. However, the situations in which hallucinations can take place are limited only to certain spaces and media, and cannot be identified with the current reality as a whole. There are structures in our culture which resist hallucinations. Merleau-Ponty is more specific when he writes: 'What protects us against delirium or hallucinations are not our critical powers but the structure of our space.'[15] The structure of space has its source, as we have seen, in the depth of our situated existence and coincides with the overall structure and coherence of our cultural world. When we speak about the coherence of the cultural world today, we refer not only to its latent background, but also to its visible manifestation, which shows a high degree of fragmentation, discontinuity and lack of wholeness.

It appears that technological thinking has to come to itself in order to understand the conditions of its own inner possibilities, mainly the limits of emancipation and disembodiment and by implication the ambiguous nature of the technologically constructed illusion of wholeness.

> The wholes established by technology do not make us feel complete or satisfied, they are still experienced as splintered wholes. Here and there, man recognises and greets a fragment of his former universe, integrated in a functional but alien and anonymous whole, in which he nevertheless must live. There is no other. Against that feeling and splintering, modern man feels a keen desire for all-inclusiveness, for synthesis. But, alas, any synthesis produced by technology fails and comes to nought.[16]

The distance that separates us from the deeper levels of reality and from the sense of wholeness, is a result of the questionable development of the new means of representation. The consequences of this development are the emancipation of representation and the tendency towards self-reference. The emancipated, relatively closed world of representation raises, more radically than ever before, the question of the unity of our culture. How can one, in such a situation, understand the relation of the abstract or simulated space to the space of the everyday life? In the past this question would be answered by a reference to a sequence of levels of reality that constituted a link between the universal concepts and the particularity of individual phenomena, creating thus an articulated, communicative space of culture.[17] The fact that this space is accessible to us nowadays only by a special effort is, no doubt, a great challenge for the future.

Notes

1 Stephen Toulmin, *Cosmopolis: The Hidden Agenda of Modernity*, Chicago, IL: University of Chicago Press, 1990; Amos Funkenstein, *Theology and the Scientific Imagination*, Princeton, NJ: Princeton University Press, 1986, pp. 290–346; Martin Heidegger, 'The Age of the World Picture', in *The Question Concerning Technology & Other Essays*, trans. William Lovitt, New York: Harper & Row, 1977, pp. 115–55.

2 William J. T. Mitchell, *City of Bits*, Cambridge, MA: MIT Press, 1995, p. 167.

3 Ibid., pp. 171–2.

4 Hubert Dreyfus, *What Computers Still Can't Do*, Cambridge, MA: MIT Press, 1992; Seymour Papert, 'One AI or Many?' in *The Artificial Intelligence Debate*, ed. Stephen R. Graubard, Cambridge, MA: MIT Press, 1988, pp. 1–15.

5 Morris Kline, *Mathematics: The Loss of Certainty*, Oxford: Oxford University Press, 1980, p. 87.

6 The vision is inverted by a system of lenses which turn everything upside down and from left to right. For a detailed description of the experiment, see Paul Schilder, *The Image and Appearance of the Human Body*, London: Routledge & Kegan Paul, 1950, pp. 106–14.

7 Marius von Senden, *Space and Sight: The Perception of Space and Shape in the Congenitally Blind before and after Operation*, London: Methuen & Co. Publishing, 1960.

8 Dreyfus, op. cit, p. xlvi.

9 Ibid., p. 300.

10 Ibid.

11 Ibid., p. 227.

12 Ibid., p. 280.

13 Maurice Merleau-Ponty, *Phenomenology of Perception*, trans. Colin Smith, London: Routledge & Kegan Paul, 1965, p. 340.

14 Ibid.

15 Ibid., p. 291.

16 Jacques Ellul, *The Technological System*, trans. Joachim Neugroschel, New York: Continuum, 1980, p. 45.

17 The communicative space of traditional culture was articulated in a dialectical process known as the great Chain of Being. See Arthur O. Lovejoy, *The Great Chain of Being: a Study of the History of an Idea*, Cambridge, MA: Harvard University Press, 1976.

13 Between Architecture and the City

The main intention behind the work of our Diploma studio was to interpret architecture as a cultural discipline.[1] The intention to see architecture as part of a broader world of culture took us inevitably to the domain of the city, the place where culture has developed most explicitly.[2] However, what was true for the relation of architecture and the city in the past is not so obvious in our times. In the last two hundred years architecture has established its own professional independence and highly individualised and fragmented history. The former sense of wholeness, based on the participation of architecture in the culture of the city, has been reduced to urban planning, where participation in the complex urban culture is replaced by the knowledge available to a small group of planners, or in extreme cases, to an individual designer. The difference between the planning approach and the way cities came into existence in their long history is overwhelming.

What makes this difference overwhelming is the fundamental difference of experience and knowledge involved in the formation of the city as urban reality. The terms 'planning' or 'design', used very often in the interpretation of traditional cities, are not appropriate for two main reasons. In the past, the *a priori* chosen configuration of the city or the regularity of its layout was in most cases, only the first stage in its development, followed by an innumerable amount of individual contributions, filling the original plan in a process that, as a whole, cannot be reduced to one of explicit knowledge. The second reason was the role of the full context of culture in decisions that may appear as isolated and structured for a very specific or ideal purpose. A good example here is that of the so-called ideal or 'planned' cities. The Greek Hippodamian grid plan of such cities as Olynthos, Miletos, Priene and Piraeus is still considered in conventional literature to be the foundation of modern town planning; and yet it is known that

DOI: 10.4324/9781003272090-14

13.1 Ideal city of Venaria Reale, Turin, aerial photo.

the plan and its repetitive geometrical pattern were a representation of democratic equality (*isonomia*), based on the contemporary political thinking and Pythagorean understanding of proportional representation and justice.[3] We can find a similar disproportion between the apparent order and the often quite complex meaning, in the ideal cities of the Renaissance and Baroque (Fig. 13.1).[4] The regularity and transparent order of their layout should be seen as a symbolic representation of the essential nature of the city, expressed most often geometrically (*more geometrico*). This should not, however, be confused with modern planning.[5]

Ideal cities were, until the end of the eighteenth century, based on historical precedents as well as on contemporary literature, philosophy and political thinking. In that sense they were a result of a broad cooperation and accumulated knowledge. This gives them, despite their highly abstracted nature, a sufficient degree of integrity, legitimacy and power to represent shared values. The nature of cooperation and accumulated knowledge is obviously more complex in the case of non-ideal cities.[6] It is virtually impossible to bring to light all the individual contributions that shape the development of a city, as a whole or in its parts. It is sufficient to take as an example one street in Paris, such as the Boulevard St. Michel, and ask very simple questions such as what brought the boulevard to existence, what contributes to the richness of its life, and what preserves its identity and meaning, in order to see that the answers have no clear end (Fig. 13.2). Still, we are in a better position to approach some answers if we look at the results of the city's development. These results come to visibility as typical human situations.[7]

The virtue of situations is their ability to bring and keep together a whole spectrum of phenomena and preserve them in relative constancy of presence. The relation between phenomena and the constancy of situations can be compared with the relation between the content of a drama and its plot. Situations can be seen, in the end, as settings, where people not only do or experience something, but which also include things that contribute to the fulfilment of human life. Situations represent the most complete way of understanding the condition of our experience of the surrounding world and the human qualities of the world. They endow experience with durability in relation to which other experiences can acquire meaning and can form a memory and history. The result is a formation of relatively stable urban configurations, such as streets, squares, courtyards,

13.2 Jean François Raffaelli, *Boulevard des Italiens*, ca. 1900.

urban blocks, etc. The unique characteristic of urban configurations is their ability to support more articulated strata of culture, social and political life, as well as arts, literature, theatre and the communicative nature of everyday life. The relation between the physical fabric of the city and more articulated strata of culture is a relation of reciprocity, in which the fabric is always a potential anticipation of culture as a whole. All that is articulated is situated somewhere, in a particular place.

The embodiment of more articulated levels of culture in a particular place is illustrated well and with great subtlety by Louis Aragon in the chapter titled 'The Passage de l'Opéra' in his *Paris Peasant*:

> Let us take a stroll along this Passage de l'Opéra and have a closer look at it. It is a double tunnel, with a single gateway opening to the north on to the Rue Chauchat and two gateways opening to the south on to the boulevard [...] The gateway to mystery swings open at the touch of the human weakness and we have entered the realms of darkness. One false step, one slurred syllable together reveals a man's thoughts. The disquieting atmosphere of places contains similar locks which cannot be bolted fast against infinity. Wherever the living pursue particularly ambiguous activities the inanimate may sometimes assume the reflection of their most secret motives and thus our cities are peopled with unrecognised sphinxes which will never stop the passing dreamer and ask him mortal questions unless he first projects his meditations, his absence of mind, towards them.[8]

We can choose many more examples, not only from literature, but also from painting, film and other areas of culture, that will illustrate the same point—the intimate link between the silent fabric (body) of the city and the tissue of broader and more explicit meanings. It is this link that in the end defines the nature of typical situations, where the fabric plays the role of final embodiment and primary reference and our entry into the visible world of the city.

What we have said so far is true for the traditional city but is, in our time, only a latent possibility that has to be re-discovered and brought into the life of the contemporary city. This is obviously not an easy task. It requires an appropriate kind of knowledge and vision of urban development. After many years of concentrated effort, the knowledge that has proved to be most appropriate to our task is phenomenology, which, in its latest stage, addresses the questions of corporeality and embodiment, areas directly relevant to architecture. The term that plays a critical role in phenomenological thinking is the decisive aspect of human situations, the horizon.

The intriguing nature of the horizon as an imaginary line is revealed in its power to define the boundary of our visible world, as well as in the invitation to transcend that boundary.[9] By defining the limits of visibility, receding with our movement but not disappearing, the horizon is an integrating vehicle of reference and continuity for everything in the visible world. Because the horizon belongs to the human way of seeing the world, it is a decisive aspect of human situations, in that it holds them together and gives them coherence and meaning: 'In the sphere of human understanding, we also like to speak of horizons, especially when referring to the claim of historical consciousness to see the past in terms of its own being, not in terms of our contemporary criteria and prejudices.'[10] The horizon of a situation represents, in a global sense, the relation of parts and whole, the primary operational notion of modern hermeneutics in terms of understanding. This answers to a great extent our own question about the role of individual contributions to the life of the city.

Before we go any further, we should take into consideration the difference between the nature of architecture as the most typical contribution, and the nature of the city. Architecture, more often than not, is designed by individuals or small teams, and usually has a client. This gives it a basic level of transparency and the possibility of some degree of explicit understanding. Cities, on the other hand are not as transparent. They are created by an indeterminate number of contributions, of which only part are architectural and the rest are institutional, while many are made by non-professionals and generally by those who participate and intervene in the everyday life of the city. Everyday life includes politics, economy, transport, services, etc. This rather complex picture illustrates the nature of culture, of which the city is an embodiment. If we agree that architecture, regardless of where it is situated, is directly or indirectly conditioned by urban culture, then we may also agree that the city is a framework and measure for what architecture can or should be, in order to play its proper and expected role in culture. The relation of architecture and city should be seen as a relation of reciprocity, in which the city can receive a higher level of articulation and subtlety from architectural design, and architecture can receive a higher level of culture from the life of the city. That such a reciprocity is not obvious and easy to achieve is illustrated by the fact that the dominant tendency today is to see the city as a result of planning, or as a design problem on a larger scale. This is clearly expressed in the recent fashion to speak about 'the architecture of the city', reflecting an older, rather problematic statement, that the city is like some large house and the house is, in turn, like some small city.[11] It is interesting that in more intelligent recent projects, architecture does not dominate the city, but is subordinated to its nature and life.

A good example is the recent restoration of the Rue des Cascades in Paris. Not only the street but the whole area, which is part of the neighbourhood called Belleville, was planned for development in a similar way as the surrounding areas, dominated by blocks of social housing. However, due to a successful intervention, the development was fundamentally altered.[12] The topography of the street was preserved, the buildings worth keeping were restored, while the rest and any empty sites were replaced by new buildings, each given to a different architect to design.

This is an approach similar to that followed in the Diploma projects in the Department of Architecture in Cambridge from the 1980s to 2006. Most of those projects, even the smallest, were articulated in reference to the culture and life of the contemporary city. The main intention was to see the limits of what can be designed, but also what else should be taken into consideration, even if it might be addressed only by approximation (Fig. 5.4). In a typical large-scale project, the most appropriate configuration of urban structure was established collectively as an initial hypothesis. In the next stage, the site was divided into individual projects that could be designed as any other medium-size project. The individual solutions were discussed, modified and adapted so that they would create a plausible, coherent solution for the site as a whole. This process was motivated by the attempt to overcome the limits of individual experience and knowledge, and the desire to come closer to the complexity of urban culture and its collective nature. The gap between architecture and the complex nature of the city reflects a much deeper gap between individual experience and consensus about what we can share as common. This deeper gap has been discussed in modern art and architecture as the problem of the fragment and the sense of wholeness. In the reality of the modern city, individual architectural projects are most often fragments, but they are not the only ones. We should take into consideration all the other individual contributions mentioned earlier.

The main characteristic of the modern fragment is its ambiguity, manifested in one sense as negative fragmentation, but in another sense as a reference to a potential whole. In the first case, the fragment has achieved in modern times a high degree of autonomy and self-reference, cultivated particularly in the Romantic era. Friedrich Schlegel writes that 'a fragment, like a miniature work of art has to be entirely isolated from the surrounding world and be complete in itself like a hedgehog.'[13] And elsewhere in his writings he adds: 'Many of the works of the ancients have become fragments. Many modern works are fragments as soon as they are written.'[14] It was the fragment, understood in the second, restorative sense, that contributed to the recovery of latent meaning and to the more explicit sense of wholeness. In order to see the restorative role of the fragment we need only to think of the works of Synthetic Cubism, Surrealism, the art of collage, or similar tendencies and achievements in contemporary literature, poetry or music (Fig. 13.3). In all of these, the fragment opens a relation to other fragments in a sequence of references, based on the principles of similarities, metaphoricity, or, in a more explicit sense, analogy.

In the thinking of the Surrealists, the restorative power of the fragment was closely linked with the notion of poetic analogy. In Breton's words, 'poetic analogy [...] transgresses the deductive laws in order to make the mind apprehend the interdependence of two objects of thought situated on different planes, between which the logical functioning of the mind is unlikely to throw a bridge, in fact opposes *a priori* any bridge that might be thrown.'[15] Poetic analogy here refers primarily to the art of collage illustrated by Max Ernst's commentary on the 'mechanism' of collage: 'I'm tempted to see in collage the chance meeting of two distant realities on an unfamiliar plane, or to use a shorter term, the culture of systematic displacement and its effect.'[16] The 'culture of systematic displacement' is only a more explicit version of the sequence (passage) of metaphorical steps that structured the non-perspectival space of early Cubism.[17]

In the Cambridge studio, the shared vision of the overall urban configuration was to see an individual project as a vehicle or tool for creating positive fragments oriented towards their potential contribution to the urban character of the site. The vision of the urban configuration was based on the individual experience of the participants to begin with, but, in the end and as far as possible, they were based on consensus and shared vision, drawing from focused investigations. The existence of the MPhil course in the History and

13.3 David Weston-Thomas, Cambridge diploma studio, 1993. Political foyer.

Philosophy of Architecture was a great advantage of the Cambridge curriculum. It was there that we could concentrate on investigations for which there is usually no time or space in the studio. Among the main topics of investigations were the key architectural principles of design, and the cultural history of the relation of architecture and city. The investigation of the nature of design, in a dialogue with philosophical enquiry, brought us closer to a better understanding of the latent levels of the accumulated historical experience, structured in culturally prominent situations, known better as institutions.

In the still prevailing understanding, institutions are linked almost exclusively with social, political or cultural associations, and generally with human affairs, regardless of the place and conditions in which they are situated and embodied. And yet it is clear that institutions are always situated somewhere, that family asks for a home, local government asks for a town hall or some form of office space, and so on. Is it not, then, true that the embodiment of institutions belongs to their nature, and even more, that it is the foundation of their institutional character? This becomes clearer once we look more closely at the formation of institutions. In most cases they are not a result of arbitrary decision or invention. They have a history, and the more important they are, the less clear, usually, are their origins, and the true motives informing their formation and development. Some institutions can be established as new by convention, and yet it is difficult to always claim their novelty in view of the broader history of the same or similar institutions to which they directly or indirectly relate. A good example is the internal street in Le Corbusier's Habitation at Marseilles, in comparison with the typical urban street on the ground (Fig. 13.4).

13.4 Le Corbusier, Unité d'Habitation, Marseilles, interior corridor (left); and view of street in Prague.

This is a problem that, in the recent past, was investigated under the name of the history of types.[18] The results remain inconclusive and problematic, mainly because the investigation is based on the dichotomy of human activities and physical fabric, usually seen as separate. This illustrates the need to see institutions and their embodiment as one continuum that may be described as the architectonics of institutions. How should this term be understood? The answer is potentially present in the genesis of institutions.[19] Institutions originate in the typicality and relative stability of human situations, based on continuity of reference to the natural, historically mediated conditions. It is most of all the phenomenon of stability that is very much enhanced in institutions. This is possible due to the more universal nature of a particular institution, its longer history and relevance for contemporary life. The strength of institutions depends on their ability to preserve the continuity of their identity. A good illustration is the life of an urban street, where many things are constantly changing; people coming and moving away, shops changing hands, old buildings demolished and new ones built, while the street remains preserved, very often for generations. This is the virtue and power of institutions. It is not sufficiently appreciated how important their stability is for the continuity of cultural tradition as a source of genuine cultural creativity.[20]

The relation of creativity and tradition is revealed in the accumulated experience that institutions endow with high level of durability in relation to which a whole sequence of other experiences acquire meaning, and, as a result, constitute a continuum of history. It is the durable dimension of institutions that serves as an invitation to the sequel of the past and future. This makes institutions important spheres of mediation between our contemporary life, the depth of history and the anticipation of future creative possibilities.

What appears to be true for the street may be extended to other urban spatial settings. The nature of the street has its roots in the natural conditions of its own history and, what is equally important, cannot be treated as an isolated element, but only as part of the situational structure of the city as a whole. In the situational structure of the city, the street plays a mediating role. It mediates between individual buildings by creating a space they can share. This mediation continues, usually in a hierarchical sequence, from urban segment to district or quarter, and finally to the city as a whole. There is a close link between the hierarchical sequence of mediation and the phenomenon of sharing. We share that which is common, what we can participate in and what is equally accessible. This defines a natural tendency towards centrality, where what is most common is usually situated. This is a tendency we shall discuss in some detail later. The process of mediation not only follows the sequence of streets but engages the fabric of the city in all its depth. This leads to an important distinction, to begin with, between urban exterior and interior, consisting of secondary streets and spaces, courtyards, gardens, etc. The investigation of the longer history of the layout and detail configuration of European cities shows a remarkable correlation between the nature (purpose) of a particular place and its spatial configuration (arrangement).

The frequently complex spatial layout of such cities creates a sequence of different conditions appropriate for shops, agencies, restaurants or cafés on the street, workshops or studios in the secondary streets and courtyards, intimate space in the gardens, etc. The process of mediation can be seen as a process of communication. What is communicated takes place on the level of the urban fabric, but this must be seen only as a mode of embodiment of city life. The street and other urban spaces are settings similar to stage sets for the events of everyday life, for markets, theatres in the open, processions, ceremonies, etc. This brings us to the most important role of communication, the mediation between the more articulated forms of life and their embodiment in the fabric of the city.[21]

A better understanding of this mode of communication can, in turn, help us to better understand not only how a particular urban configuration contributes to the enhancement of urban life, but also how it can be included in design. The results of investigations represent explicit knowledge that can be used in the first stage of design. The most important step is the use of the knowledge in the formation of typical situations, the main tools of design. As we have already seen, situations represent the most complete way of understanding the condition of our experience of the surrounding world and the human qualities of the world. The experience of the surrounding world is not limited to architecture. We can learn about the nature of design tasks, such as the design of a library, gallery, concert hall, residential building, but also of urban spaces, from the memory of our everyday experience, as well as from painting, literature, theatre and other areas of culture.

This extended version of experience is always potentially available because situations, as they should be understood, are formed in all areas of culture. However, they appear in different forms of visibility that must be translated to the visibility specific to architecture. The key to the translation is metaphor, which tells us not what things are, but what they are like. A good example illustrating the formation of a design situation is the case of a cabaret, a new phenomenon of the twentieth-century for which there are no direct precedents.[22]

Cabaret is like a night club, bar, café or theatre, but, in a real sense, it is none of them. In the preparatory stage of the project, the likeness with all these possible references can be treated as a series of metaphorical images brought together as a collage in which the role of individual images and their contribution to the specificity of the result, the convincing character of the cabaret, can be judged (Fig. 13.5). The judgement is not so much conceptual as visual. This step illustrates the shift from explicit knowledge to visual knowledge, sometimes referred to as visual intelligence. Visual intelligence is the level-horizon that brings together explicit knowledge and the spontaneous level of design, and turns them into visibility specific to architecture. This particular turn answers the question of how the individual components of the design situation, understood as positive fragments, can be related to a corresponding sense of wholeness.

This can be illustrated by the problem of how to bring to visibility the richness of the well-developed design, in view of the established convention of representation in the form of plans, sections, elevations, perspectives, axonometrics, etc. In our studio work we have tried to answer the problem using 'composite' drawings, in which the qualitative richness of a situation is represented on a level that represents the material texture, light and events of the situation, overlaid on a different level with the geometric outline of the situation (Fig. 13.6). The result is a dialogue, in which the conceptual and visual aspects of design are integrated in the visibility specific to a particular architectural setting. The journey from metaphorical studies to composite drawings represents a thinking applied in a similar way to the link between the concreteness of individual projects and the configurations on the scale of the city. This brings us back to our earlier discussion of the urban hierarchy related to the degree of sharing. As we have seen, because sharing is closely linked with what is common, there is a natural tendency towards centrality, where what is most common is usually situated.[23]

This was certainly true in the past, but is it still true today? In most cases the centrality in contemporary cities is obscured if not intentionally negated. And yet the central part of our cities was, and potentially still is, the heart of city existence, where the political activities,

13.5 Biba Dow, Cambridge diploma studio, 1993. Political cabaret.

in their broader sense, the virtues of coexistence, the enhancement of public life and shared culture, but most of all the formation of consensus and common values, can take place and be cultivated. It was with this in mind that in most of our Cambridge studio projects we tried to restore or create first of all the part of the city where the

13.6 David Thompson, Cambridge diploma studio, 2005. Film resource centre.

common interests and values can be harmonised (Fig. 13.7). This harmonisation was not seen as a goal or as an accomplished formation of public life, but only as a precondition for such a goal. In the current state of our cities, dominated by private interests and negative fragmentation, it is not possible to restore public life directly. What is possible, on the other hand, is the creation of conditions in

13.7 Cambridge diploma studio, Rue Menilmontant project, 2005. Site plan.

the existing city fabric under which the restoration of public life will become not only possible but also realistic. This is, I believe, the most important task for future intervention in the fabric of cities and, by implication, in the meaning of architecture itself.

Notes

1 Vesely taught diploma studio in the Department of Architecture at the University of Cambridge from 1979 to 2006.
2 Lewis Mumford, *The Culture of Cities*, New York: Harvest Books, 1970; Giulio Carlo Argan, *Storia dell'arte come storia della città*, Rome: Editori riuniti, 1983.
3 Pierre Leveque and Pierre Vidal-Naquet, *Cleisthenes the Athenian: An Essay on the Representation of Space and Time in Greek Political Thought*, Amherst & New York: Prometheus Books, 1997; Plato, *Gorgias*, 208.

4 The best examples, to mention a few, are Sabbioneta, Palmanova, New Breisach and Richelieu. See Helen Rosenau, *The Ideal City: Its Architectural Evolution*, Worthing: Littlehampton Book Services Ltd, 1975; Ruth Eaton, *Ideal Cities: Utopianism and the (Un)Built Environment*, London: Thames & Hudson, 2002.

5 Keith Lilley, *City and Cosmos*, London: Reaktion Books, 2009.

6 The relation of planning and design is ambiguous. They frequently overlap but, nevertheless, remain different. In design, we take into consideration the concrete, specific conditions of the task, pay attention to detail, take care of the finishing stages and maintain a dialogue with the broader, given cultural context and very often with the client. In planning, on the other hand, we take into consideration mainly the general, anonymous principles of urban configurations that can be, and frequently are, detached from the context of culture, reducing the sphere of knowledge to *a priori* knowledge. Such knowledge reflected, in the past, the inherited tradition as universal, but in modern times it does so only as general and abstract, representing the experience and knowledge of a small group of people and occasionally only that of a single individual. Modern planning turns out to be a monologue of decisions, based on the abstract construct-model of the urban reality to which design is subordinated. The subordination of design to planning leads to a victory of abstract monologue over a creative dialogue with the given urban reality.

7 For a discussion of the nature of situation, see Dalibor Vesely, *Architecture in the Age of Divided Representation*, Cambridge, MA: MIT Press, 2004, pp. 369–77.

8 Louis Aragon, *Paris Peasant*, trans. Simon Watson-Taylor, London: Pan Books, 1971, pp. 29–30.

9 Didier Maleuvre, *The Horizon: A History of Our Infinite Longing*, Berkeley, CA: University of California Press, 2011.

10 Hans-Georg Gadamer, *Truth and Method*, trans. William Glen-Doepel, ed. John Cumming and Garret Barden, London: Sheed and Ward, 1975, p. 269.

11 Leon Battista Alberti, *On the Art of Building in Ten Books*, trans. Joseph Rykwert et al., Cambridge, MA: MIT Press, 1988, Book I.9, p. 23, and Book V.14, p. 140. This became most explicit in the movement known as Tendenza, represented most prominently in the works of Aldo Rossi; see his *The Architecture of the City*, trans. Diane Ghirardo and Joan Ockman, Cambridge, MA: MIT Press, 1982; and Aldo Rossi, *Scientific Autobiography*, trans. Lawrence Venuti, Cambridge, MA: MIT Press, 1981.

12 Antoine Grumbach, *Rue de Cascade*, unpublished report, Paris, 2004.

13 Friedrich Schlegel, 'Athenaeum Fragments', in *Philosophical Fragments*, trans. Peter Firchow, Minneapolis: University of Minnesota Press, 1991, p. 45.

14 Ibid., p. 21.

15 André Breton, 'Signe ascendant' in *La clé des champs*, Paris: Editions Pauvert, 1979, p. 13 [trans. Vesely].

16 Ibid.

17 See Dagmar Motycka Weston, 'Corporeal Spatiality and the Restorative Fragment in Early Twentieth-Century Art and Architecture', in *Phenomenologies of the City*, ed. Henrietta Steiner and Max Sternberg, Abingdon: Routledge, 2015, pp. 195–212.

18 Nicolaus Pevsner, *A History of Building Types*, Princeton, NJ: Princeton University Press, 1979; Dalibor Vesely, 'From Typology to Hermeneutics in Architectural Design', in special issue 'Heaven and Earth: Festschrift to Honor Karsten Harries', *International Journal of Architectural Theory*, 12, no.1, August 2007, https://www.cloud-cuckoo.net/openarchive/wolke/eng/Subjects/subject071.htm (accessed November 2021).

19 Mary Douglas, *How Institutions Think*, New York: Syracuse University Press, 1986; Maurice Merleau-Ponty, *Institution and Passivity: Course Notes from the Collège de France, 1954–1955*, trans. Leonard Lawlor and Heath Massey, Evanston, IL: Northwestern University Press, 2010.

20 Culture is a result of the process of cultivation in which the new should enhance and not negate that which is already there; see the discussion of invention and creativity in Dalibor Vesely, 'The Nature of Creativity in the Age of Production', in *Scroope: Cambridge Architectural Journal*, 4, 1992, pp. 25–30.

21 Juliane Rietzsch, *All the world's a stage – Selbstdarstellung auf sozialen Netzwerkseiten: Eine Analyse der kommunikationswissenschaftlichen Literatur*, Munich: Grin Verlag, 2012; Peter Brook, *The Empty Space*, London: Penguin Modern Classics, 2008; Ian Macintosh, *Architecture, Actor and Audience*, London: Routledge, 1993; Edward Glaeser, *Triumph of the City*, London: Macmillan Publishers, 2011.

22 Peter Jelavich, *Berlin Cabaret*, Cambridge, MA: Harvard University Press, 1996; Alan Lareau, *The Wild Stage: Literary Cabarets of the Weimar Republic*, London: Camden House, 1995; Manfred Reuther, *Nolde in Berlin: Dance Theatre Cabaret*, Cologne: DuMont Literatur und Kunst Verlag, 2008.

23 Dalibor Vesely, 'In Defence of Architecture', originally published in *Scroope: Cambridge Architecture Journal*, 16, Cambridge, 2004, pp. 15–19; slightly reworked for *Compendium: The Work of the University of Cambridge, Department of Architecture*, Exhibition Catalogue, Cambridge, 2006, pp. 28–33.

Illustration Credits

Index